THE PRICE OF GENDER EQUALITY

Gender in a Global/Local World

Series Editors: Jane Parpart, Pauline Gardiner Barber
and Marianne H. Marchand

Gender in a Global/Local World critically explores the uneven and often contradictory ways in which global processes and local identities come together. Much has been and is being written about globalization and responses to it but rarely from a critical, historical, gendered perspective. Yet, these processes are profoundly gendered albeit in different ways in particular contexts and times. The changes in social, cultural, economic and political institutions and practices alter the conditions under which women and men make and remake their lives. New spaces have been created – economic, political, social – and previously silent voices are being heard. North-South dichotomies are being undermined as increasing numbers of people and communities are exposed to international processes through migration, travel, and communication, even as marginalization and poverty intensify for many in all parts of the world. The series features monographs and collections which explore the tensions in a 'global/local world', and includes contributions from all disciplines in recognition that no single approach can capture these complex processes.

Also in the series

(En)Gendering the War on Terror
War Stories and Camouflaged Politics
Edited by
Krista Hunt and Kim Rygiel
ISBN 0 7546 4481 2

Women, Migration and Citizenship
Making Local, National and Transnational Connections
Edited by
Evangelia Tastsoglou and Alexandra Dobrowolsky
ISBN 0 7546 4379 4

Transnational Ruptures
Gender and Forced Migration
Catherine Nolin
ISBN 0 7546 3805 7

'Innocent Women and Children'
Gender, Norms and the Protection of Civilians
R. Charli Carpenter
ISBN 0 7546 4745 5

The Price of Gender Equality
Member States and Governance in the European Union

ANNA VAN DER VLEUTEN
Radboud University Nijmegen, the Netherlands

Routledge
Taylor & Francis Group
LONDON AND NEW YORK

First published 2007 by Ashgate Publishing

2 Park Square, Milton Park, Abingdon, Oxfordshire OX14 4RN
52 Vanderbilt Avenue, New York, NY 10017

Routledge is an imprint of the Taylor & Francis Group, an informa business

First issued in paperback 2020

British Library Cataloguing in Publication Data
Vleuten, Joanna Maria van der, 1960-
The price of gender equality : member states and governance in the European Union. - (Gender in a global/local world)
1. Sex discrimination in employment - Economic aspects - European Union countries 2. Sex discrimination in employment - Government policy - European Union countries
3. Europe - Economic integration - Social aspects
I. Title
331.4'133'094

Library of Congress Cataloging-in-Publication Data
Vleuten, Joanna Maria van der, 1960-
The price of gender equality : member states and governance in the European Union / Anna van der Vleuten.
p. cm. -- (Gender in a global/local world)
Includes bibliographical references and index.
ISBN-13: 978-0-7546-4636-5 (alk. paper) 1. Women--Government policy--European Union countries. 2. Equality--European Union countries. 3. Women's rights--European Union countries. 4. European Union countries--Social policy. 5. European Union. I. Title.

HQ1236.5.E85V54 2006
305.42094'09045--dc22

2006025035

ISBN 978-0-7546-4636-5 (hbk)
ISBN 978-0-367-60574-2 (pbk)

Contents

Series Editors' Preface

In many ways *The Price of Gender Equality* by Anna van der Vleuten presents a continuation of the direction taken by the other ten books in the Gender in a Global/Local World series which focus on the gendered impact of globalization and contingent international processes from a multidimensional perspective. While situated in this general context, this volume goes beyond in its attempt to contribute to both feminist and International Relations scholarship. Directing the gaze toward the European Union and its formulation and implementation of gender policies, the volume raises an interesting set of 'puzzles.'

Van der Vleuten elaborates upon three such puzzles. First, the accomplishments in gender policies contrast sharply with the elaboration of EU social policy which has generally been very poor. Second, the formulation of gender equality policies at the EU level seems to go against the general tendency of a neoliberal project, as exemplified by the European Union's quest for the liberalization of markets in goods, services, capital and, to a certain degree, labor. The third puzzle deals with the question of why during certain periods advances were made in the formulation and implementation of gender policies while in others this was not the case.

In her analysis of these three related puzzles, Anna van der Vleuten is dealing with a multi-tiered political system that characterizes the EU and its member states. To understand how gender policies are formulated and implemented it is important to understand the institutional dynamics within the EU, for instance relations between the Commission, the European Parliament and the European Court of Justice. However, this only provides part of the picture. In addition, one needs to understand and analyse domestic politics in respective member states, as well as state-society relations and relations of non-state actors, in particular women's organizations, and EU institutions. What results is a complex web of interrelated decision-making arenas with multiple actors operating at different levels. How come, then, that states have gone against their immediate 'calculated' interests and implemented gender equity policies? According to van der Vleuten, states have often found themselves in a 'pincer situation' in which pressure from 'above' (the Commission and the EU Court) and from 'below' have forced them to adopt or implement certain gender policies. In her analysis, the financial and ideological costs of not adopting or implementing these policies outweighed the costs of implementation.

The Price of Gender Equality thus not only provides an interesting contribution to the series, but also offers an innovative example of how one can 'gender mainstream' integration theories in International Relations.

Marianne Marchand
Pauline Gardiner Barber
Jane Parpart
November 2006

Acknowledgements

I would like to acknowledge a generous grant from NWO (The Netherlands Organization for Scientific Research), No. P 43–263, which has enabled the translation of the relevant part of my research and the editing of the text. Charles Frink and Toby Adams accomplished this task with care.

I would like to thank Bob Lieshout who taught me how to do research and Bob Reinalda who taught me how to write a book. I am grateful to my colleagues Bertjan Verbeek and Mieke Verloo for their friendship and support. For comments and support, I would like to thank all members of the *Nijmegen Research Group on International Relations* (WOIB) and *Shifts*, the research group of Political Science and Public Administration at Radboud University Nijmegen.

At Ashgate, I am grateful to the Series Editors and an anonymous reviewer, whose comments encouraged me to do better, and Kirstin Howgate and Margaret Younger for their patience and guidance.

I thank Nicole and Nil Annabell, the latter for technical assistance, and both for sharing daily stress and happiness. I dedicate the book to my father.

Anna van der Vleuten
Nijmegen, 2006

List of Tables

List of Abbreviations

ASF	Arbeitsgemeinschaft Sozialdemokratischer Frauen
BGB	Bürgerliches Gesetzbuch (civil code)
CAP	common agricultural policy
CBI	Confederation of British Industry
CDA	Christen Democratisch Appèl
CDU	Christlich-Demokratische Union
CEEP	Confédération Européenne des Employeurs Publics
CFDT	Confédération française démocratique du travail
CGT	Confédération Générale du Travail
CNPF	Conseil National du Patronat Français
COPA	Comité des Organisations Professionnelles Agricoles de l'Union Européenne
Coreper	Committee of Permanent Representatives
CREW	Centre of Research on European Women
CSU	Christlich-Soziale Union
DG	Directorate-General (of the European Commission)
DGB	Deutscher Gewerkschaftsbund
EC	European Community
ECSC	European Coal and Steel Community
EEC	European Economic Community
EOC	Equal Opportunities Commission
EP	European Parliament
EPA	Equal Pay Act
ETUC	European Trade Union Confederation
EU	European Union
EU-15	Austria, Belgium, Britain, Denmark, Finland, France, Germany, Greece, Ireland, Italy, Luxembourg, the Netherlands, Portugal, Spain, Sweden
EURATOM	European Atomic Energy Community
EWL	European Women's Lobby
FDP	Freie Demokratische Partei
FGTB	Belgian socialist trade union
ICFTU	International Confederation of Free Trade Unions
ICSC	International Confederation of Christian Trade Unions
IGC	Intergovernmental Conference
ILO	International Labour Organization

ILO-100	ILO Convention No. 100 (Equal Pay)
MAE	Ministère des Affaires Etrangères
MEP	Member of European Parliament
MLF	Mouvement de la Libération des Femmes
MP	Member of Parliament
MVM	ManVrouwMaatschappij
NCCL	National Council for Civil Liberties
NVV	Nederlands Verbond van Vakverenigingen
PCF	Parti Communiste Français
PS	Parti Socialiste
PvdA	Partij van de Arbeid
QMV	qualified majority voting
RPR	Rassemblement pour la République
SAP	Social Action Program
SDA	Sex Discrimination Act
SER	Sociaal-Economische Raad
SPD	Sozialdemokratische Partei Deutschlands
TUC	Trade Union Congress
UN	United Nations
UNICE	Union of Industrial and Employers' Confederations of Europe
VVD	Volkspartij voor Vrijheid en Democratie

Chapter 1

Puzzling Policies: Gender and European Governance

The process of making and implementing gender policies within the European Union (EU)[1] constitutes a fascinating puzzle. In spite of feminist critiques of a 'European super-state' which supports a neoliberal slim-down of the welfare state and reduces gender issues to mere equality in the labour market, fifty years of EU gender policies have had quite some impact. 'I don't think that we would have agreed to this measure if we had known about the implications that it would have to the government now over the Equal Pay Act', remarked a British diplomat when in 1982 his country was declared guilty of non-compliance with European legislation (Pillinger 1992, 88). Germany amended its Constitution because 'Luxembourg' required it to do so. EU legislation and jurisprudence have spilled over beyond the realm of equal rights to include issues such as parental leave, pregnancy, positive action and sexual harassment. The Treaty of Amsterdam (1999) introduced the concept of gender mainstreaming and the commitment to incorporate a gender dimension into *all* EU policies and institutions.

In spite of a wealth of research on European 'women's policies' (Buckley and Anderson 1988; Elman 1996; Hoskyns 1996a; Liebert 2003; Rossilli 2000), many questions remain unanswered. Why has a neoliberal project, which was conceived to eliminate barriers for the free movement of goods, services, capital, and workers, gone on to develop policies that introduce new regulation? If women inside and outside the institutions are the main actors pushing for supranational gender equality policies, how can we explain the varying degrees of success of their actions? Why would states approve supranational agreements introducing ideas that clash with domestic frames and produce political resistance and economic costs? The underlying crucial question is how state and non-state actors define and defend their interests in a multi-tiered political system. We will address these questions, offering a theoretically guided empirical analysis of the process of making and implementing gender equality policies in and by the EU and four of its member states[2] between 1955 and 2005.

---

1 The Treaty on European Union (1993) established the European Union as the overarching structure for cooperation in Western Europe. When referring to the organization in general, I will use the current denomination EU, but in the empirical chapters describing events before 1993, the historical name European Economic Community (EEC) is used.

2 Britain, France, Germany and the Netherlands.

This chapter introduces the main questions and the tools we will use to look at them. First, the achievements in the field of gender equality are presented against the background of the low profile of 'social Europe' and the EU as a neoliberal project. The second section deals with flaws in mainstream integration theories. Next, the EU is investigated as a multi-tiered system with a specific identity. The fourth section presents the theoretical framework that enables us to deal with the questions mentioned above. The last section of Chapter 1 offers an overview of the subsequent chapters of the book.

Gender Equality Policies as a Theoretical Problem

The field of EU gender policies constitutes a puzzling case for at least three reasons. First, the achievements in this field contrast strongly with the poor development of EU social policy in general. Second, they do not seem to fit with a supposedly neoliberal project. Third, the history of gender equality has been characterized by ups and downs.

'Social Europe'

The first puzzle concerns the fact that gender equality policies[3] belong to the domain of social policy, where states are reluctant to accept supranational policymaking. After all, the welfare state is a construction typically rooted in national traditions and culture (Hantrais 1995). Research into how welfare states respond to globalization has shown a 'continued dominance of national institutional traditions' (Esping-Andersen 1996, 6).

Every policy change has potentially far-reaching financial consequences since in all member states spending on social security amounts to a significant percentage of total government spending.[4] In addition, it is not only governments that are involved, but employers, trade unions, and other public and private actors also have their parts to play in the development and implementation of social policy. As a result, proposals for policy change may easily threaten the positions, interests or ideas of certain groups and provoke resistance. States are, therefore, reluctant to accept supranational harmonization in this domain. They will prefer to avoid making binding international agreements and will rather approve symbolic policy in the form of non-binding instruments.

---

3 The terms 'gender equality policy' and 'equal rights policy' are used here for all policies that aim to eliminate discrimination based on sex by treating equal cases equally (such as equal pay for equal work) and to redress inequalities by treating disadvantaged groups 'unequally' (such as positive action programmes).

4 The expenditure of EU Member States (EU-15) on social protection as a share of GDP amounted to an average of 27.5 percent in 1999, with spending ranging from 33 percent in Sweden to 15 percent in Ireland (Commission 2002, 6).

And, indeed, when we examine the development of EU social policy, these expectations are confirmed. The member states 'jealously protect their prerogatives in social policy' and are reluctant to relinquish control over 'one of the most important remaining domains of national authority' (Leibfried and Pierson 1995, 46). The original ambition of achieving harmonization of national social policies was replaced in the 1980s by the aim of 'convergence'. In the 1990s, it was stripped down even further to the concept of 'active subsidiarity'. This left governments, employers and trade unions free to determine if (and how) they wanted to realize this 'convergence' (Hantrais 1995). In spite of recurrent public criticism of the poor social profile of the EU, for instance during the 2005 referenda on the Constitutional Treaty, social policy remains a predominantly national affair.

Gender equality policy, by contrast, is cited in the literature as an interesting exception to the meagre results of 'social Europe' (Leibfried and Pierson 1996). Far-reaching EU gender equality policies have been established, whereby 'the Community delivered a "shock" to national policy systems' (Mazey 1998, 131). What makes 'gender' different? Some researchers have argued that member states would not dare to reject a principle such as 'equal rights' (Milward 1992, 214). The implicit assumption is that in the area of equal rights, as opposed to other social policies, the 'ideological benefits' offset the economic costs. We will show in the empirical chapters that this reasoning is incorrect. It has not been high principles and noble aims which have dominated negotiations, but the material and immaterial consequences of policy change.

In fact, every change in the socio-economic rights of women (equal pay, access to the labour market, entitlement to social security and pension schemes) has had far-reaching economic consequences and has been heavily contested by previously privileged groups who have felt they stood to lose out. Even if there were ideological benefits to be gained, these might inspire symbolic policy making, but they could not explain the approval and implementation of strong and binding legislation. So what makes gender different? We will come back to this in the concluding chapter of the book.

Common Market Europe

The achievements in the field of gender equality also contrast strongly with the EU as a neoliberal project, conceived by transnational business and political elites. At first glance, liberalization and privatization conflict with the notion of regulating gender, but a closer look reveals that EU gender policies have remained limited to the labour market.

The EU 'excludes most of women's lives, in particular, the complexity of the connections between family, work, welfare, and the labour market' (Hanmer 1996, 143). EU policies focus on equality between women and men, deliberately ignoring underlying structural differences that distort the outcome of equality policies and mean only limited benefits for the women targeted. EU gender policies have been justified by referring to the ensuing benefits for the internal market. For instance, the

EU tackles sexual harassment in order to make workers perform better, not because it cares for all citizens. We might conclude that the way in which the EU deals with gender fits its neoliberal identity rather well. However, even if labour market concerns explain the approval of regulation in favour of equal rights, they do not explain the binding character of this regulation nor its scope, introducing novel concepts against the preferences of member states. In the concluding chapter of this book, we will formulate three complementary explanations of this apparent anomaly.

Ups and Downs

The third intriguing aspect of the history of EU gender equality policy is that it has been characterized by very mixed progress. Between 1955 and 2005, both the output of the policy process and the implementation of policies have varied considerably. We can observe a fluctuation between periods of progress and stagnation (Ostner and Lewis 1995; Hoskyns 1996b). This oscillation between standstill and progress raises the question of how to account for policy development in this domain.

Several authors credit the women's movement with the success of EU policies (Elman 1996; Hoskyns 1996a), as well as the women in the EU arena and the EU institutions, the so-called femocrats or *feminae in machina* (Reinalda 1997). Why then has their activism met with such varying degrees of success? Intensive pressure has not always resulted in progress, and progress has not always been the result of intense pressure. The EU has appeared to open up certain possibilities while blocking others, which has resulted in a pattern of governance different to a strictly national or strictly intergovernmental one. As Lene Hansen points out, 'How to negotiate the relationship between women and the nation-state takes a new and interesting spin when conducted in the context of the EU' (Hansen 2000, 131). Therefore, the EU needs to be analyzed as a multi-tiered political system, in which state and non-state actors pursuing power, ideas and interests interact and produce outcomes that generally reflect a mixture of conflicting ideas and unintended consequences.

Gender and Integration Theory: Alternative Approaches?

From its very beginning, the European integration process has been the focus of intense theoretical debates. From a chronological perspective, different waves of theorizing may be differentiated, which developed in parallel with the progress and stagnation of the integration process itself. During the 1950s and 1960s, Ernst Haas' neo-functionalism and Stanley Hoffmann's intergovernmentalism occupied central stage. The 1970s and 1980s have been portrayed as a 'Dark Age' for integration theory (Caporaso and Keeler 1995). During the 1990s, new strands of functionalism (Sandholtz and Stone Sweet 1998) and intergovernmentalism (Moravcsik 1993; 1998) manifested themselves. Comparative and institutionalist approaches came to the foreground (Marks et al. 1996; Pierson 1996). Most recently, constructivist and discursive approaches have developed (Christiansen et al. 2001; Schimmelfennig 2001; Diez 1999).[5]

In spite of this multiplicity, these mainstream theories are unsatisfactory from a feminist point of view. Feminist scholars rightly criticize integration theories for their gender-blindness, their treatment of states as black boxes and their rudimentary view of power. For this reason, integration theories fail to answer convincingly the questions raised in this book. Approaches belonging to an alternative paradigm could offer a possible way out (Hoskyns 2004). However, in order to enable and enrich the debate with the mainstream, we will follow the suggestion by Annika Kronsell and investigate the possibility of including these critiques in mainstream integration theory (Kronsell 2005).

Intergovernmentalism

Intergovernmentalist approaches used to suffer from 'black boxism' as they took the unitary state as the central actor without wondering where the preferences of these states came from. Moravcsik has opened up the black box, concentrating on the way in which states defend the interests of the most powerful interest groups (transnational industry) in 'grand bargains' during the negotiations about treaty reform (Moravcsik 1993; Moravcsik 1998). His concept of the state remains one-dimensional. It is no longer a black box, but he reduces it to a 'serving hatch' for powerful interests. This closes the arena for other interests and it obscures the nature of the state and the origins of its interests.

Kronsell rightly criticizes intergovernmentalism for reproducing existing gender relations, as it takes gender power relations as given and ignores the fact that men represent 'the state' much more frequently than women (Kronsell 2005, 1025). We need to investigate state identity in order to understand state interests and varying levels of sensitivity to accusations of sexism. The question of representation becomes relevant in this book when we want to explain why it is so difficult to get certain issues on the agenda. Chapter 6 will come back to this. In the empirical chapters, we see why in 1956, an all-male cast discussed the issue of women's pay and how women made a difference when they got a voice in 'Brussels' (1974), started to be better represented in the European Parliament (1979), national governments and the top levels of the Commission (1990s).

Domestic Approach

Kronsell makes a rather positive assessment of the domestic approach, because it takes the interplay between interests as a starting point. Yet, it does not seem promising to consider women's interests as 'specific interests', as is done so often, the corollary of which is that the 'common interest' is male (Kronsell 2005, 1026).

5 For good overviews of theories concerning regional integration, see Rosamond 2000; Wiener and Diez 2004.

It is therefore necessary to widen the analysis of the domestic level to include not only specific women's groups but also their links with other actors and to take into account the varying sensitivity of a state towards the arguments and pressure from these groups. Mainstream domestic approaches often fail to theorize the crucial link between the domestic level and the supranational level. The activities of supra- and transnational actors supporting women's interests may mean that governments experience pressure from both directions and are caught in a very uncomfortable 'pincer action'. In the next section, the approach to the EU as a multi-tiered system is elaborated, aiming at a more encompassing view of EU politics than focusing on the domestic level.

Neo-functionalism

Neo-functionalism, a third strand of mainstream theorizing, has always suffered from two weaknesses: it lacks explanatory value and it ignores power. The progress of integration is explained with the concept of 'spill-over', the expansion of supranational regulation into an ever-increasing number of areas. At first sight, this seems a convincing argument, as European integration started with coal and steel, and nowadays covers almost every policy domain. Even in the field of gender equality, where a major complaint is that EU policies are limited to the workplace, some 'spill-over' has recently taken place (see Chapter 5).

Unfortunately, neo-functionalism fails to explain why 'spill-over' occurs in some domains rather than in others. A purely functional explanation – saying that where cross-border problems and external effects occur, supranational regulation will develop – would predict that issues like cross-border railway transport, purchase of military equipment, and residence permits for third-country women who are victim of domestic violence should have been settled long ago. Sometimes we see 'spill-back', like in agriculture, where a certain re-nationalization takes place. 'Spill-over' does not offer an explanation but needs explanation itself. This explanation has to include the notion of relative power: power between and within states; between states and the Commission; within the Commission; and between all the actors in the European arena.

Multi-level Governance

The multi-level governance approach is more a framework or a metaphor (Rosamond 2000, 113) than a theory, as it seems to prioritize description above explanation. It stresses the complexity and variability of the EU's policy system, where 'states are melded into the multi-level polity by their leaders and the actions of numerous subnational and supranational actors' (Marks et al. 1996, 371). Although this seems to offer room to include women's actions and interests, multi-level governance fails to specify under which conditions these actions and interests are influential. It lacks an explanatory mechanism and focuses on technical processes, ignoring the power politics hidden inside them. Therefore, it does not conceive of a hierarchy between the levels or between the actors.

We prefer to conceptualize the EU as a multi-tiered system, separating the tiers for analytical purposes. The state level is hierarchically superior to the supranational and the subnational levels and the state is the central actor. Clearly, this does not imply that the state is fully in control. It is precisely the multiple tiers which constrain states and enable other actors to squeeze it from below (by domestic actors) and from within (by femocrats), but simultaneously from above (by European and global institutions) and from the side (by other states, transnational actors).

Our toolbox will also open up the state to identify asymmetries in the state-society relationship, based on power and identity. These structures vary across time and between states. They explain the amount of pressure necessary for non-state domestic and transnational actors to become influential and the sensitivity of a state to such pressure. This enables us to explain under which conditions state interests correspond with (dominant) women's interests – and why they mostly do not.

Analysing the EU: Multiple Tiers and Multiple Identities

The Nature of the Beast

Literature on the EU often demonstrates confusion concerning the 'nature of the beast' (Risse-Kappen 1996, 53); in the words of a former Dutch minister, Europe is like a giraffe, 'an animal difficult to define, but easy to recognise' (Beyen 1968, 220). Some scholars tend to define the EU as a unique entity, as in 'The EU has developed into a unique form of political space' (Hansen 2000, 131–2). 'Uniqueness', however, is not an intrinsic characteristic of a phenomenon, but the result of a decision on theoretical grounds, in the same way that phenomena are theoretically similar. '[S]imilarity, and with it repetition, always presuppose the adoption of *a point of view*: some similarities or repetitions will strike us if we are interested in one problem, and others if we are interested in another problem' (Popper 1980ed., 420–22 [italics in original]). Therefore, treating the EU as a *sui generis* phenomenon does not take us very far.

Others consider the EU a 'state-like entity'. Still, the EU clearly is not a state since it lacks sovereignty, the crucial feature defining a political collective as 'state'. The EU 'does not claim a sovereign status and is not recognized as sovereign state by the other members of international society' (Werner and De Wilde 2001, 303) – nor by its citizens. Member states 'have handed over powers to a degree unprecedented in the history of international organizations', but they continue to claim their sovereignty before domestic and international audiences and those claims continue to be recognized (Werner and De Wilde 2001, 302). Therefore, we prefer to define the EU as an international organization composed of states and non-state actors, rather than as a state.

Of course, in many regards the EU differs from other international organizations. Here, the degree of supranationalism and intergovernmentalism is a useful gauge, as it clarifies the relationships between states and other actors within the EU as compared to such relationships in other international organizations.

Intergovernmentalism–Supranationalism Three principles characterize intergovernmental policymaking. Representatives of governments take all decisions; binding decisions require unanimity and bind only those who approve them, and finally, governments are responsible for the implementation and enforcement of decisions (Kapteyn-VerLoren van Themaat 1995, 1–2). Supranationalism comes into play when these principles are to some extent abandoned.

The first principle concerns the decision making process by state representatives. In the EU, decision making is becoming less and less intergovernmental. It is not purely supranational either, as decision making without any involvement from governmental representatives is rare and limited to technical decisions within previously agreed-upon policy frames.

The European Commission (Commission) formulates the draft proposals which form the basis of most EU legislation. Governments do not consider the Commission an intergovernmental institution, as they do not command its initiatives and actions. Yet, the Commission is not a purely supranational stronghold of 'Eurocrats' either: there is one representative for each member state and its staff is composed of officials with national and party affiliations. Although the Commission is expected to be impartial in its dealings with individual member states (Art. 213 EC), and will in general respect this rule, the preferences of individual Commissioners and officials reflect the interests of the member states from which they originate (Hix 2005). For that reason, feminists welcomed in 1995 the 'Scandinavian enlargement', introducing Swedish and Finnish Commissioners.

Until 1993, the Council of Ministers (Council), a body composed of national ministers or their representatives, took decisions concerning new legislation. Since the Maastricht Treaty (1993) and the Amsterdam Treaty (1999),[6] decision making has acquired an increasingly supranational character, as legislation covered by the co-decision procedure needs to be approved jointly by the Council and the European Parliament (EP). Shared decision making by government representatives and members of the EP has become normal practice in most policy areas concerning the regulation of the single European market, partially including social policy and gender equality (see Chapter 5).

The second principle of intergovernmentalism is the right to veto. The principle of unanimous voting guided decision making in the Council until 1987, when the

6 Treaties are dated with the year in which they came into force, after having been ratified by the parliaments (and, where required by national law, approved by popular referendum) of all member states. However, the heads of state and government have reached agreement some years before. The negotiations in Maastricht were concluded in December 1991, in Amsterdam in June 1997.

first treaty reform (Single European Act) introduced voting by qualified majority (QMV – a weighted voting system) for issues concerning the single market. When a majority in the Council of Ministers approves a European 'law', even member states that voted against it are bound to implement it.

Until 1993, it was possible for a single state to block decision making in the field of gender equality. This is what happened during the 1980s, when the UK threatened to use its veto every time the Commission proposed a new binding directive on aspects of social policy like parental leave or the rights of part-time workers. In its protocol on social policy, the Maastricht Treaty replaced unanimity with QMV in most areas of social policy, including equal rights and equal opportunities. The protocol became a full part of the Treaty of Amsterdam, when UK Prime Minister Tony Blair took a new stance on European and social matters from that of his Conservative predecessors. We will elaborate on the consequences of the shift from unanimity to QMV on gender equality policies in Chapter 5.

Exclusive state responsibility for the implementation process constitutes the third principle of intergovernmentalism. National authorities are responsible for translating EU regulation into national legislation, but the Commission and the European Court (Court) have far-reaching competences to compel them to do so. The Court has even deepened the impact of European legislation beyond what member states agreed in the Treaty of Rome. Several landmark rulings have established the direct effect and the supremacy of European law. Without pressure by the Commission and the Court, the implementation record in the field of gender equality policies would show even more serious lacunae than it does (Van der Vleuten 2005).

If we place the EU on a continuum between supranationalism and intergovernmentalism, based on these characteristics of decision making, voting methods and enforcement we will put it towards the supranationalist end. The EU is increasingly a supranational international organization, binding states in a way that other international organizations are unable to do. The extent to which the EU binds states raises the question of why member states have agreed to be bound to such an extent. Answering this question requires an analysis of the EU as a multi-tiered system within which states are still the major actors, but other actors 'below' (within) and 'above' the state also influence and constrain state behaviour to such an extent that policy outcomes differ from outcomes in national or interstate political systems.

The State in a Multi-tiered Political System In this book, we take the state as a central actor. This is not meant to reflect a normative preference and still less to suggest that the actual policy outcomes are those intended by a state. It is simply a useful methodological device, as we want to explain policy making in the EU arena. In this arena, the state occupies centre stage because in the end, the state is the actor making and enforcing rules that others have to respect. It is the focus of pressure from a host of other actors. Indeed, it is itself the enabler of such pressure from other actors, through the granting or denying of access and resources. In short, it would be difficult to understand the outcomes of European policy making without taking the state as a central actor.

Of course, we must also take into account the behaviour of other actors in order to explain policy outcomes in this multi-tiered system. We will deal with the role of sub-national and transnational actors, and with preference formation and pressure from the Commission and the Court. A multi-tiered political system is not just a 'bargaining forum' for governments: it is a pile of interconnected decision-making arenas enabling non-state actors to 'sandwich' a state.

The supranational level offers new opportunities for women to organize politically, because the EU institutions (EP, Commission and Court) offer information and access at a level above the domestic level. Political processes transcending national borders enable women to organize as a transnational actor, just as global policy making in the United Nations framework has enabled women to organize as a global actor (Meyer and Prügl 1999). But multi-tiered politics have raised new barriers to non-state actors as well, since organizing at different levels simultaneously requires important resources. In contrast to more powerful actors many women's organizations lack the necessary resources to benefit from the new opportunities.

Power In fact, power[7] is as omnipresent in multi-tiered politics as in national or interstate politics. It should not come as a surprise, therefore, that preferences and policy outcomes reflect unequal power relations between and within states, between state and non-state actors as well as between state and supra-state actors. Feminist scholars criticize the EU as patriarchal, reproducing the public-private divide that characterizes domestic politics. Leaving aside the normative issue, it follows from power relations in this multi-tiered political system that EU politics reproduce the public-private divide.

The EU is a system where member states and their (predominately male) representatives have laid out the basic structure. It consequently replicates their power positions and ideological frames. It will prioritize the concerns of the major member states, France and Germany in the first place. Multi-tiered politics also replicate power relations among women. The 'white women in paid employment' who dominate domestic politics also dominate European politics, including the European Women's Lobby (Hoskyns 1991).[8]

Multiple Identities

Accepting, then, that the EU is 'less than a state but more than a bargaining forum for states', the next question is surely where the preferences of this hybrid actor come

---

7 Power is understood here as a structure (Strange 1988) and as a means to further ends. For discussion, see Kronsell 2005.

8 When in 2000, because of the Race Discrimination Directive, black and migrant women turned out to be potentially better protected against discrimination than white women were, this caused quite a stir. It was used as an argument to improve sex discrimination legislation (see Chapter 5).

from. The Commission has sometimes taken bold initiatives in the field of gender equality, raising issues that were new for member state governments (childcare, sexual harassment). However, at other times it has been rather conservative, avoiding potential conflicts with the Council. Similarly, the Court has at times promoted gender equality, starting with the *Defrenne* cases, but in other rulings has taken a restrictive view, for instance on maternity leave (*Hoffmann*) and positive action (*Kalanke*) (see Chapters 4–5). No wonder there is disagreement when assessing EU preferences.

The EU is often portrayed as an actor that is more ‘women-friendly’ than its member states, as following a ‘pro-women course’ (Hansen 2000, 131), and encouraging member states ‘to pursue controversial policies which they may have otherwise been reluctant to adopt’ (Elman 1996, 10). Nevertheless, the EU has also been criticized for preferring ‘women-unfriendly’ liberalization and privatization to the strengthening of the welfare state, and for defending mainly the rights of workers as opposed to the rights of citizens.

When accounting for EU policy preferences, some feminist scholars point to its gendered character. However, as Jo Shaw, a feminist legal expert, argues, ‘simplistic positions seeing the EU as one-dimensionally protective of or hostile to the interests of women’ are of little assistance (Shaw 2000, 425). Even though the gendered character of the EU helps to explain the limited scope of gender equality policies, such an essentialist view cannot explain why EU institutions oscillate between ‘women-friendly’ and ‘women-unfriendly’ preferences. The question of how to explain EU preference formation remains yet unanswered.

The Identity of the EU A starting point is recognizing that the EU has a collective identity, in the same way each member state has an identity. The concept of gender equality resonates quite differently with the identities of individual states and of the EU itself, resulting in varying preferences.

A collective identity ‘refers to positive identification with the welfare of another such that the other is seen as a cognitive extension of the self, rather than independent’ (Wendt 1994, 386). It can develop when actors interact frequently and processes of socialization take place. The collective identity will be rooted in a shared experience in the past. Each state also has its own basis of identity building, rooted in important past events, both negative and positive, and enhanced and reproduced by the collective memory of the nation. The state confirms its identity every time it legitimizes its behaviour with reference to this identity (Van der Vleuten 2005).

The collective identity of the EU is rooted in the experience of two World Wars and the strong desire to avoid a third one by integrating the heavy industries of Germany and France (Lieshout 1999). Market integration and neoliberal ideas dominate all EU policy making, not only as ends in themselves but also as means of preserving peace by enabling economic recovery under supranational and interstate scrutiny and through the institutionalization of mutual interdependence.

This neoliberal identity constructed upon fundamental security concerns has enabled and constrained policy making in the domain of gender equality. It has enabled policy making concerning all areas linked in some way to non-discrimination in the labour market or to the improvement of working conditions. It has constrained policy making owing to 'the liberal understanding of equality as sameness' (Elman 1998, 225) and the inability to conceive of 'difference'. The dominant identity of the EU as 'a single market without borders' has also limited the scope of its policies. Citizens within EU borders are classified as 'workers' or 'others'. Policies mainly concern the rights of workers and ignore the interests of and consequences for the 'others'. Workers are treated as a gender-neutral category. This approach ignores structural differences between groups of workers that are rooted in their private lives. The 'others' have relatively seldom been the object of EU policy making.[9] The Maastricht Treaty incorporated the concept of the European citizen, but the division of labour between the state and the European Union remains clear; European citizenship is complementary to national citizenship and offers a very limited set of rights.

Interestingly, the European Court has fostered an identity slightly different from the dominant 'market' idea. In its interpretations of treaty articles and secondary legislation it has focused on the underlying aim of European integration, namely promoting peace and progress among all citizens. Therefore, it has very carefully and gradually – in order to avoid upsetting constitutional courts and governments – developed jurisprudence concerning fundamental human rights (Weiler 1999). This has benefited women in several cases, especially after the Court declared equality between women and men a fundamental human right in *Defrenne III* (see Chapter 4).

National Identities The apparently 'technical' identity of the market had the advantage of uniting countries with very different cultural identities through their common feature of a market economy, only excluding purely state-led economies (Eastern and Central European countries). Different national identities persist alongside this 'common market identity' and colour the behaviour of member states. Member states will value the saliency of an issue and the costs of a supranational policy proposal differently according to their identity. The outcomes of EU policy making are, therefore, not always consistent with its own 'market' identity and reveal the more profound concerns of the (major) member states.

The national identity of France has two facets that influence its behaviour in the EU. The first facet is constituted by the principles of the French Revolution – liberty, equality and fraternity. Equality is thus part of its identity, defined as the right of every citizen to be treated equally. We will see in the following chapters that France introduced legislation to guarantee equal rights for women and men relatively smoothly. Other concepts are less easy to accommodate. In spite of the value France attributes to the use of French language (the famous 'francophonie'), there is no French equivalent for the concept of 'gender mainstreaming'.

The second facet is that, since the Revolution, France feels itself to have '*le devoir de servir d'exemple*', having the duty to serve as a role model for all civilized nations (Kessler 1999, 12–13; Marcussen et al. 1999). This has inspired French

9 Some exceptions are the rules for free movement of students and the elderly.

actions especially during its periods of EU presidency. It has also made France vulnerable to accusations of incorrect implementation of social policies.

Germany does not derive its prestige from revolutionary ideals but from the protection of the fundamental rights of its citizens (Knill 2001). A democratic-constitutional identity has replaced the negative national identity produced by the Nazi regime (EURONAT 2005, 17). A crucial aspect of the German *Rechtsstaat* is the counterbalancing of central state authority by other strong actors (*Länder*, corporatism, a strong judicial review system) to avoid abuses of power. Therefore, Germany is sensitive to accusations of violating the fundamental rights of its citizens.

Nazi-past and consequent reluctance towards state interventionism make it difficult to justify interventions in the private sphere. The strong position of employers and trade unions constitutes an obstacle for the promotion of gender equality, as the role of women in the corporatist arena is not a strong one, and the state can point to the statutory respect that it owes management and labour as a justification for tolerating non-compliance.

Based on its glorious past during the Golden Age, the Netherlands identifies itself with the idea of an 'open country' for goods (trade), people and ideas (tolerance). The political system is an 'open system'; issues that are extremely controversial in other countries – like abortion, homosexuality and prostitution – have not been taboo in the political arena but openly debated, resulting in relatively 'tolerant' policies. New actors like the women's movement have been smoothly integrated (or absorbed) into politics, unlike in Germany where formal politics used to be more remote from grass roots activism. Nevertheless, the open borders have functioned as barriers to improving women's labour market position. Low women's wages and women as flexible reserve troops for the labour market served better the national interest than equal pay and equal rights.

Britain is characterized by 'being different'. It is an island, a 'natural fortress with its distinct institutions and way of life' (EURONAT 2005, 16; 126). Europe is viewed as 'somewhere else', a place and entity to which they do not really belong. This has resulted in enduring opposition to 'Europe' and supranational ('Continental') politics. In addition, there is no strong idea of 'the state'. In contrast with Continental states, self-organization and the market have dominated historically, resulting in a 'state-less society' (Knill 2001). Therefore, realizing gender equality through state intervention does not easily match British state identity.

Conclusion

In order to explain preference formation, policy outcomes and implementation in the EU, it is crucial to analyse the EU as a multi-tiered system that creates specific patterns of inclusion and exclusion for different actors. These actors interact in order to defend their interests. The system reflects and reproduces the power relations and identities of the actors involved. In the light of this argument, it is not a useful enterprise to try defining the EU as intrinsically good or bad for women. Neither the

EU and its member states nor women in the EU have a single identity or specific set of interests to defend.

The Toolbox: Power, Pressure and Identities

In order to explain the development of gender equality policies in the EU, we have to investigate the decision making process as it evolves within a multi-tiered system, involving actors at the sub-national (society), national (government) and international (states, supranational institutions, transnational groups) levels.

The political process in the EU consists of three stages: the preference formation phase at the (sub-)national level, the negotiating phase at the supranational level, and the implementation phase of joint decisions at the (sub-)national level. After the latter phase, the outputs feed back to the next round of preference formation. For analytical purposes, we will discuss the phases separately, as if they neatly follow one another; although a 'garbage can' model may offer a more adequate description of political practice, such a model is less helpful for explanatory purposes.

Preference Formation – The Domestic Tier

It seems obvious: 'Variance in preferences must first be assessed and explained before an assessment of strategic interaction is conducted' (Moravcsik 1997, 127), but theories about international decision making frequently ignore this requirement. A standard criticism of mainstream approaches in international relations, such as neo-realism and neo-institutionalism, is precisely that they assume that states have fixed preferences. States are so-called 'utility maximizers', searching for the highest utility, but these theories do not seek to explain what utility a state wants to maximize nor why states' preferences change.

What do states want when they engage in negotiations in 'Brussels'? When in 1975, the French government had to formulate a preference on the Commission proposal for a directive on equal treatment, what did it want? Where did its preference come from? As we cannot enter the heads of the negotiators to find out what moves them, a tool has been devised to deduce these preferences and explain what they wanted and why. For this, we need to assume that actors are rational actors. The assumption does not say that an actor is rational or that it always behaves in a rational way. It just supposes that actors act as if they order the options they have at their disposal according to the perceived 'costs and benefits' of each option, and that they will prefer the option with the highest perceived benefits or lowest costs.

Costs and benefits depend not only on material calculations, but also on the actor's ideas about what is valuable and appropriate. These ideas are rooted in their identity and the way they perceive themselves. The identity of an actor may make a certain option less attractive not because of the costs attached to it, but because it is not compatible with this identity: it is simply 'not done' for the actor. The action is inconceivable because it would damage the credibility of the actor and thus rob the actor of her identity.

Domestic Costs and Benefits If there is a policy proposal on the table that has originated at the supranational level, the preference of a member state concerning this proposal can be derived from the estimated economic and ideological costs of the required policy change and from the pressure that domestic actors have exercised. The more costly a proposal is estimated, the less attractive it becomes.

Why would a state support a 'cheap' proposal and oppose a 'costly' proposal? We can assume that every government aims at least to remain in power. Therefore, it will be sensitive to pressure and will try to avoid costly policies that would undermine its support base in society. A government not only wants to remain in power, it also wants to realize certain ideas. It will support 'ideologically cheap' proposals that confirm its identity and strengthen its prestige. However, in the domain of gender equality, we see the puzzling phenomenon of states approving economically and ideologically costly policies. Have they made a mistake in their calculations? Let us first elaborate on the factor of 'costs'.

The economic costs can be assessed according to the anticipated consequences of policy change on the relevant aspects of the national economy such as the GDP, the export/import ratio, price development, employment, labour costs, and social security expenditure. The economic costs of the obligation to pay women and men the same wage for the same work, for instance, vary according to the gap between men's and women's wages. Due to state worries about competitiveness, the economic consequences as compared to the economic consequences for other member states are relevant as well.

Ideological costs may vary, depending on the extent to which a supranational proposal corresponds to the ideology of the government. When a supranational proposal contains ideas that clash with those embedded in existing or planned domestic policies, the proposal would require costly ideological reframing in order to gain approval. The idea that women have a right to receive the same pay as men who do the same work clashed with the Dutch idea that women did not need the same wage as men because they did not have to feed a family with their wage (p. 39). Therefore, equal pay was ideologically costly for the Dutch government. A government will not support a proposal which requires ideological reframing of its policies.

Domestic Pressure To the extent that a proposal is perceived to entail higher economic and ideological costs, a government will be less prepared to support it. A government, however, does not function in a vacuum. The pressure from domestic actors will influence its preference. Employers and trade unions, political parties, traditional women's organizations, autonomous women's groups, advisory bodies and experts may exert pressure on the government in favour or against the proposal. As a government wants to remain in power, it cannot ignore such pressure if it comes from the political party or parties from which it is comprised and their (potential) electorate, especially if elections are planned in the near future. The British Labour governments could not ignore pressure from trade unions and women's organizations, whereas Conservative governments were not sensitive to it at all (Chapter 4).

A government also needs the cooperation of domestic public and private actors for the implementation of supranational decisions. Because others (aggrieved citizens and companies, national and supranational courts) hold the state ultimately responsible in case of negligence (Prechal 1995), the state has an interest in making sure it has sufficient domestic support beforehand. If a government is concerned that a parliamentary majority or a majority of the population could reject a European proposal, it will attempt to obtain concessions during the negotiations at the supranational level.

Power and Pressure The strength of societal pressure is related to the expected focus of the costs and benefits of the proposed policy (Moravcsik 1993). If policy change will clearly affect a specific group, this group is likely to exert pressure. However, it is expensive to do so effectively in a multi-level system which is, even more than a single-level system, biased in favour of actors with considerable resources expressed as financial means, specialized information, a high degree of mobilization, and privileged access to the government apparatus. At the national level, pressure in favour of gender equality is more effective when women's advocacy groups are informed in time, have direct links to political parties in parliament and government, offer specific expertise and innovative knowledge and are able to mobilize other actors (members of parliament, officials and trade unions) as well.

To influence EU politics, women's advocacy groups also need direct links with the supranational level: contacts with the Commission, especially the Direction in charge; with members of the EP; and with representatives of their government in the *Comité des Représentants Permanents* (Coreper). They need access to transnational expert committees and have to coordinate their actions transnationally in order to increase the effectiveness of their pressure (Keck and Sikkink 1998; Risse-Kappen 1995). They have to overcome their structurally weak power position in an arena which is dominated by actors with a strong power position (export-oriented business) and by relatively homogeneous groups with a high mobilization capacity (farmers, trade unions in transport, ports and steel). 'Women' constitute a heterogeneous group, which is difficult to mobilize. In addition, as the European common market did not seem to concern women's lives, mobilization has been far more difficult in the European arena than in the global arena. The UN addressing issues beyond the world of paid work and having an identity as an organization of nations (peoples) instead of markets has attracted more organized pressure from women's organizations than the EU.

The power position of society vis-à-vis the state also influences how effective pressure will be. Two kinds of power are relevant here: prestige and internal power. Prestige is part of the power position of a state with regard to the nation and to other states. The sources of prestige are state-specific, since they are linked to national identity (see p. 12). A state will be more or less vulnerable to pressure in favour of a proposal or against it, depending on its national identity. Keck and Sikkink show that in the realm of human rights, '(...) certain aspects of national identity or discourse may make some states vulnerable to pressures' (Keck and Sikkink 1998, 118–9). The French government is eager to defend its prestige as a social role model and could not bear to be the first state condemned to pay a fine because of non-compliance with a European equality directive (p. 122). The German government was vulnerable to accusations that it did not respect the fundamental rights of its citizens (p. 123), while the Dutch government is particularly vulnerable to accusations of hurting trade interests.

Internal power concerns the relative power position of the government vis-à-vis society. It relates to the balance between government and parliament and the balance between government and interest groups (pluralist or corporatist interest group system). If the government has a strong position, societal actors must apply much pressure to influence the preferences of the government. The relative power position of a government is strong if it commands a stable parliamentary majority and interest groups do not enjoy privileged access (pluralist as opposed to corporatist system). If the distribution of power is more equal (minority government, corporatist system) or becomes unstable (dissent among the parliamentary majority, strikes, upcoming elections), the government becomes more sensitive to societal pressure. German governments could not afford to interfere with employers' and trade unions autonomy as opposed to British governments, owing to the structurally weaker position of German governments (p. 13). Therefore, these characteristics enable us to differentiate between governments and across time in order to explain under which conditions a state is able to resist domestic and supranational pressure.

The previous argument does not mean that a government with a weakened internal power position will be an obliging messenger for societal interests. Such a state can utilize a supranational agreement to make policy changes at the national level for which it would not have the means without this supranational pressure, real or suggested ('Brussels made us do it'). In 1956–7, the Mollet government strategically used 'European pressure' to obtain approval with liberalization of the French market (p. 49). The closed character of the process of supranational policy formation makes it easier for a state to approve an agreement which deviates from what the interest groups might otherwise deem acceptable.

Negotiations – The Global and the Supranational Tiers

The EU does not float in a neutral environment. It is part of the wider global system, which is characterized by material and social structures that constrain and enable the behaviour of all actors, including states, subnational and supranational actors and the EU as an organization.

Global Anarchy, Regional Identity The global system is anarchical in the sense that it does not have an agency that can enforce compliance with agreements by all actors, even the most powerful ones. Every state has to take care of its relative power position in order to be able to survive in this system. This implies that relative power relations are important, especially when changes occur in these relations. International instability and uncertainty are valued negatively, as they make it harder to find out what the better option is (Lieshout 1995).

The influence of these structural characteristics on the behaviour of states is not constant. It varies across time and between regions. Interaction processes between states constitute a 'filter' that may soften the effects of instability in the global system (Van der Vleuten 2001). When a state is member of an international organization like the EU, it is less sensitive to external changes and instability, due to the filter effect. The direct environment of such a state remains relatively predictable. If external changes threaten to weaken the position of the international organization, the member states will approve new joint policies to strengthen the relative power position of the organization and consequently their own power position.

We will see that the member states have taken such initiatives every time the position of the EU in the world seemed to be seriously weakened or destabilized (in 1972, in 1985 and 1990) and that each time such initiatives have opened a window of opportunity for social policy and gender equality.

Preferences and Power in EU Negotiations The preferences with which a state enters EU negotiations are the result of a calculation the government has made in the light of the economic and ideological costs of a proposal and pressure from societal actors for or against the proposal. The higher the expected costs or benefits of a proposal, the stronger the intensity of the preference becomes. During the negotiations, the state 'confronts' its preference with the preferences of other member states and other relevant actors (Commission, transnational lobbies, supranational experts, EP) in an institutional context with specific intergovernmental and supranational characteristics. The preferences of states, the intensity of these preferences, the relative power positions of states, and the institutions, together determine the outcome of the negotiations.

The 'real engine' for the negotiations is Coreper, a – literally – permanent representation of every member state (Hix 2005).[10] These representatives liaise intensively with their own national level, the supranational institutions and other delegations (Kerremans 1996).

Preferences, Power and Unanimity In principle, a state prefers to impose its own policy norm on all others and to prevent a higher or lower norm from becoming established as European 'law'. After all, a higher European norm would imply costly modification of national policy, while a lower European norm would result in a costly competitive disadvantage (Hix 2005). The probability that a state will nevertheless

10 In the Coreper working groups, approximately 70 percent of Council business is agreed, the permanent representatives themselves deal with 15–20 percent and only the most controversial issues, the remaining 10–15 percent, have to be resolved by the Council of Ministers (Hayes-Renshaw and Wallace 1997).

approve higher or lower norms depends primarily on its power position in relation to the other member states.

When the Council of Ministers votes according to the unanimity procedure,[11] the relative power position of a state determines whether it can threaten to veto the proposal. The material power of a state includes variables such as gross national product, military power, demographic characteristics, geographical location, climate, and available natural resources (Lieshout 1999). Its 'immaterial' power is constituted by its prestige. Large states have a stronger bargaining position than smaller states with an open economy. These more vulnerable states have in general the most to gain from European agreements. They are therefore more likely to make concessions on specific agreements and could prefer almost any agreement to no agreement at all.

By contrast, if the participation of a member state is crucial to the success of European cooperation (Britain, France and Germany) and this state has an attractive unilateral alternative, it will take a very demanding position during the negotiations. It will threaten to cast a veto in order to arrive at a decision at the level of the 'minimum common denominator', that is, a decision that goes no further than what the most reluctant partner is prepared to accept (Haas 1964, 111). If the state is in no danger of being excluded from the other advantages of the organization, the most reluctant state might also prefer constructive abstention ('opt-out'). This opt-out strategy leaves other member states the possibility of making an agreement that is above the minimum common denominator. As Britain in 1991 could not accept a treaty including a strong social chapter whereas Germany and France could not accept a treaty without it, and British participation was not essential for the potential success of monetary union, the impasse was solved by a British opt-out (p. 141).

Preferences, Power and QMV If the Council decides by QMV instead of unanimity, coalition formation is essential to reach or block a decision. In this procedure, relative power is also an important asset. Despite the weighting of votes in favour of the smaller member states, the larger states simply have more votes and need less coalition partners to build a blocking minority or create a majority (Hix 2005).

If the blocking coalition is more reluctant to accept the negotiation proposal than the other member states, it will prevent an agreement above the level of the minimum common denominator. If, by contrast, the blocking coalition prefers a higher norm than the one proposed by the other member states, this could result in an upgrading of the norm, thus imposing higher costs on the other states than they had initially been ready to accept.

Intensity of Preferences Not only is the relative power position relevant here, but also the intensity of preference. The negotiating position of a state with an intense

11 Until the Treaty of Maastricht (1993), all decisions concerning gender equality were taken by unanimity with the exception of the directive on pregnancy and maternity, which was presented as a health and safety issue and therefore had a different treaty base. Since 'Maastricht', for some decisions QMV applies, for others unanimity (see Chapter 5).

preference is relatively weak (Moravcsik 1993). A state with an intense preference in favour of a specific agreement will not risk a failure to reach agreement and will be ready to make concessions in order to save it. Depending on the domestic process of preference formation, each state will have more or less intense preferences across issues. This fact explains the potential attraction of issue-linkage and package deals, where the outcome of the negotiations contains a beneficial element for all participants (Bueno de Mesquita and Stokman 1994, 69).

In the EU, where countless parallel negotiations are taking place and the Commission takes the role of 'broker', it is relatively easy to link negotiations about various proposals. The package deal that results could make an agreement acceptable to a state even though it is itself costly, because another agreement in the package provides benefits (the Netherlands and Article 119, see Chapter 2). Issue-linkage is not always feasible or attractive as the internal power position of the government must be sufficiently strong and its sensitivity sufficiently low before it will disregard the resistance of aggrieved groups, or the government must have sufficient means to compensate these groups.

In order to enable compensation at the national level, proposals are usually linked within a single policy sector, but rarely between sectors (Hayes-Renshaw and Wallace 1997, 64). Therefore, it is difficult to reach package deals in policy areas where very few decisions are made. In the domain of gender equality, such deals are hardly ever feasible. Treaties and treaty reforms are exceptions to this 'rule'. These 'grand bargains' often contain progressive articles on social policy, including gender equality issues, in order to gain the approval from national parliaments and the population (relevant in countries with ratification by referendum) for the other market-oriented sections of the treaty. The Single European Act enabled qualified majority voting (QMV) on health and safety, the Treaty of Maastricht extended the scope of gender equality policies and the use of QMV, the Treaty of Amsterdam introduced gender mainstreaming.

Power, Preference and Supranational Institutions Let us shift our attention to the role of supranational institutions. What difference does the institutional framework make for the outcome of the decision-making process? Cox and Jacobson found that international institutions could only exert some autonomous influence in policy areas of a more technical character (Cox and Jacobson 1973). However, they did not consider the unintended influence resulting from the delegation of authority and path-dependent developments.

The European Council, composed of the leaders of states and governments, decides on the delegation of powers and the rules which govern policy making by the other institutions. In terms of a 'principal-agent' analysis, states (the principals) delegate authority to an organization (an agent). This can result in 'bureaucratic drift' in the organization instead of the 'neutral' delegation of authority intended by the states. The agent 'is able to use its policy discretion to move final policy outcomes closer to its ideal position' (Hix 2005, 29).

The Commission, the European Parliament and the Court have all developed their own vision of their mandates based on their own interests and preferences. They aim at expanding their means and their influence, using procedures and rules to their own advantage. They become the target of lobbying by private interest groups, which offer attractive incentives, and they seek support among domestic dissatisfied groups to strengthen their own position vis-à-vis the Council.

Principals, once they have delegated authority, can no longer exert strict control over the way in which this authority is exercised (Pierson 1996; Scharpf 1988). 'After all, states grant autonomous powers to International Organizations precisely so that supranational enforcement will be shielded from state manipulation and interference' (Sandholtz 1996, 410). They cannot easily take delegated powers back. Member states have the theoretical option of limiting the authority of the Court, but they can only do so by changing the Treaty, for which unanimity is required. Smaller member states will not agree with any limitation of the authority of the Court, because only a strong and independent Court gives them the assurance that they will be treated equally to the larger states. Furthermore, states do not always correctly judge the precise implications of new rules and cannot predict exactly how the institutions will interpret them. Consequently, delegation can lead to different outcomes than might be expected purely based on state preferences and state power.

The European Commission The Commission consists of a core executive (the College of Commissioners), a bureaucracy (the directorates-general, the equivalent of ministries at the national level) and a network of committees and agencies.[12] It has two core responsibilities: to initiate legislation and to monitor the implementation of European 'law'. Here we focus on its role in the legislative process.

The Commission is the 'agenda-setter'. It decides how a problem is formulated and framed. Even if the EP or the European Council requests the Commission to take action, the form and content of a proposal are its exclusive responsibility. In addition, the Commission chooses the legal basis of its proposal, which determines the decision-making and voting procedures, and influences the framing (see the directives on equal treatment, p. 95 and pregnancy, p. 156).

The relevant directorate-general (DG) prepares the decisions, supervised by the commissioner's cabinet. Gender equality belongs to the portfolio of the Commissioner for Employment and Social Affairs.[13] The DG 'Employment, Social Affairs and Equal Opportunities' prepares the policies.[14]

It is the Commission's duty to be impartial to the interests of individual member states and it attaches great value to maintaining this reputation, which is the basis of the legitimacy and effectiveness of its actions. This does not mean that it formulates and selects proposals in a neutral, non-political fashion. In general, the Commission

12 For a detailed description of the functioning of the Commission, see Hix 2005.

13 In the Barroso Commission (2005–09), Vladimir Špidla (Czech Republic) holds the portfolio called 'Employment, social affairs and equal opportunities'.

14 Formerly DG V, also DG Employment, Industrial Relations and Social Affairs.

is in favour of more supranational decision making and the expansion of its tasks, budget and staff (Cram 2001). Therefore, the Commission's proposals for regulation often have common ground with the preferences of 'pioneer states', member states that already have a high national norm and are in favour of a far-reaching joint policy. In this way, the Commission influences the relative power relations because it strengthens the negotiating power of the states that have the greatest interest in joint policy, and, for exactly this reason, have the weakest bargaining position on that point.

The Commission also plays an influential role as an 'honest broker' between divergent standpoints (Pollack 1997). It consults the EP and formulates an amended proposal which becomes a basis for further negotiations. The Council can amend the Commission proposal by unanimity (consultation procedure, now Art. 250 EC) or QMV (cooperation and co-decision procedures, now Art. 252 and 251 EC).[15] Therefore, the Commission needs allies in the Council to keep a far-reaching proposal on the agenda. A strong Commissioner will be able to convince the Council if she or he is supported by the presidency or a 'pioneer' state. The equality directives from 1975–8 all benefited from support by pioneer states refusing to accept amendments to the Commission proposals (Chapter 3).

The chances of success for the Commission increase if the member states are dissatisfied with the status quo; if 'no policy' seems to be more costly than some policy and there is no clear idea yet about how to deal with this unattractive situation (Pollack 1997). The status quo is unattractive if the position of the EU is contested or if there is time pressure to reach a decision (treaty stipulations, national elections). This was the case, for instance, in the 1970s, when a global UN conference was planned in 1975 and communist countries accused the EU of backwardness because women did not enjoy equal rights with men (see Chapter 3). In such a situation, it is too costly to negotiate all alternatives or to postpone the final decision. If the Commission itself has an explicit preference in such a situation or has access to specific information and expertise, it can take a leadership role and authoritatively propose how to frame the issue. In such cases, member states can agree to a proposal without understanding all its ramifications, only discovering in the implementation phase what the proposal really entails.

The European Parliament The EP initially held a limited advisory and monitoring role.[16] The Council was required to consult the EP, but could reject its amendments without explanation. The influence of the EP therefore depended entirely on the

---

15 The original numbering of the treaty articles was changed in 1999 (Treaty of Amsterdam). I will use the 'old' numbering when discussing the developments before 1999, especially in Chapters 2–4. Chapter 5 also deals with 'post-Amsterdam' policymaking and will use the new numbering, where relevant adding the old numbering between brackets.

16 The EP also acquired the right to amend the budget concerning 'non-compulsory expenditure' (Article 272 EC). It used this right to open budgetary lines for new policies, but it had no direct influence on the further legislative process.

willingness of the Commission to accept its amendments or to take an initiative following an EP resolution.

The introduction of the co-decision procedure (Treaty of Maastricht) substantially strengthened the role of the EP. It has become the co-legislator in an increasing number of areas. If the EP amends the agreement reached in the Council (common position), the Council has to accept the amendment or negotiate with the EP until they reach agreement. If Council and EP do not reach an agreement, no decision is made. The consequences of this enhanced role of the EP on policy making in the field of gender equality will be discussed in Chapter 5.

Conclusion The chances for far-reaching gender equality policies increase when the proposal is part of a package deal that contains other attractive proposals, or when the status quo is unattractive for member states and they have no intense preferences. In the latter case, the preferences of the Commission and the EP can influence the outcome of negotiations, especially when time constraints play a role. The support of the presidency or of a pioneer state may help the Commission in keeping an issue on the agenda.

In addition to these structural elements, individuals make a difference. A committed Commissioner, an active Equal Opportunities official, an ambitious President of the Commission will seize opportunities which more reluctant persons might miss.

Implementation

Far-reaching policies are useless if they remain words on paper, but a state will not implement joint policy enthusiastically if this requires far-reaching policy changes (ideological costs), encounters a great deal of resistance, or has negative economic consequences (economic costs). Under what conditions will a government implement a costly supranational policy? The EU has no 'bailiff' and no supranational police force that comes knocking at a government's door. Nonetheless, governments cannot escape costly implementation easily. There are two strong disincentives to opportunistic behaviour: the interest that states have in their credibility and the double pressure that sandwiches a government in a multi-tiered system.

Credibility A state values its credibility, because it will have a stronger bargaining position when its partners believe that it is prepared to keep its promises and carry out its threats (Keohane 1984). When a state, despite the value it attaches to its credibility, prefers not to implement an agreement, it may initially ignore it and hope that its non-compliance will remain unnoticed. If this strategy fails, it can attempt to 'immunize' its credibility (Lieshout 1995), explaining that information about its non-compliant behaviour is inaccurate and that it has in fact complied with the agreements according to its own standards. If this strategy fails too, it faces a dilemma between the costs of a damaged reputation and the costs of implementation. How it will proceed then depends on the pressure exerted on it at national and supranational levels.

In the EU, it is much more difficult for a state to play ignorant or to immunize its credibility than in other international organizations. Here, the multi-tiered system has opened up possibilities unknown in the international system. Member states have granted enforcement powers to the Commission and the Court, which are authorized to supervise the implementation of policy and intervene in cases of non-compliance. Since the beginning of the 1990s, political scientists and legal experts have debated whether this delegated authority results in greater willingness on the part of states to implement supranational legislation (Alter 1998; Burley and Mattli 1993; Garrett 1995; Mattli and Slaughter 1998). This is indeed the case. Firstly, a strong monitoring system reduces the likelihood that non-compliance will remain unnoticed and increases the risk of damage to state credibility. Secondly, the links between the supranational and national levels mean that non-compliant member states will find themselves caught between 'pincers'.

The Commission Under the supervision of the EP, the Commission has the task of monitoring implementation, to which end it compiles reports based on the information it receives from governments, sub-national actors, and its own research. Action depends on the willingness of the responsible commissioner to take the initiative and order the directorate-general to investigate (non-)implementation of a specific European law and start an 'infringement procedure' (Art. 226 EC). Until 1973, all social affairs commissioners recoiled from starting such procedures concerning the non-implementation of equal pay, fearing repercussions on their position vis-à-vis the Council (Chapter 2–3). Citizens or companies may also take their grievances to the Commission when they feel they have lost out because a state has not complied with a European agreement. This may precipitate action on the part of the Commission.[17]

After the Commission receives a complaint or suspects a violation, it initiates a dialogue with the permanent representative of the member state. The government is required to admit, justify, or refute non-compliance. States can attempt to immunize their credibility by feigning ignorance, arguing that non-compliance was the result of a misunderstanding or a difference in interpretation, but after this first discussion with the Commission, they can no longer use such arguments. Moreover, the Commission's reports inform other member states about the non-compliance.

If the matter is not resolved, the Commission sends a 'letter of formal notice' to the member state. If the government does not respond or the response is inadequate, the Commission will send a 'reasoned opinion'. Most cases are settled during these two stages, but if the issue is still not resolved satisfactorily, the Commission refers the case to the Court.

---

17 The number of complaints from individuals registered by the Commission for EU 15 was 1080 in 2004. The number of violations detected by the Commission was 285 (Commission 2005a, 4).

The Court The Court's judgment is binding for the member state. Prior to the Maastricht Treaty the Court had no powers to enforce its judgments and in theory, member states could ignore Court decisions. In practice, however, they avoid open conflict with the Court because they generally benefit from a strong and impartial legal system. They want the Court to be able to rein back the Commission and to protect states' interests against the actions of other states. For this reason, at Maastricht, the member states decided to strengthen the enforcement system. If a state did not comply with a Court ruling, the Commission could start a second infringement procedure (Art. 228 EC). If the Court finds that a member state has not complied with its previous judgment, it may impose a penalty payment on that state. Of course, such financial sanctioning seriously damages the prestige of any state.

The Pincers The Commission, on the one hand, is quite eager to undertake action in order to maintain its credibility as guardian of the treaties. On the other hand, in its agenda-setting role, it wants to make new policies. As it depends on the cooperation of at least a majority of the member states to obtain approval for its proposals, the Commission wants to avoid overt confrontation with member states (Cram 2001). It will seek support among domestic actors in the defaulting state to strengthen its position vis-à-vis the government. To that end, it has created transnational networks of judicial experts and societal actors, which provide it with information and offer indirect access to the domestic process. In the field of gender equality, the directorate-general has created a Network of Legal Experts and an Advisory Committee, and supported the creation of a European Women's Lobby and a European Women Lawyers Association. The Network of Legal Experts actively monitors the implementation of gender equality regulation at the national level.

The Court organizes support at the domestic level as well. It has made creative use of the procedure for preliminary rulings (Art. 234 EC) to establish transnational links with domestic courts. This procedure gives national courts the right to refer questions concerning the interpretation of Community law to the Court. It was created so that courts in all member states would apply European law uniformly. As a result, however, the Court came to possess an instrument with which it could interpret treaty articles and European legislation according to its own views.

Accordingly, the possibility of establishing a link with the national level was implicitly present in the treaties, but this only became visible when the Court made use of its authority to strengthen its mandate and the position of European law with respect to national law – and to national politics (Alter 1998). This has created two 'pincers' squeezing unwilling governments between the supranational and the domestic levels. The first is the construction of a transnational legal community, and the second is the direct effect of European law.

A Transnational Legal Community In order to be able to utilize the instrument of preliminary ruling, the Court depended on input from national courts, which would refer cases to it for interpretation. The Court did not wait passively for them to come up with questions; it actively searched for their cooperation by inviting legal experts to Luxemburg. It was particularly the lower national courts which accepted invitations from the Court, since they were eager to strengthen their position with respect to the higher domestic courts (Weiler 1993). A transnational legal community subsequently developed that was willing to bring questions before the Court and to accept the far-reaching legal interpretations of the Court as opposed to the more restricted political interpretations of their governments. In the field of gender equality, for instance, the activism of the British courts in asking the Court for interpretations has improved women's rights against the wishes of Euro-sceptic British governments (Chapter 4).

Due to the Court's interpretations, the scope of European legislation may be more far-reaching than the member states intended when they initially approved it. However, a state cannot ignore the broad interpretations of the Court because it is the domestic courts which apply them. The Dutch government lost several 'battles' concerning the rights of married women and social security reform against national courts which preferred to follow the Court (Chapter 4).

The Direct Effect The second 'pincer mechanism' was established in the 1960s and 1970s through such preliminary rulings (Case 26/62, *Van Gend & Loos*; Case 43/75, *Defrenne-II*; see Chapters 3–4). It is a prime example of how delegation of authority can have unintended consequences and of the way in which an institution extends its mandate.

The Court, mandated to ensure the uniform application of European law in all member states, ruled that the provisions of Community law are directly effective and that they create 'individual rights which national courts must protect'. This means that individuals and companies can file a complaint with a domestic court when their government has not correctly implemented European legislation. When the government has harmed their interests, the court can award financial compensation. Accordingly, the state faces a dilemma: ignore the ruling and risk further court cases and damage claims, or start implementing the European legislation, even if this was not its original intention. Hence, by forging this link with the domestic courts, the Court has increased the likelihood that unwilling states will implement European legislation.

Conclusion Whether enforcement by the Commission and the Court will be successful, ultimately depends on the collaboration of domestic societal and judicial actors and on the prestige of a government. An unwilling government will implement a Court ruling only when domestic actors apply simultaneous pressure or when its prestige is at risk.

If domestic actors oppose implementation, the government faces a dilemma. It does not want to harm the credibility of the Court, but it does not want to take costly measures either. Governments' time horizons seldom stretch beyond the next elections. They will opt for lip service or rhetorical compliance, for instance legislation without sanctioning mechanisms or deadlines, which neither damages the Court's reputation nor entails costly measures. In this way, the French government escaped costly implementation of the equal treatment directive in the 1980s (Chapter 4).

We can conclude that in a multi-tiered political system, states will often comply with costly agreements because they can be placed between the 'pincers' of the domestic and supranational levels in various ways. If such double pressure is lacking or if their prestige is not at stake, a government will escape 'real' implementation and limit itself to symbolism and rhetoric.

The Boomerang Effect Once a state has undergone the experience of having to implement a costly European policy, it will make a higher estimate of the costs of new agreements in the relevant policy area and adopt a more reluctant position. The probability of agreement concerning new joint policy is therefore lower than during the previous round of negotiations. The affected interest groups will in future also be more aware of the costs and benefits of supranational policy. They will mobilize earlier and further increase the intensity of state's preferences.

A 'boomerang effect' takes place in the sense that the successful approval and implementation of one supranational policy hampers further supranational policymaking. This 'boomerang' hits the actors (member states, interest groups, the Commission, EP) that have an interest in the development of new joint policy that goes further than a 'minimum common denominator' standard.

Some Methodological Remarks

We will apply the toolbox to the development of gender equality policies. In Chapters 2–5, the decision making processes regarding gender equality instruments are reconstructed by using a form of 'process tracing', defined as a 'close processual analysis of the unfolding of events over time within the case' (Collier 1993, 115).

Sources

The analysis is based on primary and secondary written sources. Primary sources include documents from the European Union Archives in Florence (Italy), parliamentary documents from the Netherlands and Germany, official journals, documents from the European institutions (Council, Commission and EP),[18] transnational organizations (CREW, ETUC, EWL, the Legal Experts Group on Equal Treatment of Men and Women) and national advisory commissions. The archival material consists mainly of notes prepared by governmental delegations and trade unions for the negotiations about the Treaties of Rome (1955–7), notes and reports prepared by officials in DG V, and letters from governments, employers' organizations and trade unions to the Commission (1958–68). Autobiographies by Willy Brandt, Barbara Castle, Richard Crossman, Françoise Giroud, Roy Jenkins, Robert Marjolin, Paul-Henri Spaak and Margaret Thatcher have been consulted.

18 Documents from the European institutions are available in print in European Documentation Centers; since 1996, most documents can be found on the web, <http://ec.europa.eu/comm/>.

We have cited articles from Belgian, French and Dutch newspapers and from the Brussels daily edited by Agence Europe.

Four Periods

The empirical analysis is split into four periods: 1955–68, 1969–78, 1979–91 and 1992–2005. Each period is delimited by a significant change in the development of social policies. In 1969, stagnation was ended; in 1979, progress stalled, and in 1992, stagnation broke again (for similar periods, see Ostner and Lewis 1995). For each period, we will analyse the processes of preference formation, bargaining and implementation concerning gender equality policies. We will assess the economic and ideological costs of policy change, the amount of domestic, transnational and supranational pressure, and the role of identity and prestige, in order to explain why EU gender equality policies are what they are.

Selection of States

A major inconvenience of the toolbox is the amount of information needed for its full application. It was impossible to investigate preference formation in all member states. There were six of them during the first period, nine during the second, twelve during the third period and fifteen (1995) to 25 (2004) during the last period discussed.

We have opted for an analysis of preference formation, bargaining and implementation in four member states; France, Germany, the Netherlands and Britain. France and Germany constitute the basic ‘tandem’ of the EU that set the whole cooperation process in motion in the 1950s. Because of its material power position, Britain is the third crucial state. It joined in 1973. The Netherlands is the largest of the small states and one of the founding members.

Importantly, these four states all played key roles in the development of joint gender equality policies. In spite of its image as a progressive and liberal country, the Netherlands was notoriously slow, conservative and reluctant when it came to gender equality policies (see Chapters 2–3). Britain has a reputation for blocking all supranational social policies, but preliminary rulings by the British courts have strengthened the impact of EU gender equality policies (Chapter 4). In Germany as well, we see active courts but unwilling political actors, whereas France has combined political ambitions in the field of social policy with judicial silence. These states comprise an interesting selection to study under what conditions member states approve and implement costly policy in the area of equal rights.

Costs

In order to compare the attractiveness of policy proposals between countries and across time, we have chosen to calculate the economic and ideological ‘costs’ of those proposals.

'Costs' do not imply easily quantifiable indicators. The economic costs are the only category for which it was possible to use figures. Even for this category, it was impossible to arrive at exact calculations because figures could not be compared between the various countries or between various periods. This fact was used for political ends in the 1960s, when endless discussions between national experts began with the question of how to calculate 'pay' and what to include when assessing men's and women's wages (see Chapter 2).

We have assumed that interdependent member states in a common market are concerned with relative economic costs. Depending on the proposal, a relevant indicator was taken (wage gap, social security) and the scores compared, labelled low costs (1), medium costs (2) and high costs (3). A proposal for establishing equal pay, for instance, was considered to entail relatively low costs for France, as its gender pay gap was much smaller than in other states.

To calculate ideological costs, we compared the extent to which a policy proposal fitted the existing domestic policy frames. A country where unequal pay is justified because women are supposed to have different needs than men, incurs high ideological costs when a proposal prohibits establishing pay according to the sex of the worker. Again, we distinguished between low (1), medium (2) and high costs (3).

The scores for economic and ideological costs have been added up without weighting them, which would have implied a level of sophistication unwarranted by the calculations and unsupported by theory. The sum enabled comparison of the relative domestic costs of a policy proposal for the member states: high costs (5–6), medium (3–4) and low (1–2). We would expect a government to oppose a relatively costly proposal.

Pressure Support for and opposition to the proposal were calculated. We assumed that pressure from political parties participating in government has a greater effect on governmental preferences than pressure from opposition parties. Pressure from several actors increases the score. Again, we distinguish between limited pressure (1), rather limited (2), rather strong (3) and strong (4).

Totalling the scores for support and opposition, we decide whether an issue is salient. We assume that a government is able to ignore pressure and follow its own preference when an issue is hardly salient (0–3), whereas it feels more constrained when an issue has some saliency (4–5) and feels highly constrained when the issue is highly salient (6–8). When we deduct opposition from support, we see the net level of support for the proposal.

Sensitivity Whether a government feels constrained by the costs, the pressure and the saliency of a proposal is also related to the internal power position of the government. Its sensitivity is high if it has a weak or unstable position: if it lacks parliamentary support (minority government), elections are coming up and pressure comes from the governing parties' support base. Its sensitivity is low if the government has a comfortable parliamentary majority, there are no elections in the near future and pressure comes from groups which do not belong to the governing parties' support base.

These calculations have been summarized in several tables for preference formation concerning new policies and concerning the implementation of previously agreed policies.

Outline of the Book

In this chapter, we have presented EU gender equality policies as a fascinating set of puzzles, we have introduced the EU as a multi-tiered political system with a particular, neoliberal identity and we have developed a toolbox that helps us to explain why unwilling states sometimes have approved and implemented costly gender equality policies.

Chapter 2 covers the period 1955–68. An equal pay obligation was included in the Treaty of Rome (1957) against fierce opposition from Germany and the Netherlands. Member states succeeded in avoiding the implementation of equal pay, despite 'peer pressure' and pressure from the Commission, the EP, women in parliaments and in trade unions. Archive materials show how inventive member states were when it came to slowing down any action by the Commission and saving their reputations.

Chapter 3 explains the remarkable changes of 1969–78. Member states finally implemented the equal pay obligation. Still more significantly, this period saw the approval of strong, binding directives in the field of equal pay, equal treatment in the labour market and in social security. States agreed to broaden the norm of equal pay for equal work to equal pay for work of equal value. They accepted the inclusion of the brand new concept of indirect discrimination in the directives. Combined developments at the subnational and supranational levels explain how stagnation suddenly changed to swift progress.

Chapter 4 analyses the apparently contradictory events of 1979–92. Supranational policymaking in the field of gender equality came to a standstill. The Treaty on European Union even contained a protocol weakening the equal pay obligation contained in the original 1957 Treaty. Stagnation and decline are puzzling considering the strong pressure in favour of gender equality at both domestic and supranational levels. Governments were able to ignore all pressure for new policy initiatives, but, to their dismay, they could not ignore double legal pressure for implementation of the 'old' directives. The experience of costly compliance resulted in a 'boomerang effect'.

Chapter 5 assesses further progress and stagnation of EU gender equality policies. Contrasting developments again mark the period from 1992 to 2005. On the one hand, the widening of the Treaty base for gender equality policies and the approval of new procedures enhancing the role of the EP, have increased the chances of progress. On the other hand, policymaking has shifted towards non-coercive instruments, prioritizing symbolic measures over binding rights and entitlements. The outcome of these institutional changes is not a clear-cut set of strong, costly gender equality policies. Still, certain member states have on occasion approved and implemented costly policies.

Chapter 6 summarizes the main empirical findings and links them to the theoretical toolbox. It explains under which conditions states in a multi-tiered system have approved and implemented gender equality policies that went further than existing national regulations, and why the output has shown so much variation between swift progress and stagnation. We discuss the question of why pressure by women's groups has met with such varying success. Finally, we investigate the empowerment of women in the EU and the question: 'what makes gender different?'.

Chapter 2

The Price of Equal Pay (1955–1968)

The Treaties of Rome, which in 1957 created the European Economic Community (EEC) and the European Atomic Energy Community (EURATOM), contained a single article on social policy placing a direct obligation on the member states and even specifying a deadline for its implementation. This was the famous article on the principle that women and men should receive equal pay for equal work (Article 119, now Article 141 EC). Other treaty articles on social policy had no such imperative character. Nobody would have expected this in 1955 because the topic of equal pay was not included in the initial proposals for a customs union and from the moment it figured on the agenda, it was highly controversial.

This chapter will show how equal pay ended up on the agenda for negotiations on customs union, why it was so controversial, why member states approved a treaty containing an obligation on equal pay for men and women, and why they did not subsequently fulfil this obligation.

National Preference Formation: The Price of Equal Pay

Equal Pay on the European Agenda, 1955

The creation of the European Coal and Steel Community (ECSC) in 1951 was the source of inspiration for proposals to extend cooperation into the fields of defence, transport, agriculture, health care and other sectors. These proposals failed at an early stage (Urwin 1995), but in the spring of 1955, two new plans circulated. The first originated from the 'father' of the ECSC, Jean Monnet, and the Belgian Minister of Foreign Affairs, Paul-Henri Spaak. They proposed expanding the ECSC to cover the areas of energy and transport and to establish a new organization for nuclear energy. The Dutch Minister of Foreign Affairs, Jan-Willem Beyen, suggested the establishment of a customs union. Spaak and Beyen decided to link their proposals (Spaak 1969).

Their colleague Joseph Bech of Luxembourg supported the plan. This 'Benelux Memorandum' was discussed by the Ministers of Foreign Affairs of the six ECSC member states[1] at their meeting in June 1955 in Messina (Italy). The meeting did not produce any spectacular results. The ministers agreed only on the formation of an intergovernmental committee to study proposals for a common market and sectoral

1 Belgium, France, Germany, Italy, Luxembourg and The Netherlands.

integration in transport and atomic energy. The committee would draw up a report for the heads of state and government.

On 18 July 1955, the Intergovernmental Committee began its activities under the leadership of Spaak. During the first meeting, Spaak and the delegation leaders discussed proposals from the member states in order to formulate guidelines for the different commissions that would investigate specific areas. Because of the discord that existed between governments on the issue of social harmonization, a Sub-commission on Social Problems was established to address that issue. Social harmonization implied that national legislation in the field of social policy would be adapted to a common 'European' standard.

In his original proposal, Beyen made no mention at all of social policy; he believed that trade liberalization would automatically result in social harmonization. The German proposal to the Spaak Committee was also silent on the issue. Belgium and France, on the other hand, considered social harmonization 'extremely important' (MAE/SEC 13/4, 26 July 1958). In its very creative interpretation of the 'Messina agreement', the French proposal noted 'with satisfaction' that all governments had agreed that freedom of movement must be accompanied by social harmonization. To this end, it proposed the compilation of existing research about the consequences of divergent social costs and an assessment of the implementation of relevant International Labour Organization (ILO) conventions (MAE 51 f/55). The Belgian proposal was even more specific, listing the topics for further investigation.

The delegation leaders adopted the Belgian proposal and gave the Sub-commission on Social Problems five areas to study. One of them was the 'harmonization of wage systems, including women's wages'.[2] It is at this point that women appear for the first time on the agenda. The idea of specific attention for wage systems originated in the Belgian proposal, but the addition of the words 'including women's wages' had not been mentioned in any of the national proposals. Since the French delegates had received 'strict instructions' about the 'priority that they were to assign to this problem of social costs', they must have introduced the topic during the meeting (CM 2/1958, *Rapport Abelin*, No. 5296, 39).

Once on the agenda, the issue of women's wages would remain there for the next 20 months, due to French stubbornness and German and Dutch resistance.[3] The origins of these divergent standpoints are to be found at the domestic level.

---

2 The four other topics were: 1. Free movement of persons; 2. Harmonization of legislation concerning working hours, compensation for extra work, holidays; 3. Harmonization of social security systems and the creation of a European centre for social security (French proposal); 4. Policy coordination concerning other international agreements and institutions (MAE 65f/55 mj).

3 From the beginning, Italy and Luxembourg would hardly ever participate in the discussions on this topic as they had no intense preferences concerning equal pay. Belgium partially supported the French position, but was willing to compromise and preferred any agreement to no agreement at all (MAE documents).

The Price of Equal Pay

In the international political arena, equal pay for women and men was a familiar demand. As early as 1870, the Swiss feminist Marie Goegg formulated the equal pay demand for the first time at the international level (Reinalda and Verhaaren 1989). After the First World War, lobbying by women's organizations ensured that the equal pay claim was on the agenda of the committee that drew up the so-called 'labour section' of the Versailles Peace Treaty. International trade unions supported their claim because they feared that employers would prefer to keep the cheap female workers who had replaced men during the war. In this way, the principle of equal pay for work of equal value was included in the constitution of the ILO in 1919 (Reinalda and Verhaaren 1989).

After the Second World War, the ILO, which from this point on was a specialist organization of the United Nations (UN), once again focused attention on women's rights. After all, the role played by women during the war had rendered a number of widely held prejudices about women and work untenable (Reinalda and Verhaaren 1989). In February 1948, the World Federation of Trade Unions placed equal pay for women on the agenda of the UN Economic and Social Council (ECOSOC). Denmark, Britain, the Netherlands and New Zealand made so-called 'technical' objections to introducing the principle, but a Dutch proposal to conduct a preliminary study was voted down and ECOSOC passed a resolution requesting member states to apply the principle of equal pay (Blok 1978).

Following extensive preparations, the ILO approved *Convention Number 100 concerning equal remuneration for men and women workers for work of equal value* (ILO-100) by a vote of 105 in favour, 33 opposed and 40 abstentions (Reinalda and Verhaaren 1989). The convention came into force on 23 May 1952. The statutes of the ILO required its signatories to submit the convention to the competent national bodies for ratification. In the 1950s, ILO-100 thus placed the principle of equal pay on the national agendas of all ILO member states.

France: The Price of being a Pioneer From the beginning of negotiations in the Spaak committee, France held firm on its insistence that agreement should be reached on equal pay, believing as it did that its 'head start' in this area would lead to a competitive disadvantage in a liberalized market. French experts considered the ratification by the other member states of ILO conventions such as ILO-100 as a precondition for complete liberalization (*Année Politique* 1955, 128). France (and Belgium) had already ratified ILO-100, but the other ECSC countries had not.

French industry, expressing its viewpoint via the *Conseil National du Patronat Français* (CNPF), feared the negative effects of liberalization. Compared to its major trading partners, French industry enjoyed more protection by means of tariff barriers, quotas and state support (*Année Politique* 1956, 129). Progressive social legislation had led to relatively high labour costs. Therefore, the CNPF was willing to support economic integration only on condition that the other member states accepted 'safeguard clauses'[4] and harmonized their social legislation 'upwards' to the French standard. It believed that equal pay was one of the issues for which harmonization was essential.

As far back as 1900, French women were able to convince the communist trade union to support the principle of equal pay. In the 1920s, they had been successful in achieving equal pay in the areas of pre-school and primary education and in the national postal service (Hantrais 1993). The Second World War had led to a breakthrough. The communist party (PCF) and the socialist party (PS) had established women's groups within the resistance movement. When women were given the right to vote in April 1944 in return for their role in the resistance, the women's groups of the PS and PCF were viewed as 'vote organizers' and their demands were placed high on the political agenda (Lovenduski 1986). The PS and PCF regarded equal pay also as an instrument to reduce the poverty of the workers (Hoskyns 1996a).

In July 1946, a governmental decree prohibited employers from cutting women's wages in comparison to men's. The preamble of the new constitution of October 1946 guaranteed equal rights for women 'in all areas' – in conformity with the equality principle of the French Revolution. In February 1950, the statutory minimum wage was introduced with a single wage scale for both women and men, and in March 1953, France ratified ILO-100.

Table 2.1 Equal pay in France, Germany and the Netherlands (1955)

	France	Germany	the Netherlands
Women's wages compared to men's wages (percentage)	86	63	58
Women in labour force as percentage of total female population	37.1 (1931)	34.2 (1933)	19.2 (1930)
Legislation concerning equal rights (as of 1 January 1955)	Decree, 1946 Constitution, 1946 Minimum Wage Law, 1950 ILO–100, 1953	Constitution, 1949 Works Councils Constitution Act, 1952	–

Source: MAE 102f/55 jv, 21 July 1955

4 A safeguard clause allows a government to suspend liberalization measures in order to protect the interests of the national industry.

The statutory stipulations had a clear effect. In 1938, women's wages were 20–25 percent lower than men's wages. This difference was reduced to less than 10 percent under the controlled wage policy of 1944–50 (Commission 1961, V/1289/61). The wage gap was therefore significantly smaller in France than it was in Germany and the Netherlands (see Table 2.1). Particularly in sectors that employed many women, such as the textile industry, paper processing, clothing and food, the CNPF feared competition from member states where women were poorly paid. The French government therefore regarded the equal pay demand as a means of obtaining domestic approval for economic integration.

Germany: The Court Decides The German resistance to French demands for equal pay was not directed against the principle of equal pay, but against the proposed instrument for achieving this aim: the mandatory equalization of social legislation. The Minister of Economic Affairs, Ludwig Erhard, supported by German industry, resisted every form of social harmonization. One of his characteristic statements was that 'Sicily is not the Ruhr'; differences in wages and social costs were the consequence of differences in productivity (Collins 1975, 5). Erhard agreed with Beyen that social harmonization was not a precondition for economic integration; instead, it was the probable result of such integration. The *Deutsche Gewerkschaftsbund* (DGB), the German trade union federation, however, feared that economic integration would undermine acquired rights and therefore demanded the harmonization of social policy on the condition that norms would be adjusted upwards and that trade unions would be given a voice in European decision-making on social policy (Behrendt et al. 1968; Köpper 1982).

In the area of equal pay, the government believed that adequate arrangements had already been made, particularly since its authority regarding wage determination was limited by the statutory wage autonomy of employers and trade unions. The new West German constitution contained an article that gave equal rights to men and women (Constitution of 23 May 1949, Articles 3.2–3.3).

Initially, the constitution did not refer to the equality of men and women. Elisabeth Selbert, a Member of Parliament for the social democratic SPD, proposed to add the assertion that 'Men and women have equal rights'. The Christian-Democratic parties (CDU/CSU) disagreed, because they believed that men and women were different and should therefore be treated differently. Selbert's proposal was supported by a parliamentary majority only after she had mobilized the press, the Democratic Women's League (*Demokratische Frauenbund Deutschland*), Catholic and Protestant women's organizations, and these groups had persuaded enough Members of Parliament to change their minds (Nödinger 1983).

Article 3 of the Constitution made it necessary to modify the sections in the civil code that stipulated the privileges of husbands and fathers. This modification was resisted by the CDU/CSU, who viewed the protection of marriage and family as a 'Barrier against a tidal wave of equal rights' (Plantenga 1993, 34). The Constitutional Court ruled in 1953 that the civil code had to be modified, yet it interpreted equality in accordance with the Christian viewpoint: difference was allowable if there were 'objective grounds' for this. This led to the conclusion that married men were responsible for the work that took place outside the home, and married women for housekeeping and childcare. Consequently, the civil code stipulated that women were allowed to work outside the home if this did not interfere with their marital and family duties (§1356 civil code) and were required to work if their husband's income was not adequate to support the family (§1360 civil code). Men and women did not have an equal right to work.

The parliament was of the opinion that 'equal rights' in Article 3 also meant that men and women 'should be paid equally for equal work' (Menschik 1971, 123). However, legal experts believed that Article 3 did not apply to individual and collective labour agreements (Menschik 1971). As a result, employers did not feel obliged to apply the principle of equal pay and continued to classify work that was primarily done by women within *Frauenlohngruppen* (women's pay scales) which stipulated very low wages.

As far back as 1947, the trade unions had demanded equal rights for women 'in view of their contribution to the rebuilding of the German economy and the German state' and called for the abolition of *Frauenlohngruppen* (Krasnogolovy 1968, 582). In October 1949, the DGB included the demand 'equal pay for equal work and equal performance' in its manifesto. Female union members repeatedly brought up the problem of discrimination in wage classification, and in 1954 the DGB congress instructed the unions to stop approving collective labour agreements that allowed lower wages for women (Krasnogolovy 1968). Nevertheless, most collective labour agreements included *Frauenlohnabschlagsklauseln* (women's pay scale reduction clauses) which allowed women to be paid 20–30 percent less than men for the same work.

After many complaints from the women's committees in the DGB, a breakthrough finally came because of two decrees from the Federal Labour Court in January and April of 1955. Following a complaint about the wood processing industry, where the collective labour agreements stipulated that women were to be paid 75–80 percent of the wages for men, the court ruled that Article 3 of the constitution was also binding for the parties involved in collective labour agreements. Wages could only be determined based on the work itself, regardless of who performed that work (Krasnogolovy 1968). From that moment, *Frauenlohngruppen* and *Frauenlohnabschlagsklauseln* became unconstitutional and female employees had a formal right to equal pay for equal work.

The German government did not want an expansion of this court-imposed obligation of 'equal pay for equal work' to the ILO-norm of 'equal pay for work of equal value' and its representatives on the Spaak Committee resisted all supranational obligations concerning social harmonization.

The Netherlands: The Breadwinner Endures Women in the civil service, including health service and education, faced dismissal when they married. Not until 1957 was the law changed. Not surprisingly, labour market participation of women was much lower in the Netherlands than in neighbouring countries. Equal pay was so much an international affair that until the 1970s, government, members of parliament, employers and trade unions used the English term to refer to equal pay rather than the Dutch '*gelijke beloning*' (Eijl 1997).

An equal pay stipulation was in direct conflict with Dutch wage policy. In contrast to France, the Netherlands alleviated poverty among workers not by providing equal pay for female workers, but by paying all male workers, whether married or not, a 'family wage'. Until 1963, the Netherlands had a controlled wage policy; after receiving advice from the bipartite Labour Foundation, the Board of Government Mediators issued binding wage regulations. This Board controlled all collective wage agreements, meaning that the Dutch government, unlike its German counterpart, had a major influence on wage development.

The Labour Foundation found lower pay for women appropriate because women did not have to support families. Only in the case of work carried out by both sexes, the workers group wanted equal pay to prevent men from being replaced by women. For work that was primarily carried out by women, but was equal in value to work carried out by men, the workers group asked 80–90 percent of the pay for men while employers asked 60–70 percent. For specifically 'female work', a level of 60 percent could be maintained. Despite protests from female trade union members, trade unions approved such recommendations (Eijl 1997).

Women in the trade unions attempted to move equal pay higher up on the trade union agenda, but encountered stubborn resistance. In the ILO, the Dutch trade union representatives had voted in favour of ILO-100, but in the national context they wanted to avoid conflict with their predominantly male membership. This membership would not accept the limited latitude in wage negotiations being used to increase women's wages (Eijl 1997).

The Dutch government believed that lower pay for women was 'not justified in principle', but that the costs of equal pay were so high that in practice it was 'highly objectionable, if not impossible, to introduce the principle of equal pay for the time being' (*Handelingen* 1973–4, 13031, 4). In the Netherlands, an international norm takes precedence over a national norm with which it is in conflict (Constitution, Articles 93–4). In the ILO, the Dutch government representatives therefore abstained during the voting about ILO-100. The government asked the tripartite Social and Economic Council (SER) whether the Netherlands had to ratify ILO-100.

According to a majority in the SER, ratification was not desirable because the 'need element'[5] justified unequal pay. The SER was unanimous in its recommendation that any possible implementation of equal pay had to take place in stages, while taking account of the capacity of industry to absorb this change (SER 1953). In view of the 'significant repercussions on the labour market situation', the government decided to delay ratification of ILO-100 for an unspecified period (*Handelingen* 1973–4, 13031, 5). The Parliament approved a motion in which they asked the government to submit ILO-100 for ratification, but this was in vain (*Motie-Tendeloo*).

5 The 'need element' referred to the idea that women had other needs than men because they did not have to support a family with their wages.

Dutch employers had voted against ILO-100, opposing not only the costs of equal pay, but also the principle. They argued that the principle did not take account of the 'need element' and the higher production costs resulting from the 'nature of female workers' (Blok 1978, 142). In the 1950s, the labour market became so tight that the business community began to employ married women and to introduce part-time work for them. However, the scarcity of workers did not mean that women would now be given equal pay:

> The famous principle of 'equal pay', an hourly wage equal to that of men, will not be applied. This is partly because there would be resistance on a psychological level from male staff and partly because the government mediator (and therefore the government itself) is opposed to equal pay (*De Zakenwereld*, 26 November 1955, in Blok 1978, 138).

Meanwhile, Dutch employers enjoyed a competitive advantage with respect to France due to low wage levels in general and especially the very low wages for women (see Table 2.1). In the Spaak Committee, the Netherlands therefore took the same neoliberal standpoint as Germany: the operation of the market would bring about harmonization automatically. The Dutch government resisted any equal pay provision because it believed that the costs would be excessive.

Conclusion

In July 1955, the points of view of the member states on the introduction of a supranational equal pay provision as part of the harmonization of social legislation diverged greatly (see Table 2.2).

In Germany and the Netherlands, the economic costs were estimated to be high since equal pay would lead to a sharp rise in wage costs and could erode the competitive position of sectors with many female workers. The ideological costs were also significant. Equal pay was incompatible with both the Dutch policy paradigm, where wages were determined according to the 'breadwinner' and 'need' philosophies, and the German one, which was based on 'objective differences' and non-interference in the free negotiations of employers and trade unions. For France, a supranational equal pay provision was compatible with its existing policy.

In view of the high costs, Germany and the Netherlands were not expected to approve a treaty that contained a supranational equal pay provision, whereas France, considering the intensity of its preference for high social standards, would not approve a treaty without such a provision.

Intergovernmental Negotiations: French Weakness as Strength

The negotiations between the ECSC states, which ultimately resulted in the Treaties of Rome, would take 20 months. It was only when the international situation became very unstable that France and Germany were able to reach a compromise. A binding equal pay provision was part of this compromise.

Table 2.2 Equal pay: domestic costs and pressure (1955)

	France	Germany	the Netherlands
1. Relative economic costs: gap women's pay – men's pay	Low costs (1): difference of 14 percent	High costs (3): difference of 37 percent	High costs (3): difference of 42 percent
2. Ideological costs: compatibility with domestic policy frame	Low costs (1): compatible with statutory equal rights, social role model	High costs (3): incompatible with tariff autonomy, objective differences ideology	High costs (3): incompatible with family wage, different needs ideology
Relative domestic costs of equal pay (1 + 2)	Low (2)	High (6)	High (6)
3. Domestic opposition to a supranational equal pay provision	Limited (1): Gaullist party	Strong (4): Employers, CDU/CSU, FDP (governing parties)	Strong (4): Employers, Christian Democrats, liberal party
4. Domestic support for a supranational equal pay provision	Strong (4): Employers, most political parties, trade unions	Limited (1): Women in DGB and SPD, Deutsche Frauenbund	Limited (1): Women in NVV and PvdA
Saliency (3+4) and relative domestic pressure (4–3)	Medium saliency (5), rather strong support (3)	Medium saliency (5), rather strong resistance (–3)	Medium saliency (5), rather strong resistance (–3)
Sensitivity	High	Medium	Low
Expected preference	In favour	Opposed	Opposed

From 'Messina' to 'Paris' (July–November 1955)

From its very first meeting, opinions within the Sub-commission on Social Problems were diametrically opposed. The discussion focused on the issue of 'distortions', differences in labour costs that could be the source of unfair competition in a common market. France and Belgium considered low women's wages a source of distortion. They proposed to ratify the ILO conventions and to develop higher European norms. The Netherlands viewed such proposals as 'entirely premature' (MAE 81 f/55). The British representative, who attended the negotiations until November, wondered why wage differences between men and women were a source of distortion, while wage differences between farm workers and cotton weavers were not (MAE 363 f/55). The Sub-commission reported that equality of men and women 'results from an uncontested principle of equity' (MAE 167 f/55). Research into why only Belgium and France had ratified ILO-100 and whether unequal pay would distort the operation of the common market had to be carried out (MAE 202 f/55).

There were repeated discussions in the Sub-commission on the question of whether legislation had to be harmonized before the creation of a common market – as the French claimed – or whether market effects would lead automatically to harmonization – the view taken by Germany and the Netherlands (MAE 324 f/55). According to France, they had all agreed in Messina that liberalization and harmonization should go hand in hand to prevent 'social dumping'. Otherwise, French employers would be forced to cut women's wages (MAE 386 f/55). When its preference for general harmonization turned out to be untenable, France proposed in any case to eliminate six specific distortions, including equal pay (MAE 421 f/55).

The Commission on the Common Market adopted the French position that the market effect was insufficient to eliminate specific distortions such as equal pay. However, it proposed only to conduct a study during the transitional period to a common market (MAE 425 f/55), which was too meagre for France (MAE 477 f/55). In November 1955, the activities of the Spaak Committee came to a halt because the French government fell. At that time, the delegations had reached agreement on all reports except agriculture, overseas territories – and distortions.

On 31 January 1956, a new French government came to power under the leadership of the socialist Guy Mollet. The government had shaky foundations, the socialist party having only 100 of the 594 seats in the parliament. Mollet governed with the support of an unstable coalition of ten small, centrist parties, while the opposition was comprised of the strong, anti-European Gaullist and Communist parties.

Mollet declared that he would support a common market on condition that the necessary measures would be taken to prevent unfair competition (*Année Politique* 1956). Christian Pineau, the Minister of Foreign Affairs, assured the parliament that he was aware that the French public was worried about the variation in social costs between France and other member states, 'especially the existing inequality between men's and women's wages'. He promised to consult regularly the trade unions and the employers (*Année Politique* 1956, 463).

From 'Paris' to 'Venice' (February–April 1956)

In February, the delegations resumed their work. The Commission on the Common Market reached agreement about an ingenious procedure for correcting specific distortions, including equal pay. If the future supranational executive, the European Commission, detected distortions, it could propose measures. Unanimity on the Council of Ministers would be required to approve such measures during the first stage of economic integration; after this stage, the measures could be approved with a qualified majority. If the Council rejected the proposal, the European Commission could provide a safeguard clause for the disadvantaged industry.

The procedure was a clever compromise because the required unanimity gave Germany and the Netherlands the possibility to block every proposal that did not suit them during the first stage, while France was satisfied for the time being with the promise that the European Commission could always provide a safeguard clause to a disadvantaged industrial sector.

On 21 April 1956, Spaak presented the final report of his Intergovernmental Committee.[6] The section on the harmonization of social costs combined the various national viewpoints:

- Differences in social costs were in themselves not a source of unfair competition;
- Harmonization of social costs could emerge from the operation of the market;
- Intervention was only necessary to compensate for specific distortions, such as the effect of unequal pay (according to the procedure discussed above);
- Governments were required to make extra efforts to harmonize working conditions in an upward direction regarding equal pay for men and women, working hours, payment for overtime, and holiday leave (MAE 120 f/56, 60–6).

The first two points accorded with Dutch and German preferences, and the third point with the wishes of the French. Moreover, the combination linked up with the results of an ILO study which stated that the advantages of liberalization would exceed the disadvantages of the high social costs and that no general measures for harmonization were required. However, harmonization was justified if one sector had lower social costs than other sectors in a country, for instance sectors with many female employees in countries where women's wages were much lower than men's wages. The report recommended that the relevant ILO conventions be ratified and that research be conducted into the small number of states having ratified ILO-100 thus far (ILO 1956). The fourth point in the Spaak Report linked up with earlier French and Belgian remarks, which urged the inclusion of social progress as an aim of the treaty in order to gain the approval of public opinion, trade unions and employers.

In spite of this, French reactions were negative. In the *Assemblée* of the ECSC, Michel Debré, a French member of parliament, fiercely attacked Spaak over the weak social section (*Année Politique* 1956). The French newspaper *Le Monde* warned that the European Commission would force its will upon national governments by acting as a European 'super ministry' of economic affairs (*Le Monde* 1956, 6 May). The majority of high-level French officials rejected the Spaak Report and the Mollet government was divided (Snoy et d'Oppuers 1989).

On 29 May 1956, the foreign affairs ministers met in Venice to discuss the report. In order to avoid a defeat, Spaak had emphasized that they would not take any definitive positions with respect to the *content* of the report. They would only decide whether further negotiations could take place. The French Minister of Foreign Affairs Pineau chaired the meeting in Venice. Since none of the other delegations took the floor, Pineau had to present the French position first. To the relief of the others, he opened his presentation by stating that his government proposed to move

6 The *Rapport des Chefs de Délégation aux Ministres des Affaires Etrangères*, better known as the Spaak Report (MAE 120 f/56).

on to the second phase of the activities, working out the content of the treaties. He then expressed a number of reservations about the report. The crucial issue appeared to be whether a fixed schedule would be established for the transition from the first to second stage or if the transition would depend on the achievement of specific aims. He made clear his preference for the second possibility and proposed making the transition dependent on the elimination of customs duties and the simultaneous harmonization of social costs (MAE 126 f/56).

Walter Hallstein announced that the German government had a number of reservations, including the correction of the distortions. Beyen also had reservations concerning the harmonization of social costs and legislation. Hallstein and Beyen both emphasized that their governments did not feel bound by the details of the report, but that further negotiations could take place (MAE 126 f/56). Pineau was given the assurance that the transition to the second stage would only take place when 'the proof was given that the programme for the first stage had been realized, especially the harmonization of social costs between the countries' (*Année Politique* 1956, 309).

The ministers thus reached agreement in less than two hours. The weather was beautiful and they spent the remaining time sight-seeing (Beyen 1968). In both Messina and Venice, Spaak's approach had allowed the discussions to proceed without the member states having to commit themselves. This changed during the second phase, when the real negotiations started.

From 'Venice' to 'Paris' (June–September 1956)

Under the leadership of Hans von der Groeben, the *Groupe du Marché Commun* drew up the texts concerning the common market. In the first draft of the treaty, Chapter 2 addressed the thorny topic of the 'correction of distortions and the harmonization of legislation'. The procedure for the correction of distortions was copied from the Spaak Report. The text was more explicit regarding the desirability of extra efforts on behalf of social progress; it included the statement that harmonization resulting from the market effect 'must be supplemented by special efforts of the governments' in the areas of equal pay, overtime, and holiday leave. Moreover, the European Commission was given the mandate to make proposals for measures in these areas to benefit social progress (MAE 131 d/56). This mandate disappeared during the first meeting of the delegations.

From the first meeting of the *Groupe* on 27 June 1956, the relatively ambitious draft treaty led to disagreements between France on one side and Germany and the Netherlands on the other. Alfred Müller-Armack (Erhard's right-hand man) described French arguments for social harmonization as obsolete. Although the Netherlands understood the 'psychological and political motives of the French delegation for hammering away on this point', it rejected the arguments. Then Robert Marjolin from the French delegation proposed establishing a group of experts to study the issue of distortions. The other delegations believed this was a waste of time. They did not reach agreement and passed the problem on to the next meeting (MAE 141 f/56).

At the next meeting, Germany and the Netherlands, to 'show their good will', agreed to establish a group of experts (*Sous-groupe pour le problème des charges sociales*) on condition that their mandate was limited (MAE 174 f/56). During the following meeting, there was a discussion about the mandate, since the experts themselves had not reached agreement. The *Groupe* failed to reach agreement as well, because France stated it could not support a mandate that did not include an investigation into equal pay, overtime pay and holiday leave, while the other delegations could not support a mandate that included these aspects (MAE 190 f/56). At France's request, the issue was passed on to the delegation leaders. Following a long discussion under Spaak's leadership, even the leaders were unable to reach agreement (MAE 208 f/56).

Following the summer recess, negotiations resumed on 6 September. Maurice Faure then reported that, to save time, France dropped its demand to establish a group of experts. He also proposed speeding up the negotiations by meeting more frequently, even though it had been decided in June at Marjolin's request to meet only two days per week so that France could always be represented by high-level officials (MAE 141 f/56). What was the reason for this sudden haste? Since the debate in the French parliament about EURATOM in July 1956 (332 votes in favour and 181 against), the Mollet government had become more confident that France would be capable of ratifying the future treaties. At the same time, Mollet feared that the parliamentary debate about EURATOM had awoken the opponents of the treaties and that the mood could become negative if the negotiations took too long (MAE 209 f/56).

Faure again emphasized that liberalization and harmonization of social costs had to take place simultaneously. The procedure in the Spaak Report offered inadequate guarantees because every country could veto the European Commission proposals. After this, he presented the French conditions, which seemed to be dictated by employers (Girault 1989). The treaty had to contain provisions to achieve equal pay during the first two years and measures had to be taken with respect to overtime pay and holiday leave. France accepted the proposals for the correction of distortions on the condition that the Council of Ministers would approve the Commission proposals with a qualified majority instead of unanimously. Finally, general labour costs had to be approximately equal in the six member states by the end of the transitional period (lasting 12 to 15 years) (MAE 236 f/56). Spaak saw the dismay and disapproval on the faces of the other negotiators (Spaak 1969). No progress was made during the following meeting either.

Crisis in 'Paris' (October 1956)

Spaak took the negotiations to a higher level. On 20 October, the ministers of foreign affairs met in Paris to get the negotiations back on track. 'The conference took a dramatic turn' (Carstens 1976, 594) and 'ended badly' (Spaak 1969, 94).

The Conference At the top of the agenda was the transition from the first to the second stage of the common market. Pineau continued to insist that this transition should not take place automatically after four years, but had to depend on the extent to which specific aims, including those in the area of social harmonization, were realized. The other member states could agree to this on the condition that the decision of whether the aims had been achieved or not was taken by a qualified majority. Pineau continued to insist on unanimity. The delegations ultimately approved a compromise, which stipulated that if no agreement had been reached after four years, the vote could be taken by qualified majority after one year instead of after two years. Pineau emphasized that this was a 'very important concession' of France (MAE 460 f/56).

The second point on the agenda was the harmonization of social costs. Spaak explained that there were problems with equal pay because not all countries had ratified ILO-100, and the French government believed that it was ahead of the others on this issue. He proposed to solve the problem by including a safeguard clause for industries that employed many female workers.

During the afternoon session Heinrich von Brentano, the German Foreign Minister, said that his government could accept a formula 'which for that matter would correspond with the principle of ILO-100', that every government 'should strive during the first stage to apply the principle of equal pay for identical work and identical performance'. Pineau agreed. However, Joseph Luns, the Dutch Foreign Minister, expressed a reservation, remarking that the problem of equal pay was 'of great importance' to the Netherlands, especially to the textile industry. They decided to have the experts draw up a text based on which the discussion would be reopened. The following day, they discussed and accepted a text comparable to the German proposal: 'the principle of equal pay for the same work and same performance' (MAE 460 f/56).

A German 'Concession' Due to domestic developments, this ostensibly important German concession to France no longer had much significance for Germany. In response to the ruling of the Federal Labour Court that 'reduced wages' for women were unconstitutional (see p. 38), German employers had countered that an increase of 25 percent for women's wages was unacceptable. The trade unions agreed, as they feared that their demands for a 40 hour working week and holiday pay had little chance of success if they 'would insist without compromise on the abolition of *Frauenlohngruppen*' (Wiggershaus 1979, 82). The court offered an escape clause by accepting separate wage categories for physically lighter and heavier work – even though in practice it meant that women were placed systematically in the lowest-paid category (Plantenga 1993).

In 1956, the IG Metall trade union reached an agreement with the employers on the introduction of *Leichtlohngruppen* (light work wage groups), a pay bracket to be placed below the lowest one on the existing pay scale (Wiggershaus 1979). In other sectors as well, 'women's work' was redefined as 'light work'. Formally, women were entitled to the same pay for the same work, but in practice, their work was usually defined as 'not the same' as men's work. They could therefore be paid substantially less without breaching Article 3 of the Constitution. Of course, these practices were in breach of the right to equal pay for work 'of equal value' in ILO-100. In February 1956, the German parliament had ratified ILO-100 following years of pressure from the National Women's Conference of the DGB and the Democratic Women's League (Nödinger 1983). However, international norms were not binding in Germany if they were in conflict with national law. Article 3 of the Constitution therefore took precedence over ILO-100.

As a result, in Paris in October 1956, Germany was able to approve an equal pay provision on the condition that there was no requirement to reform the job classification system or to provide equal pay for comparable jobs. In contrast to what he claimed, Brentano's formulation 'equal pay for identical work' was much more limited than the ILO-100 norm. Von der Groeben, the German negotiator, explained later that he had deliberately avoided using the term 'of equal value' when formulating Article 119. This kept open the option of continuing to pay women less as long as they did not do identically the same work as men, certainly while the labour market continued to be characterized by strong sex segregation and women were often doing work for which there was no direct equivalent done by male workers (BAC 008/1966, Memorandum to Dörr, Von der Groeben, 1959).

In exchange for this 'concession' to France, Brentano primarily intended to acquire a concession concerning overtime pay, because he feared that the French proposal would strengthen the German trade unions in their demands for better pay for overtime and for a 40 hour working week (CM 3/NEGO 095, Minutes of the meeting, 26 October 1956). Brentano said he was unable to make any concessions on this point, due to the statutory guarantee of autonomy for employers and trade unions in wage negotiations (CM 3/NEGO 185, *Auswärtiges Amt*, 19 January 1957). The discussions stalled. After adjournment, Müller-Armack explained the German position again. Brentano repeated that his instructions did not allow him to make concessions. Pineau answered that he was forced to withdraw his earlier 'very important concession' for the transition to the second stage, at which point the meeting was dissolved (MAE 460 f/56).

Dramatic Breakthrough Immediately after the crisis in Paris, two dramatic events destabilized the international political situation. On 4 November 1956, Soviet troops crushed the Hungarian uprising. At the same time, there was an escalation in the Suez crisis. On 26 July, Nasser had nationalized the Suez Canal, and on 4 November, Britain and France decided to intervene militarily. They were sharply criticized by the American government. The Soviet Union even threatened to retaliate with force.

The German Chancellor Konrad Adenauer was very conscious of the vulnerable position of Western Europe with respect to the Soviet Union and the United States. Under these conditions, 'European disintegration was irresponsible' (Carstens 1976, 595), especially when 'the great political importance of the integration process' was compared with the 'limited material significance of the remaining points of contention' (Hentschel 1998, 394). Adenauer decided to finally participate personally in the negotiations and use the already planned visit on 6 November to Paris to discuss the issue with Mollet.[7]

On 6 November, Adenauer encountered a tense French government, which had deliberated throughout the night about the Soviet threat. Mollet and Adenauer decided that a working group would address the unresolved issues, while they discussed the international situation. They reached agreement on all points. Regarding the 'especially difficult issue of the harmonization of social costs' (Carstens 1976, 599), they agreed on a compromise text that would become Article 117 of the treaty. Harmonization was no longer a condition for the transition to the second stage, but became a common aim. Regarding equal pay, they kept the formulation agreed by Foreign Ministers in October.

From 'Paris' to 'Rome' (November 1956–March 1957)

The delegations in Brussels went back to work based on the French-German compromise (MAE 522 f/56). With regard to equal pay, there was still the question of what to do if some sectors had achieved equality at the end of the first stage and others had not. Should the member states then move on to the second stage, and if so, should they establish safeguard clauses for the disadvantaged sectors? (CM 3/NEGO 149, *Note rapide*, 9 November 1956). On 16 November, the delegation leaders met to take stock of the situation. The majority of the delegations approved the equal pay provision, but the Netherlands had reservations about the expansion of the principle to the ILO-100 norm of equal pay 'for equal work and work of equal value' (MAE 612 f/56).

On 4 January 1957, the delegation leaders decided to send the text of Article 46 concerning equal pay to the Groupe de redaction with a request to revise the article to correspond as much as possible with ILO-100 (MAE 58 f/57). In the *Groupe de redaction*, the Netherlands proposed limiting the ILO formulation 'equal pay for work of equal value' to 'equal pay for equal work'. Due to a disagreement in the *Groupe de redaction*, they submitted Article 46 to a *Comité d'experts en matière sociale*. The experts were asked to find a solution to the problem that was 'apparently' caused by the translation into French of 'für gleiche Arbeit und gleiche Leistung' (for the same work and the same performance – the text agreed in Paris), but was 'possibly' also related to a more 'fundamental issue' (MAE 527 f/57).

The experts translated the crucial concept as 'pour un même travail' (for the same work), in accordance with the Dutch and German preferences (MAE 562 f/57). The *Groupe du Marché Commun* and the delegation leaders approved this translation (MAE 588 f/57; MAE 701 f/57). The *Groupe de rédaction* reworked the first paragraph of the equal pay provision as well, after which the definitive text of Article 46 read as follows:

7 See Segers 2006 for a detailed account of German preference formation.

> Each Member State shall during the first stage ensure and subsequently maintain the application of the principle that men and women should receive equal pay for equal work. For the purpose of this Article, 'pay' means the ordinary basic or minimum wage or salary and any other consideration, whether in cash or in kind, which the worker receives directly or indirectly, in respect of his employment from his employer.
>
> Equal pay without discrimination based on sex means: a. that pay for the same work at piece rates shall be calculated on the basis of the same unit of measurement; b. that pay for work at time rates shall be the same for the same job (MAE 649 f/57, 25 February 1957).

In the meantime, the French parliament had debated the issue of the common market in January 1957. Pineau emphasized that the French delegation had acquired 'significant guarantees' in the area of social policy. MP Pierre Mendès-France, unconvinced, pointed out that 'our partners want to maintain the trade advantage that results from their retarded social development' (Marjolin 1986, 287). In a dramatic speech, he painted an image of how unemployed Italians would flood into France, and investment would flow to Germany and other low cost countries (*Année Politique* 1957). Faure warned the parliament that it had to choose between 'Europe' and 'the uncertain future of an isolated France' (*Année Politique* 1957, 284). The parliament approved the motion for the common market on 23 January with 322 votes in favour and 207 votes against it. This gave the French government the mandate to continue negotiating on condition that agreements on the harmonization of social costs would be explicitly confirmed and that France would be given guarantees concerning agriculture and French overseas territories (CM 2/1958, *Rapport Savary*, No. 5266, 1957).

The other member states took the wishes of the French parliament into account out of fear that the treaty at the last minute would be put in jeopardy by rejection in the French Parliament. Domestic instability in France meant the negotiators were under pressure to conclude, fearing 'that the EEC might not happen with a different government in power in Paris' (Urwin, 1995; *Handelingen* 1956–7, 4725, 4). Spaak also put pressure on the negotiators because he wanted the treaties approved before the German parliamentary elections in the autumn of 1957; he feared that a SPD majority would reject the treaties because they viewed them as obstacles to German reunification. His remorseless pace led to 'incremental decision-making' because the governments no longer had time to realize the overall consequences of their decisions (Griffiths and Asbeek Brusse 1989, 491).

However, the time pressure cannot explain why the member states approved the equal pay provision; this stands in contrast to Hoskyns' assertion that 'many of the loose ends and anomalies in the treaty (and certainly the inclusion of the provisions on equal pay) can be attributed to these pressures' (Hoskyns 1996a, 45). Equal pay was not a 'loose end' or an 'anomaly', but was part of the 'liberalization-harmonization debate' that had been waged since the 1950s in France, the ILO and the Spaak Committee. Women's wages were on the agenda from the first meeting of the Spaak committee in June 1955 and negotiations about the exact formulation of the equal pay article and its position in the treaty continued until the very last. The crucial moment for equal pay was the approval by Brentano on 21 October 1956.

In March 1957, negotiations were completed and the treaty texts only required a *toilette juridique* (Snoy et d'Oppuers 1989). Von der Groeben and Pierre Uri of the *Groupe de redaction* made a thorough revision of the chapter on 'mutual adaptation of legislation', which until then included Article 46 (equal pay). To strengthen the social outlook of the treaty, 'equal pay' was moved to the 'Social Provisions' chapter and became Article 119. They condensed the rest of the section about distortions into a single article (Article 101) (MAE 776 f/57, 5 March 1957). On 11 March, the delegation leaders approved the treaty texts although working groups were still discussing amendments until the day of the signing.

In Rome on 25 March, the foreign affairs ministers signed the Treaties which established the EEC and EURATOM. The Netherlands added an interpretive declaration concerning the application of Article 119. It stated that 'the Netherlands shall not be required to go further in this matter than that which has in fact been realized in France at the end of the transitional period' (*Handelingen* 1956–7, 4725, 31; MAE 945 f/57). The result of the negotiations was a customs union as the first stage of a common market, with transition to the second stage dependent on, among other things, the implementation of the equal pay provision.

Women's Interests in the Negotiations for a Customs Union

The right of women to equal pay was inserted into the treaty to prevent the French parliament from blocking further integration. France was able to put the issue on the agenda by referring to the international obligation of ILO-100 and the 'distortion'-argument. Germany accepted a limited equal pay provision – for equal work, not for work of equal value – only after the economic costs had decreased due to domestic developments. The Dutch government could not block the provision without German support, but at the last minute, it succeeded in unilaterally weakening its obligation to implement it and thus reduced the potential costs. None of the governmental representatives was motivated by a genuine interest in women's rights or the issue of equality between women and men.

Transnational actors were only indirectly involved. The international trade unions complained that they were kept away from the negotiations and sent notes to inform Spaak of their position. The International Confederation of Christian Trade Unions (ICSC) was of the opinion that equal pay for work of equal value should be realized in stages. At the same time, it stated that fair pay should be complemented by a family wage for the head of the family and equal pay be accompanied by 'measures to avoid women being given work that is improper for them' (CM3/NEGO, Ref. JK/LV-1610, 4 June 1956). This view tended more towards the interests of breadwinners and conservatives than the interests of women workers.

Women themselves had no direct access to the negotiations and no channels of influence. Discounting interpreters and secretaries, only men were present at the negotiation table in Messina, only male delegation leaders in the Spaak Committee, only men in the *Groupe du Marché Commun* and as ministers of foreign affairs. In the *Sous-commission des problèmes sociaux*, there was one German woman expert, Dr Lenz, among the 26 members. The Political Affairs Committee of the ECSC Assembly[8] counted one woman, the Dutch Christian-Democrat Marga Klompé, who pleaded as rapporteur for 'the progressive harmonization of social policies' in the framework of harmonization (CM 2/1958, AC 1562, Doc 43:4, 20 June 1955).

Although in the following decades Article 119 would become a powerful instrument to improve working conditions for women, this was not the intention of the negotiators. Article 119 would only reveal its potential from the moment that women attained the position and the power to use it.

No Implementation of Article 119 (1958–1961)

Ratification of Article 119 by the National Parliaments

France had striven for a customs union that included guarantees concerning social harmonization, including equal pay. It had obtained what it wanted, and on 10 July 1957, the parliament ratified the treaties by a vote of 342 in favour and 239 against (Gaullists, radicals, and communists) (*Année Politique* 1957, 73).

In Germany, both the parliamentary *rapporteur* for social affairs Sabel and the government confirmed that the German concession made on Article 119 was of minor importance. The government explained that the implementation would not cause problems for Germany because 'Article 3 of the Constitution, especially due to recent court decisions, already stipulates the equality of men's and women's wages' (CM 2/1958, *Bundestag* 1957, 208. *Sitzung*). On 5 July, the *Bundestag* ratified the treaty with a large majority, followed two weeks later by the *Bundesrat*.

In the Netherlands, there was more discussion about Article 119. The government itself was disappointed with the treaty. If wages, terms of employment, and social provisions had to be raised to the highest level in the EEC, 'the industrialization of our country and the welfare of our population could even be endangered' and Article 119 alone could have an immediate inflationary effect of 2.5–3 percent (*Handelingen* 1956–7, 4725, 7). However, the government was not dissatisfied with what had been achieved 'in view of the necessity to compromise, at least to some extent, due to the French aspiration to achieve social harmony that was deeply anchored in the public opinion of that country' (*Handelingen* 1956–7, 4725, 31). The harmonization had been limited to equal pay and holiday leave, the European Commission had not been given any decision making authority regarding social policy, and the Netherlands had been able to stipulate that it did not have to go any further than France concerning the implementation of equal pay.

In the Dutch parliament, opinions on Article 119 were divided. 'Many members' of the preparatory committee approved of the principle despite the expected difficulties

8 The Assembly was the predecessor of the European Parliament, not directly elected but composed of representatives of the six national parliaments.

for some sectors of industry. 'Other members' pointed out that the consequences for industries with many female workers were much more serious than the government believed. In the ready-to-wear clothing industry, there would be wage rises of 30 percent. They did not show concern about the discrimination of women workers but about the economic costs of paying women correctly. 'Various members' believed that Article 119 was illogical because the market would automatically create social harmonization, but they reluctantly accepted the article as 'a compromise to get out of a remarkably thorny negotiating position' (*Handelingen* 1956–7, 4725, Nr. 9, 53).

According to the liberal party, while in the Netherlands regulations were promptly and rigorously adhered to, in other countries they were not; the wage system in the Netherlands was 'different' (family wage); some industries would be badly hit; and the equal pay obligation restricted opportunities for 'wage increases and other and better social provisions that are preferable from the Dutch viewpoint'. 'Of course, it is inherent to a treaty such as this that one is required to give up certain aspects of one's sovereignty, but … in the haste [to complete the treaty], the aim of a harmonious improvement of working conditions and social provisions has been incalculably damaged' (*Handelingen* 1957–8, I, 72).

The government answered that it was 'very aware' of the danger of price increases and 'was resolved to not be drawn into an unreasonable pursuit of social harmonization' (*Memorie van Antwoord*, 16 September 1957, 7). However, equal pay applied only to professions and companies where men and women did exactly the same work and not to traditional women's professions. There Article 119 deviated from ILO-100. This meant that 'that to which the Dutch government now obligates itself is less far-reaching than that to which we would have obligated ourselves if we had ratified the relevant ILO convention'. This was 'an important limitation to the concession made to France' (*Handelingen* 1957–8, I, 133). The business community itself would be responsible for implementing the principle because 'the government … should preferably not impose anything on the employers in this respect' (*Handelingen* 1957–8, I, 168). In the event that difficulties should occur in some industries, then the government would 'not hesitate to make an appeal to the escape clause' (*Memorie van Antwoord*, 16 September 1957, 35).

Gerard Nederhorst, MP from the PvdA, formulated a minority standpoint with his criticism of this limited interpretation of Article 119. In vain, he reminded the government (and parliament) that three years earlier, a parliamentary majority had approved the principle of equal pay for work of equal value in the *Tendeloo*-motion (*Handelingen* 1957–8, 4 October 1957, 154–5). In the end, a large majority of the Dutch parliament voted in favour of the treaties.

The Deadline Becomes a Dead Letter

On 1 January 1958, the treaties on the EEC and EURATOM came into force. The member states had to implement Article 119 before the end of the first stage of the customs union on 31 December 1961; if not, then the transition to the second stage could not take place (Article 8 EEC Treaty).

Equal Pay at the National Level (1958-61) In formal terms, France had already implemented Article 119. The principle of equal pay was included in the new constitution of 1959 and it applied to all labour contracts. The trade unions and the labour inspectorate were responsible for enforcing compliance. The French trade unions denied that there was any kind of systematic discrimination. They attributed the nine percent wage difference between women's and men's wages to women's lower trade union membership and lower educational level resulting in women holding lower level jobs (BAC 008/1966, *Letter Louet to Van Tilburg*, 13 March 1961).

In view of the French battle for Article 119, one would expect that the French government would actively monitor the compliance in the other member states. However, when Charles de Gaulle came to power in 1958, the electoral and economic motivation for Article 119 disappeared. De Gaulle made changes in the constitution, such as to make French governments structurally less sensitive to parliamentary pressure. The French economy grew, and it quickly turned out that French industry did not suffer from its head start in social policy.

German employers believed that equal pay had been achieved and that the 25–30 percent difference in men's and women's wages was the result of age differences, marital status and seniority (Commission 1961, V/6120/61). In June 1961, three female members of parliament (CDU) asked about the state of affairs concerning Article 119. Minister Blank assured them that 'the principle of equal pay for men and women for equal work has been realized and is applied in the Federal Republic of Germany' (BT Drs, 2793, 7 June 1961; BT Drs, 2899, 21 June 1961).

However, a major discrepancy existed between the formal right to equal pay and the wages that were in practice paid to women and men. Job classifications were determined in accordance with so-called 'objective' scientific criteria. Such criteria differed between regions and companies, but all systematically assigned a lower value to work done primarily by women (Commission 1960, V/7154/60). Female employees had no judicial recourse because the courts had ruled that women could be paid less if their work was not identical to the work done by men in the same company. Furthermore, women could be paid a lower piecework rate because their productivity was thought intrinsically lower than male productivity. In some sectors, 'sub-categories' for 'typical women's work' were created. Remuneration in these categories was 25–35 percent below the lowest pay scale. Some companies paid women less than men because women were not allowed to do night work or because they were not given family supplements and overtime premiums. A study conducted by the European Commission confirmed that women's work was systematically undervalued (Commission 1960, V/7154/60).

The German trade unions complained that equal pay was only being applied in a formal sense and that women's wage groups had disappeared in name only. It had even become more difficult for women to file a complaint because discrimination was no longer visible in separate tables for men's and women's wages, and a female employee now had to prove that her job had been incorrectly classified as 'light work' by using 'objective criteria' (BAC 008/1966, DGB, Press release, 7 July 1961). But despite their protests, trade unions continued to approve collective agreements with separate, lower women's wage scales (Commission 1962, V/6286/62).

Of all the member states, the Netherlands was the most backward concerning equal pay. There was no statutory equal pay provision. Collective labour agreements fixed women's wages 25–30 percent lower than men's wages for the same work (Commission 1962, V/6286/62) and the Board of Government Mediators accepted this situation without protest. Women who felt disadvantaged had no legal means whatsoever of fighting wage discrimination. With the simple step of amending the guidelines of the Board of Government Mediators, the government could have eliminated wage differences. However, the Dutch government feared that its state-controlled wage policy would mean that implementation would then go further than other countries and export interests would be harmed.

Consequently, in December 1960 the government only sent an 'invitation' to the Board of Government Mediators to 'pay special attention to the gradual implementation of the principle of equal pay for mixed jobs' (jobs performed by both men and women) (BAC 006/1977, Memorandum Dörr, 10 June 1963). Anxious to avoid accusations of disregard for Article 119, the government defended its actions from criticism from France and the Commission with the argument that the gender-based wage gap in other member states was larger than shown by the figures. Men in other countries were paid higher wages than those in the collective labour agreements, while Dutch employers were required to stick closely to the stipulated wages (Commission 1959, V/4847/59).

The Dutch trade unions association (NVV) protested against the limitation of equal pay to 'mixed jobs'. At the request of female trade union members, the NVV had even established a committee for equal pay. However, this committee alleged that the NVV's concern for equal pay was primarily symbolic since the association never insisted on this point during wage negotiations. The NVV defended itself with the argument that there were too few female members (30,000 women compared to 485,000 men) and that the male members were opposed to using the limited financial bargaining space to obtain an increase in women's wages (Eijl 1997).

Delay at the Supranational Level The European Commission had the task of monitoring the transition to the second stage of the customs union. However, the Social Affairs Commissioner, Giuseppe Petrilli, was reluctant. He answered critical questions in the European Parliament and the Economic and Social Committee by replying that the Commission still had three years to solve the equal pay problem and first ordered a study into the Commission's authority concerning Article 119 (BAC 008/1966, Petrilli, *Memorandum*, 23 April 1959, III/a/3954; Dörr, *Letter to Leleux*, 28 April 1959). The legal service of the Commission interpreted the Commission mandate in a strict sense. It believed that the Commission could only formulate non-binding recommendations to remind member states of their obligations. If a member state had not fulfilled its obligations at the end of the first stage (December 1961), the Commission had the right to bring the matter before the Court. However, the legal service did not recommend this procedure in order to avoid an open conflict with member states (BAC 008/1966, *Note service juridique*, 11 May 1959).

The Directorate General of Employment and Social Affairs (DG V) disagreed with the legal service. It believed that the Commission could propose binding measures to the Council based on Article 101 of the EEC Treaty because wage differences distorted competition, or based on Article 100 of the EEC Treaty to harmonize national legislation in the area of equal pay (BAC 008/1966, Toffanin, *Memorandum*, 14 May 1959). However, Commissioner Petrilli took a cautious approach and decided that the Commission should limit itself to collecting judicial and statistical information with the aid of national experts, employers and trade unions. Even these extremely modest activities encountered resistance.

UNICE, the European employers' organization, and the European offices of the international trade union federations ICFTU and ICSC met regularly under the auspices of the DG V. They steadfastly disagreed about the selection of sectors for a study regarding equal pay (Commission 1959, V/4903/59). They also preferred to be consulted separately and were unable to draw up joint national reports (BAC 008/1966, Reports, 24 July 1959 and 22 December 1960). The unions thought it was pointless to limit the reports to mixed jobs since only 2–3 percent of women worked in such jobs. The employers' priority was to prevent expanding the research to include non-mixed jobs (traditional women's professions) (Commission 1960, V/5274/60). As a result, the monitoring work of DG V was delayed (BAC 008/1966, Reports, 31 March 1960 and 24 November 1961).

The 'national experts' who assisted the DG V in collecting information were not independent experts, but officials of the Ministries of Labour or Social Affairs who defended the standpoint of their government. Most experts were men. During the first major meeting of experts on 7–8 October 1959, Mrs Ledru from Belgium made the following intervention:

> Please allow me to say, by the way and in all courtesy, that in fact it is rather astonishing that, for a problem which is of such big interest for women, I am here the only woman represented. And I am not sure whether this is always a good thing, because I believe that it would be useful that in discussions on equal pay women should be represented with a much more comfortable majority (Commission 1959, V/4847/59, 203 [original in French, translation AvdV]).

This was her reaction to an Italian colleague who explained that it was a good thing when the man works and the woman stays at home. None of her colleagues responded to her suggestion to invite more women around the table.

Continuing disagreements about the scope of the 'equal work' concept further delayed the work of DG V. Days of discussion were necessary to determine whether women who produced small automobile tyres and men who produced large automobile tyres did the same work or not, and whether men could be paid more because they were allowed to turn on the machinery in the morning (Commission

1959, V/4847/59). It took three years before German and French experts agreed that Article 119 also applied if a man and a woman did the same job in the same company, but not at the same time (Commission 1961, V/5529/61). Many arguments were used to justify pay reductions for women: work was not 'equal' because women received one day off per month to do household duties, or because women needed time off to give birth; women were not allowed to do night work; women were assisted by men to repair the machines once or twice a year (Commission 1959, V/4847/59).

The Dutch government insisted repeatedly on the importance – because of its interpretive declaration in Rome – of reliable statistical data (BAC 008/1966, *Letter to Hallstein*, 17 September 1959). However, it simultaneously delayed the statistical research of the Commission and refused to submit the requested information (BAC 008/1966, S/4853, 1959). Member of European Parliament Nederhorst asked the Commission if the member states were frustrating its efforts to supervise the implementation of Article 119. In the final version of its reply, the Commission wrote that it had not ascertained a lack of cooperation from any member state. The first version of the Commission's answer had criticized France, Germany and the Netherlands, but the Committee of Permanent Representatives (Coreper) edited all these criticisms out (BAC 001/1962, Question submitted by Nederhorst; S/4853, First version of answer, 20 July 1959; Second version, 24 July 1959).

The Deadline Approaches In November 1959, the Council invited the Commission to make recommendations on accelerating the implementation of the treaty. The Commission recommended advancing the deadline for the implementation of Article 119. It drew up a recommendation which proposed setting 30 June 1961 as the deadline for the complete implementation of equal pay. To put an end to the continuing disagreement between member states about the precise meaning of Article 119, the Commission provided its official interpretation. Equal pay for equal work meant not only that direct wage discrimination was forbidden, but also that classification systems had to contain the same criteria and categories for men and women. 'Equal work' did not necessarily have to be 'identical work'. As a result, the Commission interpreted the concept of 'equal work' in a broader way than Germany and the Netherlands had. However, in his accompanying letter, President of the Commission Walter Hallstein made it clear that the issue of 'equal pay for work of equal value' still fell outside the area of application of Article 119 (Commission 1960, V/4900/60). Earlier versions of the recommendation were more ambitious, but employers and governments had weakened the text (BAC 008/1966, Pro-memoria, 21 June 1960).

When the deadline approached, the Netherlands complained that the recommendation lacked factual supporting evidence because the statistical information from the various member states was not comparable. The Council then established a Special Working Group for Article 119 with two representatives from each member state. This Working Group would have the task of collecting comparable data with the assistance of trade unions and employers organizations (*Bulletin* 6–

1961, 45). The group was led by Lionello Levi-Sandri, the new Commissioner for Social Affairs, succeeding Petrilli in October 1960.

The first meeting of the Working Group became bogged down in a long discussion about the interpretation of 'equal work' because the Netherlands and Germany considered the Commission's interpretation too far-reaching (Commission 1961, V/5536/61). During the second meeting, Levi-Sandri proposed to limit matters to the collection of information 'without interpretations'. The delegations accepted Levi-Sandri's proposal.

In September 1961, four months before the deadline of Article 119, the Commission published a report that was based on the information collected. It ascertained that the index figures showed a certain amount of progress because women's wages had increased more quickly than those of men had, but that in *all* member states the

Table 2.3 Wage gap for equally qualified men and women

	France		Germany		The Netherlands	
Sector	Women workers (%) of all workers	Difference women's – men's wages (%)	Women workers (%) of all workers	Difference women's – men's wages (%)	Women workers (%) of all workers	Difference women's – men's wages (%)
Textile	55.7	12–13	60.1	21	30.2	25–30
Food	30.1	7–12	–	38	20.7	27
Chemical	–	8–14	29.4	35	22.1	–
Electrical	33.7	7–10	37.7	28	–	–
Clothing	82.2	10–16	84.9	29	60.4	27–31
Mean industry	27	9.2	24	10–20	23	31

Source: Commission (1961), V/1289/61 and V/6120/61

application of the equal pay principle was inadequate. Some stipulated that equal pay applied only to '*identical* work carried out by men and women at the *same* company at the *same* time' (Commission 1961, *Draft Report*). As a result, Article 119 had a very limited effect. Statistical data clearly showed the discrepancy between the approval of the principle and its implementation (see Table 2.3).

The Council had a problem. Before 31 December 1961 it had to make a decision on the transition to the second stage, but as long as the conditions for this transition had not been satisfied, the Council could not pass to the second stage without damaging 'the political authority of the treaty' (EP 1961, Proceedings, 314–18). The transition to the second stage had become stuck on equal pay and the common agricultural policy. Regarding equal pay, the member states had violated the deadline of Article 119. Various parties were exerting pressure on the Commission to take firm action against the member states. Maria Weber, the only woman on the Board of the DGB, warned the Commission to be sceptical about the German government's assertion that equal pay had been completely implemented (Commission 1961, V/6286/61). The international trade unions urged the Commission not to accept any compromise (BAC 008/1966, Doc. 1500/61 SOC132) The EP vigilantly followed the events (Official Journal 1961, 1417/61, Resolution; 1544/61, Resolution; 1556/61, Resolution).

On 28 November, the Special Working Group reached agreement on a compromise text in which member states promised, before the end of December 1961, to 'begin taking measures' to assure the right to equal pay; the complete implementation would be spread across three years. After an extensive discussion, the Council approved the general terms of the draft resolution on 4 December (BAC 008/1966, Memorandum for Levi-Sandri, 8 December 1961). During a marathon session that lasted from 18 December 1961 to 14 January 1962, the ministers reached agreement about the common agricultural policy. They approved the resolution on equal pay and predated the document to 30 December 1961. The Netherlands repeated its declaration from 1957, clinging to the limited interpretation of Article 119 and insisting on an application that did not go further than the other member states.

In the resolution, the member states promised to reduce the differences between men's and women's wages to 15 percent by 30 June 1962, to 10 percent by June 1963, and to eliminate the differences entirely by 31 December 1964. The interpretation of Article 119 was extended by defining the 'systematic under-classification of female workers' as a violation of the principle of equal pay. However, the postponement of the full implementation of Article 119 until the end of 1964 meant that the Commission could not begin a procedure against member states that were in breach of the article until 1965.

No Pressure, No Implementation (1962–68)

Much Paper, No Pressure

Due to the above events, there were three new deadlines for implementation of Article 119. The resolution also stipulated that discrimination in job classifications was impermissible and that the right to equal pay had to be judicially enforceable.

Equal Pay at the National Level (1962–65) In March 1962, the French government responded by calling on employers and trade unions to modify any collective labour agreements that were not in accordance with the resolution. In contrast to the period up to 1961, the trade unions had become more critical than before. They had ascertained inconsistencies in collective labour agreements. In the paper and footwear industries, women and men in the same job category were paid differently. In the gas and electricity sector, jobs performed exclusively by women were classified as 'work for the handicapped'. In regions where the employment opportunities for women were limited to a single sector (such as the canning industry in coastal regions), women's wages were very low (BAC 006/1977, Commission 1963, Draft Report). Married male workers received a family and child supplement, but married female workers did not because they had 'other needs' (Commission 1964, V/13206/64).

When it became clear that policy change was also necessary in France, the government became less cooperative towards the Commission. It tried to prevent the Commission from including *effective* wages in its report. The collective labour agreements only stipulated minimum wages, which were indeed the same for men and women, but the effective wages above the minimum wage level differed for men and women (Commission 1962, V/5394/62). The government disagreed that systematic wage discrimination was also prevalent in France (Commission 1963, V/3479/63).

It was very important to France to be the only member state that had correctly implemented Article 119. Due to the criticisms in the Commission report, the government therefore prepared a law that the parliament was supposed to approve in December of 1964, before the final deadline of the resolution had passed. According to the law, every wage agreement that did not respect the principle of equal pay should be declared void (Commission 1964, 10760/V/64). The bill was never discussed in parliament, but the government was able to save its reputation merely by referring to its intention to implement Article 119 correctly.

In February 1962, the German government requested the Ministries of Labour of the *Länder* and the employers and trade unions to implement the resolution. Members of parliament from the SPD questioned Minister Blank about the differences between the effective wages of women and men. Blank stuck with his opinion that equal pay had been achieved and that 'unequal pay' was not the result of discrimination, but of 'unequal work'. The fact that women found themselves in the lowest pay scales in all sectors came about, he believed, not because women's work was valued less than that of men, but 'very simply' because women were incapable of working in highly paid jobs, such as those in the mining industry. He did not answer the question from the *Bundestag* about how he could then explain the differences in sectors other than mining (BAC 008/1966, *Bundestag*, 15 March 1962).

The fact that equal pay was not applied as thoroughly as Blank believed was shown by the judgements of the Federal Labour Court, which declared various collective labour agreements void based on a violation of Article 3 of the Constitution (BAC 006/1977, Dörr, Memorandum, 10 June 1963). Still, all collective labour agreements in the leather industry maintained separate wage categories for women. In other sectors, women were placed into categories where the wages were 15–20 percent lower than the categories reserved for men (BAC 006/1977, Commission 1963, Draft Report).

According to a study of the Commission, in the Netherlands there was a 'historical difference' between men's wages and women's wages and this difference was 'quite generally accepted' based on the 'need' element (Commission 1962, V/10993/62). The trade unions warned the Commission that this conclusion only reflected the opinion of Dutch employers. The companies involved in the Commission study had prevented their employees from participating because they were concerned that 'asking questions about the topic of equal pay for men and women would cause unrest. For such simple people, this could lead to unjustified or premature expectations' (BAC 006/1977, Neirinck, *Letter to Overlegorgaan*, 1964). The Dutch trade unions appealed to the Commission to force the Dutch government to adopt a more activist policy with regard to employers (BAC 006/1977, Van Tilburg, *Letter to Levi-Sandri*, 31 August 1964). However, at the domestic level they did not protest against collective labour agreements that violated the equal pay obligation (Eijl 1997).

The government informed the Labour Foundation that it would limit the application of the resolution to mixed jobs, because it did not want to go further than other countries and first wanted to have statistical material on implementation in the other member states (BAC 006/1977, Veldkamp, *Letters to the Labour Foundation*, 18 January and 21 February 1962). Because of the Commission report on the state of affairs, the government made a proposal on 8 January 1963 to the Labour Foundation to increase wages of women in mixed jobs to 90 percent of men's wages. This guideline had to be carried out within the available space for wage increases.

The parliament asked the government to accelerate application of equal pay as a means of easing the tight labour market. In November 1963, the government therefore recommended the Labour Foundation to accelerate the implementation of equal pay and to increase the pay of women in non-mixed jobs as well. The Foundation informed the government that the employers were opposed to accelerated implementation because of negative consequences in certain industries (BAC 006/1977, Labour Foundation, *Letter to Veldkamp*, 4 December 1963). The government took no further steps. It even approved an agreement of the Labour Foundation that stipulated a minimum wage for male workers only. Women in mixed jobs could earn no more than 90% of the minimum wage, and those in non-mixed jobs had no right to a minimum wage at all (BAC 006/1977, Coppes, *Letter to DG V*, 27 July 1964). Some months later, the government informed the Labour Foundation that 'if [the] Foundation believes that further implementation of equal pay must be limited', it was prepared to negotiate with the European Commission on this issue. It agreed with the employers that insufficient data was available about other countries and the data that was available 'did not indicate that clear progress is being made in other countries of the EEC' (BAC 006/1977, Veldkamp, Letter, 1 December 1964).

Pressure at the Supranational Level The three deadlines in the resolution offered the Commission three opportunities to take stock of the implementation of the equal pay principle. However, there was no effective supranational pressure on member states.

After every deadline, the Commission drew up a report based on the data it obtained from governments, employers, and trade unions. In its first report of 30 June 1962, it ascertained that 'in all countries of the Community, sometimes remarkable progress has been achieved', although it also noted inadequacies and the fact that Article 119 was still interpreted differently in different countries (*Bulletin* 2–1963, 58; Commission 1962, V/COM(62)321).

In the second report on 30 June 1963, the Commission was initially more critical. In the draft version, it complained about the lack of adequate judicial protection in France. It also criticized Germany on the grounds that employers had a great deal of freedom to classify jobs whilst female employees had no defence against this arbitrary classification and the conditions for correctly implementing equal pay were unfavourable due to the freedom of the parties in collective bargaining. The Netherlands had not sent any data (Commission 1963, *Draft Report*).

The report appeared to indicate that the Commission would act more firmly in the future, and the member states responded immediately. They wanted to gain more control over the contact between the Commission and the trade unions and asked to see all information that the Commission received from the trade unions before this was included in its annual report (Commission 1963, V/3479/63). In the final version of the report, in Germany, 'the conditions for correct application of the principle' had suddenly become 'remarkably beneficial' (Commission 1964, V/COM(64)11).

Every time a deadline approached, the European Parliament noted the member states' lack of political will and the restriction of equal pay to mixed jobs (*Bulletin* 5–1963, 68). Commissioner Levi-Sandri agreed with the criticism of the EP. He confirmed that he did not accept the interpretive declaration of the Netherlands: a member state could not justify non-fulfilment of its treaty obligations by pointing to treaty violations by other member states. However, he did not take any steps against the Netherlands (EP 1962, *Handelingen*, 333).

The Final Deadline? When the final deadline for implementation of the resolution (31 December 1964) approached, the DG V had prepared a recommendation with detailed criteria that applied to national legislation and collective labour agreements. It also contained new ideas, such as proposals for improving the professional training of women, establishing supervisory bodies, and launching a campaign to inform the public (BAC 006/1977, Commission 1964, Draft). However, the Commission did not submit the recommendation to the Council, because it feared it would not be approved (BAC 006/1977, Toffanin and Leleux, Notes of discussion, 1964).

Levi-Sandri sent a separate letter to each government and to the European employers' organizations and international trade union associations. He made specific recommendations for each of these bodies and included a general warning that 'the Commission was very concerned that it would ascertain violations at the end of the year which would have legal consequences in accordance with the norms and procedures in the treaty' (BAC 006/1977, Levi-Sandri, Draft letter, 15 May 1964). France, Germany and the Netherlands urged the Commission to include only a survey of the state of affairs in its final report, to make no suggestions for further strategies, and to draw no conclusions. The Commission responded by pointing out that the content of the report was its sole responsibility (Commission 1964, V/11932/64 and V/11933/64).

In his letters, Levi-Sandri also reported that the Commission had relinquished its mandate from the Council to conduct statistical research into men's and women's wages. After three years of holding arduous meetings, establishing national workgroups, drawing up questionnaires, and establishing separate workgroups for each sector, the national experts had suddenly decided that the planned research was not useful. The majority of the delegations stated that they preferred to wait for the results of a study conducted by Eurostat, the EEC Bureau for Statistics, concerning the general wage structure. The Netherlands reserved the right to request a separate study of men's and women's wages if the general study did not yield the expected results (BAC 006/1977, Council 1964, 1293/64 SOC 128). On 15 October 1964, the Council decided to postpone the study and to wait for the Commission report about the implementation of Article 119.

The Third Report On 9 July 1965, the Commission submitted its third report to the Council about the implementation of equal pay after a draft version had been modified by national experts in the Special Workgroup and by Coreper (BAC 006/1977, Commission 1965, V/COM(65)270 and 931/65 SOC 106). Despite the request of the member states, the Commission also drew conclusions.

It ascertained that progress had been made, but that 'in all countries, a great deal remains to be done by the government or the organized business community' (*Bulletin* 9/10–1965, 47). In France, the differences between men's and women's wages turned out to be 10.1 percent. According to the government, this difference was related to objective differences in performance, the number of years of employment and the skill level; therefore, there was no discrimination against female workers in France. The best proof of this was that not a single woman had submitted a complaint about unequal pay in recent years. The government deliberately ignored the fact that women were unable to complain because the classification of jobs was not strictly specified, and this allowed arbitrary choices to be made. Moreover, women did not qualify for supplements for unhealthy or hazardous work, overtime, night work, and work on Sundays and holidays, 'which of course were usually added to the wages of male workers' (Commission 1965, V/COM(65)270). In Germany, the systematic undervaluation of female labour in all sectors and the use of *Leichtlohngruppen* were the most important causes of discrimination. Job valuations varied according to regional traditions and characteristics of the local labour market (Commission 1965, V/COM(65)270).

For the first time, the Commission's conclusion about the Netherlands was openly critical. The Netherlands continued to discriminate openly by continuing to stipulate different wages for men and women in collective labour agreements. For women, the wages in these agreements were between 77–95 percent of those for men. The Commission rejected the interpretive declaration from 1957. The Dutch government's argument that it had no comparable data did not release it from its obligation to implement the provisions of the treaty (Commission 1965, V/COM(65)270).

Based on this report, the Commission appeared to be justified in taking action against all member states due to their breach of Article 119. However, the Commission believed that such a procedure would only be justified if a *government* had not met an obligation imposed on it by the treaty. In Germany, the gaps in implementation were the result of the action (or inaction) of employers and trade unions. The Commission did not want to initiate a procedure against the other five countries because the situation in some of them was less serious than in Germany. 'At the present time, it appears there is no political and psycological opportunity for a procedure at the Court of Justice' (BAC 006/1977, Toffanin, *Reminder for the 324th meeting of the Commission*, 5 July 1965). The Commission therefore decided to ask the member states to establish a new deadline. The Council did not consider the report until eighteen months later, in December 1966, due to the crisis which had meanwhile broken out in the EEC.[9] The Commission certainly was not in a position of bringing a member state before the Court.

From 'Empty Chair' to Serious Unrest

Equal Pay at the National Level (1966–68) In France, a shift was taking place. Due to the increasing educational level and labour market participation of women during the 1960s, working women saw their inferior position no longer as self-evident (Mazur 1991). Due to the 'global increase in consciousness of the nation' and fearing the electoral appeal of the socialist party, the Gaullist government established a *Comité d'études et de liaison pour les problèmes du travail féminin* (Committee on Women's Work) (Commission 1966, SEC(66)1796). The Committee was not only composed of employers and trade unions, but also included representatives from women's organizations and independent experts. Although the Committee was only able to exert influence when it acquired strong political support (see Chapter 3), this was the first time non-traditional women's groups acquired formal access to decision making.

The German government disregarded the criticism of the Commission. After all, the issue of equal pay had been formally settled (Commission 1966, SEC(66)1797). In a study about equal pay, *IG Metall* admitted that it had not succeeded in removing separate women's wage groups from the collective labour agreements and showed that the effective wage gap was actually 22–28 percent.

In 1966, Germany experienced a recession. The return of women to 'hearth and home' was a cheap method of reducing the size of the active working population (Krasnogolovy 1968). It was also compatible with the findings of a study that the government had carried out – at the repeated insistence of the SPD – concerning the position of women in 'profession, family, and society'. The 641–page report defined women as 'mothers and housewives', despite figures that showed that half of all women engaged in paid work (Wiggershaus 1979, 36). In the eyes of the DGB and the SPD, the report provided proof of the 'failure to achieve statutory

9 On 15 March 1965, President of the Commission Hallstein had presented a package of proposals in which he linked the financing of the common agricultural policy (cherished by France) to an extension of the budgetary authority of the Commission and the European Parliament (unacceptable to France). On 30 June 1965, the French Minister of Foreign Affairs, Maurice Couve de Murville, broke off discussions in the Council and France no longer participated in the activities in 'Brussels'. On 29 January 1966, the 'Luxembourg compromise' ended the crisis (Lieshout 1999).

equality for women' and the 'failure to acknowledge working women' in Germany (Krasnogolovy 1968, 370). The debate on the report took place on 25 January 1967 in front of a virtually empty parliament; nearly all male members of parliament were absent due to lack of interest. The debate led to no resolutions or initiatives (Wiggershaus 1979).

In the Netherlands, as in France, societal pressure increased. In 1965, the Board of Government Mediators approved collective labour agreements for the sugar and chocolate processing industry, the footwear, cigar and leather industries, all of which were in violation of Article 119. As a result, 400 female trade union members sent a protest telegram to the government on 20 February 1965. In that year, the annual national 'demonstrative meeting' of women members of the NVV was given the theme 'equal pay, equal opportunities, equal rights, equal obligations' (Eijl 1997). Member of Parliament Hanni Singer-Dekker, who maintained close contact with the NVV women, asked the Minister of Social Affairs, Gerard Veldkamp, to use all means to achieve equality in mixed jobs and to conduct a study into equal pay for non-mixed jobs. Veldkamp then requested the Labour Foundation to implement equal pay during the next year, but only for mixed jobs, since other countries also continued to discriminate between men and women (BAC 006/1977, Veldkamp, Letter to Labour Foundation, 52.735). The Foundation decided to apply the principle of equal pay to mixed jobs as an 'experimental norm'.

On 10 January 1966, the Board of Government Mediators issued a Minimum Wage Order that only applied to men. Once again, Singer-Dekker questioned the government. As the order was in breach of Article 119, she wanted to know what action the government would take (Eijl 1997). At the same time, Henk Vredeling, a MEP, asked the European Commission to evaluate this breach of Article 119 (Official Journal 1966, 1071/66, 21 April). Owing to the double criticism, Veldkamp asked the Board of Government Mediators to expand the order so that it applied to women in mixed jobs (BAC 006/1977, Veldkamp, Letter to Levi-Sandri, 53.276). The Board agreed, but stipulated that industries could request an exemption. The laundry, footwear and leather industries asked for and received exemptions. Exceptions were also made for many other sectors (BAC 006/1977, Council 1966, 416/66(SOC 69). Nel Tegelaar, Chair of the Women's Secretariat of the NVV, repeatedly asked trade union executives for clarification when they voted in favour of such exceptions and exemptions in the Labour Foundation. They answered that they approved 'for tactical reasons' (Eijl 1997).

Minister Veldkamp asked the tripartite Social and Economic Council (SER) if it was desirable to implement a statutory minimum income for men and women as requested in the EEC resolution. The advice of the SER was that women should be granted the minimum wage only if they did the same work in the same company under the same conditions as men (SER 1966, No. 3). The European Commission, informed about this decision by MEP Vredeling, confirmed that this was a violation of Article 119. However, the Commission hoped that 'the difficulties experienced by the Dutch government in connection with relinquishing a restrictive interpretation of Article 119' would quickly be overcome (*Official Journal*, 1967, 1760-1761/67, 10

May; 208/1, 28 August). The Dutch government believed that 'the situation was not yet ripe' for equalizing the wages of men and women. The economic situation would not support such an upward pressure on the level of wages, particularly industries with many female workers (*Handelingen* 1966–7, 8606, 2).

A study of female workers conducted by the SER on its own initiative demonstrated how controversial this topic still was, especially regarding married working women. In the Netherlands, as compared to other countries, relatively few women were in paid labour. The main obstacles for women turned out to be the practical problem of childcare, the opposition of their husbands and neighbours, and the low wage level in typically female professions. Therefore, the SER's Committee on Working Women, chaired by sociologist Hilda Verwey-Jonker, proposed to revise the 'financial classification' of women's professions (SER 1966, No. 15). With this recommendation, the SER was to prove ten years ahead of government policy.

Cautious Pressure from the Supranational Level In May 1966, the EP discussed the Commission report on Article 119 of July 1965. Rapporteur Cornelis Berkhouwer, a Dutch liberal, strongly criticized the Commission's cautious approach. The Commission should involve the Court by starting legal proceedings against the member states that were in breach of the treaty (BAC 006/1977, *Avant-projet Rapport Berkhouwer*, PE 15.623). In the final version, the EP toned down his criticism, eliminating the section about the Court and approving for the sixth time a resolution which called on the Commission to publish an annual report and to make proposals concerning the implementation of equal pay (*Official Journal* 1966, 2439-2440/66, 19 July).

In Coreper, all delegates criticized the Commission report, feeling their governments were being unjustly condemned. They deplored the fact that they were unable to evaluate to what extent various states had applied the principle because the report provided no figures concerning wage differences. France wanted supplementary empirical research into men's wages and women's wages. Levi-Sandri indignantly reminded the delegates that their own national experts, after meeting for three years, had decided two years earlier that such a study was 'technically problematic'. The Netherlands stated that it had always wanted such a study, but that it was no longer necessary since the problem of equal pay would be solved in the near future by the labour market situation (Council 1966, 416/66 SOC (69) and 568/66 SOC (91)).

Member states could make no formal decision about the report because the Social Affairs Council had not met since October 1964. The EP warned that it could declare the Council 'in default' because it had not made any decisions in the area of social policy, while the urgency for a common social policy had increased. After all, social integration and economic integration were falling increasingly out of balance, while European citizens would only support an EEC with a social dimension (*Bulletin* 1–1967, 90). The Council defended itself with the argument that a crisis of trust had occurred between the Commission and 'some' member states because the Commission had been insufficiently tactful and had a tendency to exaggerate its authority in social matters. Finally, the Dutch presidency called a meeting of the

Social Affairs Ministers on 19 December 1966. The Council used the opportunity to limit the authority of the Commission to develop supranational social policy (BAC 006/1977, *Memorandum van Nederland aan de Raad*, 19 December 1966).

In 1967, the Commission again compiled a report on the implementation of equal pay. After it had heavily amended the report, Coreper submitted it to the Council and the EP (*Bulletin* 9/10–1967). Even the amended version showed that the member states were still in breach of the equal pay principle. In May 1968, the EP therefore made an appeal to the Commission to 'finally draw the obvious conclusion from this report' and initiate proceedings against one or more member states (*Official Journal* 1968, OJ C 55, 5 June). The Commission, however, took no action.

Conclusion: Equal Pay is Too Costly

Four questions opened this chapter: why did the issue of equal pay for men and women end up on the agenda of the negotiations for a customs union? Why was the issue so controversial, why did member states agree to a binding equal pay provision with a clear deadline, and why did they not implement this provision correctly?

France put forward the equal pay demand to obtain approval of the Treaty of Rome from the parliament. The equal pay demand was controversial in Germany and the Netherlands for economic and ideological reasons. It met with resistance among employers, who would have considerable economic costs, and was in conflict with government policy. German resistance to equal pay was overcome when the economic costs involved were reduced by domestic changes. Germany preferred to concede to French demands on this issue, in exchange for a French concession on overtime work – a point that had become more costly than equal pay. The Netherlands approved a treaty that included a costly equal pay provision because it was unable to prevent this without German support, and because, with its open, export-oriented economy, it did not want to be excluded from a common market with France and Germany.

These three member states all found that equal pay was too costly. In contrast to other aspects of the Treaty of Rome, such as tariff reduction, which were implemented on time or even sooner than required, their implementation of Article 119 was both reluctant and incomplete. In 1968, the Netherlands still did not have any statutory requirement for equal pay. Discriminatory collective labour agreements were not declared void in any of the three member states studied. The wage gap between men and women in collective labour agreements was still significant (10–25 percent), especially in sectors that employed many women. Women did not enjoy adequate judicial protection against unequal pay and excessively low job classification in any of these member states.

Pressure for implementation increased after 1965, but remained too weak to overcome resistance among employers and governments. The concern of trade unions for equal pay was primarily rhetorical. Governments did not reject the principle of equal pay, but they always found practical objections. German and Dutch employers rejected even the principle of equal pay. The pressure at the supranational level remained weak. The Commission drew up reports, censured by Coreper, but it shied away from taking action against member states, and did not bring a single one before the Court for fear of losing Council support for its proposals in other domains and of losing the support of the German trade unions. Some (male) officials in DG V made efforts to advance the implementation of equal pay, but the Commission was not supportive. The EP supported the Commission's criticism of the member states, but lacked any substantial power.

Yet, the member states all argued that they were not guilty of non-compliance. The Netherlands referred to its interpretive declaration and the lack of reliable data while Germany stated that the requested intervention was outside governmental authority. More generally, in both countries the idea of women and men having fundamentally different roles and needs as housewives and breadwinners respectively, persisted and resurfaced in times of recession. This idea legitimized different treatment. Only France drafted new legislation to maintain its reputation as social role model.

Meanwhile, levels of social unrest were increasing. May '68 would go into history as the month during which a rebellion of students and workers in France almost brought down De Gaulle. However, the cautious initiatives of the Commission to develop a common social policy ran aground due to the resistance of the member states. They seemed to be deaf to the argument that social progress and the support of society were necessary for the success of economic integration. In the 1970s, the Commission suddenly began to act much more autonomously, and the member states agreed to new, binding agreements concerning equal rights. How can this be explained? This question will be the central focus of Chapter 3.

Chapter 3

The Price of Supranational Gender Equality Policies (1969–1978)

During the 1960s, no new supranational policy was established in the area of equal rights for women and men. The member states did not even manage to implement Article 119. During the 1970s, the member states approved new supranational equal rights policies, which even contained norms that were more progressive than the existing national ones. How can we explain this sudden progress?

Shifts at the National and Supranational Levels

Social Policy on the National and European Agendas

At the end of the 1960s, all member states experienced a period of instability during which the foundations of the social order were questioned. The electorate made it clear that it wanted political change. As a result, governments came into power that were more sensitive to pressure for domestic social reform than were their predecessors.

In France, De Gaulle yielded his office to Georges Pompidou, a moderate Gaullist who aimed for social reform. Germany abandoned its neo-liberal standpoint when, on 21 October 1969, Willy Brandt was elected as the first social democratic chancellor. The *Leitmotiv* of his domestic policy was 'Dare more democracy' (Bundestag 1988). It also became his motto at the European level. He aimed to make the European Community 'into the most progressive social body in the world' (*Bulletin* 7–1970; Agence 1971, 23 February). Brandt wanted to open discussions with the Eastern-European states, but since he did not want this *Ostpolitik* to upset the internal balance of the EEC, he wanted simultaneously to strengthen European cooperation and expand the Community with Britain (Brandt 1977, I). However, France had vetoed British admission already twice. Consequently, new initiatives were required.

The Hague Summit In December 1969, the heads of state and government met in The Hague 'to discuss the issues facing the Community' (*Bulletin* 1–1970, 7). Pompidou agreed to begin negotiations about enlargement in exchange for guarantees provided by Brandt concerning French-German relations, monetary cooperation and the CAP. The leaders of the governments agreed that further integration required the approval of the population. They wanted to regain the support of 'political and social groups' for European cooperation (*Bulletin* 2–1970, 33–40). They therefore approved the recommendations of the Commission and the EP to add a social dimension to the economic and monetary cooperation (*Bulletin* 12–1969; *Bulletin* 1–1970). Commissioner of Social Affairs Levi-Sandri took their words seriously and drew up a social policy memorandum, but his proposals encountered resistance from the member states (*Bulletin* 12–1970; Agence 1971, 15 February).

Meanwhile, DG V had asked the French sociologist Evelyne Sullerot to conduct a study into the statutory obstacles to women's employment, especially in the area of social security (*Bulletin* 4–1969). Sullerot had become famous with her *Histoire et sociologie du travail féminin* (1968), a groundbreaking analysis of women's work. Sullerot's study for DG V was groundbreaking as well. Of the more than 200 pages in the report, she devoted only 16 to the requested summary of statutory obstacles to the participation of women in the labour market (Sullerot 1970). The other 184 pages offered a sharp analysis of many aspects of women's work, supported by a wealth of data, and many suggestions for measures.

After reading the report, the new Commissioner Albert Coppé organized a meeting of employers and trade unions concerning discrimination against women (*Bulletin* 3–1971). He hoped to gain their support for new European equal rights initiatives. However, the interest of employers and trade unions remained limited to vocational training and dissemination of information on professional choices for women and girls (Agence 1971, 22 January).

Coppé presented a somewhat less ambitious policy document to the Council than Levi-Sandri, the Preliminary Guidelines for a Community Social Policy. Coppé utilized Sullerot's critical interpretation of statistical data for the Preliminary Guidelines. The improvement of the position of the working woman should become one of the seven priorities in the EEC social policy. The 'highly significant, factual inequality between the incomes of men and women' was related to the position of women in the economic system and could only be eliminated by means of supranational policy, since national initiatives would lead to distortions. The Commission argued:

> … that women be offered access to all jobs … In this context, it is necessary to achieve completely equal pay for men and women, promote part-time work without this leading to an excessively low job classification or limitation of promotion opportunities, modify the social security regulations, offer the working woman the necessary labour protection without this leading to new forms of discrimination, promote the inclusion of women in the representative bodies of employers, and provide the essential collective provisions that make it possible to combine working outside the home with her tasks in the family (*Bulletin* S2–1971, 50).

However, the recommendations were not even discussed by the member states.

Paris Summit On 18 August 1971, three days after the US had temporarily halted the convertibility of the dollar, Pompidou decided to hold a summit meeting about the economic and monetary union (Agence 1971, 9 November). Sicco Mansholt,

President of the Commission, warned the governments that a purely market-oriented European Community would lead to serious political and social friction (Shanks 1977a; Agence 1972, 14 April).

The government leaders met in Paris from 19 to 21 October 1972.[1] Brandt and Pompidou each presented a memorandum on the social dimension. Both stressed that a common social policy was essential so that the population – workers and consumers – could identify with the EEC (Agence 1972, 12, 17 and 20 October). The member states agreed that 'powerful action in the social area is equally as important as achieving economic and monetary union'. The Commission was told to present a social action programme before 1 January 1974 which 'should primarily focus on a coordinated policy concerning employment and professional training and the improvement of working and living conditions' (*Bulletin* 10–1972, 20). To accomplish these tasks, the Commission could apply 'all provisions of the treaties ... including Article 235 to the greatest extent possible' (*Bulletin* 10–1972, 24).[2]

Women on the European Agenda

Finally the Commission had an official mandate to develop social policy. The 'Paris mandate' did not mention equal rights policy, but at its own initiative, the Commission seized the opportunity to give equal rights a prominent place, using the documents it had prepared during the decade of stagnation. Coreper eliminated the proposals for paid pregnancy leave and equal treatment in social security from the draft version, but accepted the other proposals (*Bulletin* S4–1973). In this way the equality of women and men became one of the key objectives of the Social Action Programme (SAP).

On 24 October 1973, the Commission submitted its definitive version of the SAP to the Council. It reported that it had already established an ad-hoc group to formulate proposals in the area of recruitment, professional training, childcare and flexible working hours. Even before the approval of the SAP by the Council, the Commission submitted a draft directive for equal pay to the Council. Furthermore, it announced proposals for the establishment of a community documentation centre for women's work and an information service, a contribution of the EEC to the UN International Women's Year and the establishment of a standing committee on the issue of working women (*Bulletin* S2–1974).

Surprisingly, the member states did not weaken but strengthen the SAP. They believed the SAP was a step backwards with respect to the guidelines the Commission

---

1 The representatives of Denmark, Britain and Ireland were also present in Paris. In January 1972, they had signed the admission treaties, and on 1 January 1973, they joined EEC, ECSC and EURATOM. Norway had also signed the treaties, but in a referendum, a majority of the Norwegian electorate voted against joining the Community.

2 Article 235 of the EEC Treaty (now Art. 308 EC) provided that in unforeseen cases the Council shall, acting unanimously on a proposal from the Commission and after consulting the EP, take the appropriate measures.

had been given in Paris (Agence 1973, 8 December). Commissioner of Social Affairs Patrick Hillery defended the cautious character of the SAP by pointing to the problems of the oil crisis and inflation, which had meanwhile come to dominate the political agenda (Agence 1973, 10–11 December). The Yom Kippur War in October of 1973 'pushed the western world into recession and high inflation' (Urwin 1995, 157). Hillery assumed that the member states would not be prepared to meet their commitments from Paris and had aimed lower to avoid complete rejection. However, they wanted to make progress out of fear that stagnation at the supranational level would aggravate the crisis.

In a hectic atmosphere, the member states held a series of Council meetings to realize as much as possible from the Paris programme (Agence 1973, 26 November). In his 'landmark speech' in the European Parliament on 13 November 1973, Brandt urged the Community to 'pull itself together' and he asserted that 'the Europe we want requires democratic legitimacy, an economic basis and its own social policy aims' (*Europe Documents* 1973, No. 771, 5). The Council of Ministers of Social Affairs met on 11–12 December 1973. It decided to expand the number of priority actions in the SAP, especially in view of rapidly increasing unemployment (Agence 1973, 12 December). The ministers established nine priorities, including the equality of men and women, for which the Commission had to make concrete proposals during the course of 1974. After Coreper made some textual amendments, the SAP was approved in January 1974.

The Commission as Agenda-Setter Without the Commission, equal rights would not have been included in the SAP. Why did the Commission use its 'Paris mandate' to put equal rights on the agenda? Simultaneous changes at the supranational and national levels account for this.

First, committed officials in DG V had been involved with the topic of equal pay since 1958. In spite of their efforts, they had achieved few results due to the lack of will of the member states and the lack of support from their superiors in the Commission. Their position improved when in January of 1973, a new Commission began work under the presidency of François-Xavier Ortoli. The portfolios of the commissioners were redistributed due to the expansion of the EEC with Great Britain, Ireland, and Denmark. The Irishman Hillery took over Social Affairs from Coppé. He was more ambitious, arguing in favour of a broad vision of joint social policy, including poverty alleviation and the combination of work and family. Several conservative top officials in DG V were replaced by officials who wanted to utilize optimally 'the social mandate' of the Commission (Hoskyns 1985, 79).

Furthermore, thanks to the efforts of DG V, a transnational equal rights network of national experts and supranational officials had developed. Officials in Brussels had established contacts with feminist experts such as Sullerot and lawyer Eliane Vogel-Polsky and women in the trade unions such as Maria Weber (DGB), Nel Tegelaar (NVV) and Emilienne Brunfaut (FGTB, Belgium). They had collected much information about all aspects related to equal rights and had been ready to formulate concrete proposals.

Most importantly, there was pressure from national groups 'so the Commission would resume the battle for equal pay and, more generally, equal employment rights' (Nonon and Clamen 1991, 61). Women's organizations and women in political parties and the trade unions placed equal pay on the national agendas. They organized equal pay strikes and invoked Article 119 against recalcitrant governments and employers. DG V supported their initiatives (Deshormes La Valle 1979). For Hillery, the emergence of the women's movement was an ideal opportunity to strengthen the position of the Commission with respect to the member states by acquiring the political support of a large social group that was still getting an inadequate response at the national level (Warner 1984).

The fact that the Council of Ministers approved the priority given in the SAP to developing a supranational equal rights policy can be explained, first, by domestic changes and secondly, by international time pressure.

Women on the Domestic Agenda

Social dissatisfaction during the second half of the 1960s acquired a strong gender-specific dimension. The entry of huge numbers of women into the labour market and their increased education level raised their political consciousness and opened up new possibilities for organizing themselves. Women translated dissatisfaction and awareness of discrimination into protests against their under-representation in trade unions, parliament and government. Shifts in the political preferences of women weakened the position of conservative parties and helped to bring governments into power that were sensitive to the demands of women.

France The breakthrough of the *Mouvement pour la Libération des Femmes* (MLF) occurred in May of 1968 when young people, students, women and workers protested forcefully against the authoritarian Gaullist state. The MLF was elitist and intellectual, but had access to the French political elite (Lovenduski 1986; Hantrais 1993). The movement reached a broad public with its campaigns to liberalize abortion. The weekly *Elle* organized in November 1970 a 'General Assembly of Women' in Versailles. Women demanded equal access to education and the labour market, strict application of the 'equal pay' principle, more and better childcare, easier access to part-time work, and training for women who re-entered the labour market (Albistur and Armogathe 1977). Prime Minister Jacques Chaban-Delmas promised the women in Versailles that he would take initiatives in the area of equal pay and work.

French politicians were sensitive to women's demands. Traditionally, the Gaullists had many female voters, among other things because De Gaulle had given women 'the right to vote' in 1944 (Northcutt and Flaitz 1985). Secularization, increasing education and growing political awareness in combination with demands for social change, contributed to the fact that women began to identify increasingly with the left. The shift in the female electorate led to 'a competitive bidding by party leaders for women's support' (Chamberlayne 1993, 186). During the presidential elections of

1974, 'the spotlight was on women'. The liberal politician Valéry Giscard d'Estaing won the election. T*he Nouvel Observateur* announced his victory with the headline 'Giscard, the Women's Favourite' (Albistur and Armogathe 1977, 597).

Giscard appointed more women to the government than ever before. Besides electoral motives he had also an ideological interest. For a liberal intellectual such as Giscard, the issue of women's rights was compatible with his discourse on 'equality' and 'individual liberty' (Giroud 1977). At the insistence of women's organizations and the Committee for Women's Work (see p. 63), Giscard appointed a Secretary of State for Women's Issues. In the 1960s, De Gaulle had rejected a similar request with a condescending 'Why not appoint an undersecretary for knitting?' (*F-Magazine* 1981, 35, 50). Giscard asked the leftist journalist Françoise Giroud for this position. She could count on the support of Giscard, feminist experts such as Sullerot and lawyer Gisèle Halimi, and the women's movement, but she would encounter increasing resistance from the Gaullist ministers in the government (Albistur and Armogathe 1977).

Germany Like in France, the women's movement arose from student resistance. In 1968, female students organized themselves in Women's Councils, dissatisfied with their subordinate role in the Socialist Student's Alliance. Their battle against capitalism and patriarchy took concrete shape in campaigns for childcare and liberalization of abortion. The mass demonstrations to decriminalize abortion were given a great deal of attention in the media, but in contrast to France and Britain, they obtained no support from trade unions or political parties. This strengthened the women's movement in its distrust of established institutions.

In his statement on taking office in 1969, Brandt said in very general terms only that the government was 'prepared, more than before, to help women take an equal role in the family, professions, politics, and society' (Van Ooijen et al. 1996, 195). The *Arbeitsgemeinschaft Sozialdemokratischer Frauen* (ASF) – the women's groups in the SPD – asked for a more outspoken policy. The SPD won the elections in 1972 primarily due to the votes of young women (Wiggershaus 1979; Brandt 1977, II). After the election victory, Brandt established a section of Policies for Women – as proposed by the ASF – which operated under the auspices of the Ministry for Youth, Family and Health. It was given the task of advising the government about all policy matters concerning women.

The policy of the Brandt government focused primarily on reforming marriage and family law, due to pressure from the ASF and the women's movement, and on improving vocational training for women, especially at the instigation of women in the DGB. In June 1970, SPD Minister of Justice Jahn made a proposal to reform the marriage and family law, which had not changed since the 1950s. Married women would finally be given the same right to perform paid work as men due to the elimination of the 'statutorily mandated allocation of tasks in marriage' (Bundesministerium für Frauen und Jugend 1992). The reform would not be approved until 1977 due to the fierce protests of CDU/CSU against the relaxation of divorce procedures (Menschik 1971, 93).

The Netherlands In 1968, the movement *Man Vrouw Maatschappij* (MVM) was founded. It signalled the beginning of the second feminist wave in the Netherlands (Van Rossum 1992). MVM campaigned for abortion and against sex discrimination in the areas of wages, education and taxation. The marxist-feminist group *Dolle Mina* [Crazy Mina] conducted 'happenings' in favour of abortion, equal pay (the 'Working Wives Plan'), public toilets for women and childcare. There were countless autonomous discussion groups and radical women's groups. Thanks to the activism of the women's movement, the continuing quest of women in trade unions for equality gained more attention. However, the trade unions continued to defend the interests of the breadwinner every time that equal rights meant that male workers had to make concessions.

The political arena initially did not change. The centre-right government did not want to give in to the demands of the MVM and Dolle Mina. This attitude led to increased mobilization, which was favoured by the fact that opposition parties supported the women's movement. During the 1972 elections there was a spectacular shift as women reduced their traditional support for the Christian Democratic parties and for the first time more women than men voted for the PvdA.[3] Because of this shift, in May 1973 a coalition of progressive parties and Christian Democrats came into power under the leadership of Joop den Uyl (PvdA). Contrary to its predecessors, this government was very accessible for the women's movement due to the personal contacts between women in the leftist governing parties and the MVM, *Dolle Mina* and women in the trade unions. Den Uyl's motto, 'share knowledge, power and income', offered a good framework for the demands of the women's movement.

In October 1973, the MVM conducted a postcard campaign 'Den Uyl, it's high time for emancipation policy' and formulated three demands: a national steering group for emancipation policy, an institute for statistics and research, and anti-discrimination legislation following the British-American example. In April 1974, the government established the Emancipation Commission, an advisory committee for equal rights, composed mainly of MVM-members. The Emancipation Commission benefited from the widespread consensus that 'something had to be done; but on the other hand, there was no clear idea of what needed to be done' (Outshoorn 1997).

Britain British 'Women's Lib' was characterized by the strong connections between the 'new' women's movement, Labour, trade unions, the civil rights movement (the National Council for Civil Liberties, NCCL) and the 'old' women's movement, such as the Fawcett Society which was established in 1865. The new women's movement began in 1968 with strikes for equal pay and the publication of Juliet Mitchell's essay 'The Longest Revolution' (Lovenduski 1986). In 1969, Prime Minister Harold Wilson (Labour) established a Women's National Commission that represented all women's organizations so that 'the informed opinion of women is given its due

3 Female votes for the Christian Democratic parties: 1967, 46 percent; 1972, 33 percent. Votes for PvdA: 1967, men 24 percent, women 22 percent; 1972, men 25 percent, women 27 percent (Leyenaar 1989, 222).

weight in the deliberations of Government on both national and international affairs' (Castle 1980, 141). The main demands of Women's Lib were: equal pay, equal opportunities in education and on the labour market, 24-hour childcare, free birth control, and abortion on demand. In many cities, women campaigned in favour of these demands.

Many women were active in both the women's movement and the trade unions. Starting in the 1970s, the Trade Union Congress (TUC) began to attach more importance to women's rights and the position of women in the trade unions (Meehan 1985). The TUC supported the campaigns for abortion law reform and parental leave, but their attitude towards 'bread-and-butter issues' such as equal pay was less clear due to fear that equality legislation could erode their freedom of negotiation and could divide the trade union movement (Boston 1985). Yet, the trade unions were a valuable partner for the women's movement because TUC participated in tripartite work groups (which prepared legislation) and was an influential discussion partner of Labour governments (Castle 1984; Crossman 1977).

Unlike the other three countries discussed here, Britain did not have a conservative but a Labour government during the turbulent second half of the 1960s. This gave it several years head start in equal rights policies.

The Domestic, European and International Levels Combined

The fact that all governments developed national policies for women at virtually the same time does not mean by itself that they also wanted to develop supranational policy. To explain their willingness to do so, we have to combine the levels.

First, the member states approved the initiative of the Commission to make equality one of the priorities of the SAP to avoid competitive disadvantages. In view of the strong societal pressure, policy change was highly desirable. Yet, the economic costs linked to policy change were high. Equal pay and equal treatment in social security, pensions, and taxation remained costly and could create unequal conditions for competition (*Bulletin* S2–1971). Accordingly, member states preferred joint equal rights policy instead of unilateral national policy in this area. In this way, every state would be bound to the same high norms.

Secondly, there was a certain amount of time pressure regarding the approval of equal rights policy due to the UN declaring 1975 as the International Women's Year. Its aim was 'to encourage and multiply efforts aimed at concerted action by governments and non-governmental organizations for the full application of the Declaration on the Elimination of Discrimination against Women' from 1967. In May 1973, the Secretary General of the UN requested all governments to take action on the International Women's Year (*Handelingen* 1975–6, 14030, 2). In June 1975, a World Conference would take place in Mexico, where the governments would present 'joint concrete proposals'.

At the national level, the governments were all wrestling with the question of what a suitable activity would be in the framework of this Women's Year. When she entered office in June 1974, the French Secretary of State Giroud had not realized that 1975 would be the International Women's Year and she complained about this 'poisoned gift' (Giroud 1977, 121). In Germany, the government wanted to use the Women's Year to try to calm down the dissatisfaction among women. However, even the announcement of the membership of the Committee responsible for the programme for the Women's Year (under the leadership of the former chair of the employers association Hans Martin Schleyer) resulted in new protests (Wiggershaus 1979). The discovery that the Women's Year was approaching, combined with the MVM postcard campaign, gave the Dutch government the feeling that 'it had to do something' but without knowing exactly what (Dijkstra and Swiebel 1982). In Britain, Wilson appointed the only woman in the Cabinet, his Minister of Social Affairs Barbara Castle, Vice Chair of the Women's National Commission, with the aim of giving the meetings extra importance (Castle 1980). In all member states, the half-hearted governmental initiatives functioned as a catalyst for new actions of women's groups.

Commissioner Hillery pointed out to the Council that it was important to have a joint presentation of the EEC in Mexico. After all, Western Europe could not fall behind the states in the Communist block, who boasted about the equal position of women in their countries and their head start in this area. Nor could they fall behind the 'G-77',[4] which attributed the subordinate position of women to the capitalist economic system (Stienstra 1994). The representatives of the member states agreed that the prestige of the EEC was at stake, but they had no clear idea about suitable initiatives. The contribution of 'external experts' was welcome. As a result, the Commission enjoyed a strong position to set the agenda.

Conclusion

Joint equal rights policy was placed on the European agenda thanks to the Commission. The member states approved the initiative because of the pressure of women at the national level, the economic costs of unilateral equal rights policy, and the desirability of a joint initiative in the framework of the UN International Women's Year. The Commission strategically utilized this window of opportunity to label women's rights as one of the priorities in the SAP and to submit proposals to the Council for binding directives on equal pay and equal treatment, which had to be approved before the World Conference in Mexico in 1975.

In the following subsections, we will describe for each directive how the Commission proposal came about, the preference formation at the national level, and the supranational negotiation process.

4 The G-77 is the coalition of developing countries that signed a joint declaration in 1963 in which they called for reforms to benefit fair trade between 'North' and 'South.'

Equal Pay on the Negotiating Table

The Commission: New Approaches to an Old Problem

As the Commission ascertained in its report published in June 1970, the implementation of Article 119 had reached an impasse (Commission 1970, SEC(70)2338 fin). The Commission initially did not link any consequences to this assessment. Commissioner Coppé only asked the member states to continue their periodical reports (Agence 1971, 20 April). The EP therefore called for women to take action and claim their right to equal pay before the national court. *Rapporteur* Astrid Lulling asked the Commission to negotiate a European agreement between employers and trade unions to improve the compliance with the equal pay principle in collective labour agreements. However, the employers and trade unions were not interested to make such an agreement (Agence 1971, 13 April).

The Lawyer and the Court While member states, Commission, employers and trade unions remained passive, women took action. Eliane Vogel-Polsky, a Belgian lawyer, chose the judicial way to put pressure on unwilling actors. In 1966, a long strike for equal pay had taken place at the Belgian weapons factory *FN Herstal* (Official Journal 1966, 1931–32/66, Question Troclet, 16 June). Because of the strike, Vogel-Polsky published an article in the *Journal des Tribunaux*, writing, 'you are better off as a male immigrant worker from a non-EEC country than as a female worker who is an EEC-resident' (Vogel-Polsky 1994, 42). She questioned whether Article 119 had direct effect. If this was the case, women could exercise their rights via the national courts if their government had not implemented equal pay.

This question could only be answered by a decision of the Court following a complaint to the national court. Thereupon, Vogel-Polsky and her colleague Marie-Thérèse Cuvelliez began to search for a suitable test case (Degraef 1988). The trade unions refused to cooperate because they were afraid of a precedent-setting effect and did not want to nullify any collective agreements that they had been part of (Lovenduski 1986). The stewardess Gabrielle Defrenne agreed that her case could be used to test the reach of Article 119. In February 1968 she had been fired by Sabena, the Belgian national airline, because she had reached the age of 40, even though male cabin personnel remained in service until they were 55. Vogel-Polsky and Cuvelliez began a case against Sabena on 13 May 1968.

The case remained in appeal until the Belgian court asked the European Court (Court) for a preliminary ruling in April 1975 (*Defrenne II* – see Chapter 4). In the meantime, Cuvelliez and Vogel-Polsky had initiated a case against the Belgian state that came before the Court in 1970 (*Defrenne I*, Case 80/70). In *Defrenne I*, the complaint was that stewardesses were excluded from the pension regulation for airline personnel. The French Advocate General, Dutheillet de Lamothe, argued that Sabena stewardesses had 'every right to feel aggrieved', but that statutory pension regulations did not fall under Article 119 (*ECR* 1971, 455). On 25 May 1971, the Court decided in accordance with the opinion of the Advocate General.

Despite the negative decision, the ruling had far-reaching consequences due to two of Dutheillet de Lamothe's remarks. First, he believed that pensions which were paid directly by employers were indeed covered by Article 119. Telchini, the representative of the Commission's Legal Service, disputed this viewpoint and emphasized that Article 119 had a 'stringent character' and 'did not establish any general principle for the equality of men and women'. However, the Court agreed with Dutheillet de Lamothe that 'social security payments are in principle not entirely separate from the concept of pay' (*ECR* 1971, 450–2). From this ruling, DG V deduced that its mandate concerning the implementation of Article 119 also comprised equality in the area of social security. In its report about the application of Article 119 published in July 1973, the Commission therefore announced that it would forthwith also collect information about equal treatment in social security arrangements.

Secondly, the Advocate General confirmed the presumption of Vogel-Polsky on direct effect. He reminded the member states that Article 119 imposed an obligation on them that was sufficiently precise to hold it directly effective. This would mean that Dutch women, who still did not have any legal right to equal pay, could appeal to the national court and ask to apply Article 119. However, the Court would rule on this aspect only in *Defrenne II*. The Legal Service of the Commission therefore continued to assume that Article 119 was not directly effective and that national equal pay legislation was required to provide individual rights to women. DG V therefore addressed the question of how the member states could be made to approve national equal pay legislation.

The Commission Acts In the meantime, the Commission was compelled to postpone the publication of the 1971 report on the implementation of Article 119 because the member states refused to provide data. In the report that was finally published in July 1973, the new Commission changed its tune (Commission 1973, SEC(73)3000). This report was not comprised of a description of the situation in each country, which had been customary until then. Instead, following the Sullerot report, there was a comparative analysis of the problems concerning the implementation of equal pay (Hoskyns 1996a). The Commission warned that it would start infringement procedures and use a 'new instrument'.

In October 1972, six months earlier, the Commission had been given the mandate to develop a Social Action Programme. Confronted with the stubborn unwillingness of the member states to implement Article 119, while at the national level there was pressure everywhere from women for equal pay, the Commission decided to use its new social mandate to finally achieve progress in this area. Moreover, there was very little time to prepare the SAP; as a result, the Commission fell back on proposals that were already in preparation (Shanks 1977a).

In November 1973, it presented the draft of the previously announced 'new instrument' to the Council: an equal pay directive. Until then, directives – a binding instrument, a 'European law' that has to be transposed in national legislation – had not been used for social policy, but Commission President Ortoli was positive about the idea (Hoskyns 1996a). In view of its long history and clear treaty basis, equal pay was a perfect topic to test the value of directives as a social policy instrument. For the Frenchman Ortoli, it was especially attractive because France had approved already new equal pay legislation in December 1972; as a result, France could be again the 'social role model' for the EEC.

Simultaneously, the Commission began infringement proceedings against the Netherlands and Luxembourg. Hillery was determined to achieve finally the right to equal pay, through the Court and through a directive.

Equal Pay at the Domestic Level

Due to differences in national provisions, the expected costs of a binding supranational equal pay provision diverged greatly for the member states – as well as their preferences.

France Sets the Example At the beginning of the 1970s, there were strikes for equal pay all over the country (Callet and Du Granrut 1973). Opinion polls showed that equal pay was the most popular measure to improve the status of women (Mazur 1991). The reform programme of the government under Chaban-Delmas, called 'The New Society', offered Minister of Labour Joseph Fontanet a framework for new social legislation. He raised the status of the Committee for Women's Work and appointed his assistant Claude du Granrut as General Secretary. She persuaded him to submit a draft equal pay bill, drawn up by the Committee, to the cabinet. Fontanet was unable to steer the law through the cabinet before the change of government in the summer of 1972, when Pompidou replaced Chaban-Delmas with the Gaullist 'hardliner' Pierre Messmer.

Edgar Faure became the new Minister of Labour. Faure, a conservative, had little interest in social legislation. Pressure from employers led him to weaken the draft bill by eliminating the reversal of the burden of proof.[5] In November 1972, the parliament approved the Equal Pay Act (Mazur 1991). The Act established the principle of 'equal pay for equal work and work of equal value' in the private sector, required employers to classify all jobs, specified in greater detail the criteria for job classification and provided sanctions for employers who discriminated (Callet and Du Granrut 1973).

France was a proponent of a European directive for equal pay because it assumed that it did not have to modify its own legislation, and it wanted to see the other member states bound to the same high norm. France also enjoyed the prestige it gained from its role as a 'model of social progress' and as an example of 'harmonious development of women and men towards equality' (Giroud 1977, 61, 146).

5 The principle of 'reversing the burden of proof' means that the individual who submits a complaint about discrimination is not required to show that he or she suffered discrimination, but that the accused employer must prove that there has been no discrimination.

Germany: 'Free Choice' On 31 January 1973, the last two collective labour agreements that contained separate *Frauenlohngruppen* (women's wage groups) became null and void – 18 years after the court had ruled that separate wages for women were unconstitutional. Of the 346 collective labour agreements that were in force in 1974, 104 still contained *Leichtlohngruppen* for 'light physical work' (Wiggershaus 1979). Unskilled or semiskilled work was classified only on the basis of the physical strength required. Consequently, the *Leichtlohngruppen* concerned almost exclusively female workers.

The trade unions declared 1972 as 'The Year of the Woman Worker'. The DGB demanded 'fair assessment of work and performance' (Wiggershaus 1979). Yet, the employers successfully resisted the elimination of the *Leichtlohngruppen* and the trade unions refused equal rights legislation because they feared losing their bargaining freedom (Hund 1983). As a result, their efforts had little effect on the position of female employees.

The women's movement primarily exerted pressure for the reform of marriage and family law. Moreover, part of the women's movement was reluctant to support the demands for equal rights and preferred instead to emphasize the difference between men and women (Ostner 1993). The *ASF* did campaign for equal pay, but were unable to persuade the government that Article 3 of the Constitution offered insufficient protection for women's rights. When unemployment increased rapidly in 1974, the government preferred to emphasize the *Wahlfreiheit*, the 'free choice' of women between paid and unpaid work, rather than strengthening their rights. The government opposed the EEC directive with the argument that they had to respect the autonomy of employers and trade unions. The expansion of the norm 'equal pay for equal work' to 'equal pay for work of equal value' was unacceptable, since it went further than the Constitution.

The Netherlands: Pincers Women in the trade unions, supported by the women's movement, became more and more vociferous about the equal pay demand. In 1970, women in the NVV and *Dolle Mina* organized the 'Discrimination Fair'. The event focused on equal pay partly because a recent strike for equal pay in the cigar industry had failed. In a radio programme on the Fair, Minister Roolvink of Social Affairs promised that he would ask the parliament to ratify ILO-100. He kept his word, and on 23 April 1971, the parliament approved ILO-100, which established the principle of equal pay for work of equal value (*Handelingen* 1971, *Nadere Memorie van Antwoord* 8606, 26 April). Yet, the ratification did not have any immediate consequences, since ILO Conventions did not have a direct effect (Asscher-Vonk 1995).

Real change took place in 1973. The Dutch government was 'caught in a pincer action'. At the Optilon zipper factory, women conducted an unsuccessful strike for equal pay in March 1973. The strike was given a great deal of publicity and support by Dolle Mina, but the union decided to stop the strike for tactical reasons. The NVV Women's Union protested in vain. In October 1973, the women's movement and the leftist parties pushed the Den Uyl government to take emancipation policy seriously. During the same month, the tripartite SER published a report on equal pay. It recommended adopting a generally applicable equal pay regulation in view of the number of female workers who were not covered by collective labour agreements (SER 1973, 4–5).[6] This contradicted the government standpoint that the employers and trade unions were primarily responsible for equal pay, but the Optilon case had made it clear how difficult it was to ensure equal pay by means of a collective labour agreement.

To top it all, in November 1973, the government received the official warning of the European Commission announcing infringement proceedings against the Netherlands. The Commission demanded that the Netherlands finally implement Article 119. Den Uyl and his government viewed themselves as progressive. Their credibility was at stake. They could not risk to be condemned by the Court because Dutch women were paid more poorly than men. The Commission agreed to halt the infringement procedure after the government promised to take measures (*Europa van Morgen* 1974, 628).

In August 1974, Minister Boersma presented the equal pay bill. He urged parliament to pass the legislation quickly because he wanted the act to go into force at the beginning of the International Women's Year (*Handelingen* 1974, 13031, 1738). All political parties supported the equal pay principle, although the ARP (one of the governing parties) emphasized that equal pay 'fortunately' did not mean equality. It was more important that a woman 'choose the division of tasks between herself and her husband in such a way that the family is assigned a higher priority than providing a directly paid contribution to the production process' (*Handelingen* 1974, 13031, 1725–9). Urged by the Rooie Vrouwen[7] and other women's organizations, the parliament criticized the bill because it exempted the civil service and pensions. Boersma argued that expanding the law to cover civil servants was superfluous because equal pay was 'already a fact' for the civil service (*Handelingen* 1974, 13031, 5–6). Parliament expressed its scepticism about that argument, but the amendment did not achieve the required majority. Despite the recommendations of the SER and the request of the parliament, Boersma also held firm on the exemption for pensions because of the financial consequences (*Handelingen* 1974, 13031, 5–6). The Christian Democratic parties asked for compensation for small and mid-sized companies because the law would cost the retail trade alone an estimated 400 million guilders (*Handelingen* 1974, 13031, 1725). The minister refused, as he believed that the employers had already been given sufficient time to adapt to the obligation to pay women the same wages as men.

6 The SER also recommended establishing a tripartite commission of experts, including women, to advise disadvantaged women and the courts. The SER added that the principle of equal pay should also apply to pension rights and that an equal pay law would have little effect as long as no measures were taken against discrimination in training, hiring and promotion (SER 1973, 8), but the minister ignored these recommendations.

7 The women's group in the PvdA.

On 10 December 1974, the Parliament approved the bill – mainly because this law was better than no law at all. On 20 March 1975, the Equal Pay Act went into force. Boersma assured parliament that the Dutch law satisfied the EEC directive. He was wrong about this, since the law did not apply to the public sector. As a result, the Commission would initiate another infringement procedure against the Netherlands in 1979 (see Chapter 4).

Britain: 'In these ways is history made!' The British campaign for equal pay started way back during World War II to prevent the wage scales for men from being lowered (Meehan 1985). In 1955, the Conservative government agreed to a phased implementation of equal pay for public employees (Meehan 1985). The campaign for equal pay in the private sector began in the 1960s. The TUC pointed out to the government that EEC membership would require equal pay legislation. On the occasion of the British request for admission in 1961, Prime Minister Edward Heath stated that he accepted the principle, but wanted to leave its realization to collective negotiations (Meehan 1985). Actions of individual unions, a report from the NCCL and a private member's bill from Lady Edith Summerskill all had little effect until Labour came into power in 1964.

Labour had promised equal pay legislation in its election programme. The TUC reminded the cabinet of its election promise, but the government believed that 'its application would obviously be inflationary' and that it would undermine the difficult attempt of Labour to implement a tight income policy (Crossman 1977). Some ministers resisted the idea that 'the men should hold back claims in order to let the women come into line' (Castle 1984, 97). To prevent strikes, Minister of Labour Ray Gunter set up a committee for negotiations 'in a non-committal way' in 1964 (Meehan 1985, 65). Pressure increased. In April 1965, The Sun published a series of articles on 'The Wasted Sex', which resulted in thousands of letters from women who were prepared to campaign for equal pay. The venerable Fawcett Society advised its members to join a trade union and if necessary to strike for equal pay. 'Certainly by 1968 feelings were running high', but employers rejected all demands for equal pay (Meehan 1985, 38).

In June 1968, the 'petticoat strike' broke out. At the Ford factories in Dagenham, women went on strike for equal pay and fair job classification. The strike blockaded exports worth £50 million at a time when the Labour government was desperately searching for the means to balance the British balance of payments (Crossman 1977). Castle had meanwhile replaced Gunter as Minister of Labour. She invited the women strikers to come to the Ministry for a cup of tea. They were able to reach a compromise and the women resumed work (Crossman 1977).

That same month, parliament discussed the Wage Act, which was a very sensitive issue for the Labour government. To the government's dismay, Lena Jeger (Labour backbencher) submitted an amendment that exempted wage increases from the wage freeze if such increases were intended to achieve equal pay. The amendment threatened to gain a majority, at which point Castle improvised during the session by promising to begin immediate negotiations concerning equal pay with the CBI and the TUC. Jeger's amendment was defeated by a narrow margin. 'In these ways is history made!' cheers Castle in her memoirs (Castle 1984, 471).

The TUC was 'very pleased' with the initiative (Castle 1984). It preferred the ILO-100 norm of 'equal pay for work of equal value' until it realized that the determination of the value of work would require the implementation of job classification schemes. Men's jobs would also have to be reclassified, and this could alter the wage differences between men (Davies 1987). The TUC therefore did not insist on the ILO-100 norm (Castle 1984).

The CBI protested that implementing equal pay would cost between £600 million and £1 billion and in some sectors would result in increases in wage costs of 32 percent (Rowbotham 1972a). They believed that equal pay would ruin the British export industry because 'not a single country in the Common Market is doing more than pay lip-service to it' (Castle 1984, 539). They attempted to convince Castle to postpone the legislation until the economic situation had improved. As a compromise, Castle proposed to make compliance voluntary during the first five years and placated the TUC with the promise that the Minister of Labour would, if necessary, enact a decision to bring women's wages up to 90 percent of men's wages (Meehan 1985).

In the meantime, women had lost their patience and a 'period of industrial militancy among women workers' broke out with equal pay strikes all over the country (Rowbotham 1972b, 92). Women established a 'National Joint Action Campaign for Women's Equal Rights', which organized a large equal pay demonstration in May 1969. Castle futilely attempted to get the government to approve the bill before the summer recess of 1969 (Crossman 1977, 790). At the beginning of September 1969, Castle presented her bill saying that 'we had run out of delaying excuses, though we had behaved with an inertia worthy of the Northern Ireland Government' (Castle 1984, 704). Prime Minister Wilson pointed out that 'if we went into the Common Market, we should have to adopt it anyway' and that a wave of strikes would break out if the government left the matter to the TUC. On 25 September 1969, Wilson managed to get the cabinet to approve the Equal Pay Act (Castle 1984).

Castle had attempted to include pensions in the law, but Crossman made it 'absolutely clear [to her] that we didn't want this' (Crossman 1977, 789). On 13 May 1970, only a few hours before her bill was to be addressed in the House of Lords, Castle accepted Crossman's promise that 'the Government were determined to deal with this by legislation, before equal pay becomes effective five years from now' (Crossman 1977, 919). In order to see this promise become reality, women would ultimately have to wait for Castle's Social Security Pensions Act, which would not take effect until two governments later in 1978. The Equal Pay Bill became law on 28 May 1970, two weeks before the general elections that Labour would lose unexpectedly.

The slow 'voluntary' implementation of equal pay led the TUC to demand a Ministerial Decree, but the Conservative government refused. In 1973 and 1974, an unprecedented number of strikes by women took place, supported by the women's movement and the trade unions (Meehan 1985). In February of 1974, Labour once again came into power during a period of great social unrest. The Wilson government faced high price and wage inflation, rapidly increasing unemployment, heavy pressure on the pound and resistance in the Labour party against EEC membership (Castle 1980). The government therefore could not allow wage costs to increase further, and it could not allow the anti-EEC feelings to be aggravated. Britain therefore 'had one objective and that was to ensure that the European directive fitted into the newly introduced, but not implemented, Equal Pay Act' (Pillinger 1992, 85).

Conclusion Table 3.1 summarizes the economic and ideological costs of an equal pay directive and the pressure in favour or against it.

For France, the costs were low as a directive did not seem to require any major policy changes. Although the economic costs in the Netherlands were still rather high, the ideological costs were low. The government was very sensitive to the strong pressure in favour of equal pay legislation. Pressure was further strengthened by the infringement actions of the Commission. In Germany, the costs were high and opposition was strong. In Britain, the economic and ideological costs of any expansion of the EPA were relatively high and the issue was very salient. Given these preferences, we would expect that negotiations would result in a directive based on the minimum common denominator, the strict 'equal pay for equal work'-norm, which was acceptable to Germany and Britain.

The First Directive (Equal Pay)

The Commission had based its proposal on Article 100 for the harmonization of legislation. This decision emphasized that equal pay was part of the common market. The draft directive basically committed the member states to abolish discriminatory provisions, implement job classification systems, and offer statutory guarantees enabling disadvantaged employees to submit a complaint and protect them against being fired.

The tripartite Article 119 Group, which had been created in the 1960s (see p. 57), discussed the draft. The Commission had expanded the principle of 'equal pay for the same work' to the ILO norm of 'equal pay for work of equal value' because experience had shown that due to labour market segregation men and women hardly ever did exactly the same work. The employers' representatives successfully resisted the new norm with the argument that objective job classification was impossible. For implementation, the Commission initially wanted to use the opportunity to launch collective negotiations at the European level and to place the responsibility with employees and employers (*Official Journal* 1973, C 110/38, 13 December). The trade unions were not willing to bear the direct responsibility for applying equal pay and the Commission changed its proposal.

Coreper attempted to weaken the Commission proposal so none of them would have to modify their national policies. Germany wanted Treaty Article 235 to be the basis of the directive and preferred a general obligation to 'take measures' instead of the strict wording of Article 100 calling for 'harmonization', implying the

Table 3.1 Equal pay: domestic costs and pressure (1974)

	France	Germany	the Netherlands	Britain
1. Relative economic costs: hourly wages women/men*	Low costs (1): difference 21.3 percent	Medium cost (2): difference 30.3 percent	Medium costs (2): difference 35.4 percent	High costs (3): difference 40.5 percent
2. Ideological costs: compatibility with domestic policy frame	Low costs (1): compatible with equality and social role model	High costs (3): incompatible with wage autonomy, 'free choice'	Low costs (1): compatible with redistribution of opportunities and income	High costs (3): incompatible with inflation control and wage moderation
Relative domestic costs of equal pay (1+2)	Low (2)	High (5)	Medium (3)	High (6)
3. Domestic opposition to a supranational equal pay/equal value provision	Limited (1): Gaullist party	Strong (4): Employers, governing parties SPD and FDP, CDU/CSU, DGB	Rather limited (2): Employers, small Christian parties	Rather strong (3): Employers, Conservatives
4. Domestic support for a supranational equal pay/equal value provision	Strong (4): Other political parties, employers, trade unions, women's movement	Limited (1): Women in DGB and SPD	Strong (4): MVM, Dolle Mina, majority in parliament, women in NVV, SER	Strong (4): TUC, women's movement, Labour women and backbenchers
Saliency (3+4) and relative domestic pressure (4–3)	Medium saliency (5), rather strong support (3)	Medium saliency (5), rather strong opposition (–3)	High saliency (6), rather limited support (2)	High saliency (7), limited support (1)
Sensitivity	High	High	High	High
Expected preference	In favour	Opposed	In favour	Opposed

**Source*: Saunders and Marsden (1981, 221).

introduction or adaptation of national legislation (Agence 1975, 7 June). Germany also opposed establishing a system for monitoring compliance in companies, since it wanted to leave implementation to the employers and trade unions (Agence 1973, 1 November). Coreper introduced a certain degree of flexibility and stipulated that they would achieve the aim 'in accordance with national circumstances and legal systems' (Directive 75/117, Article 6). Under this condition, Germany also approved the principle of monitoring in companies (Agence 1974, 18 December). Britain rejected every expansion of Article 119. Based on *Defrenne I*, the Commission had expanded the concept of 'wages' to social security payments (*Official Journal* 1973,

C 114/46, 27 December). Britain, apprehensive of the economic costs, eliminated the reference to social security from the directive.

The intervention of France lifted the equal pay directive above the 'minimum common denominator' level. It demanded that the norm be expanded again to the norm in the draft ('equal pay for work of equal value'), so that all member states would be bound by the same high norm as France. Britain, Germany and Denmark resisted the French proposal, but France did not want to give in.

During the second half of 1974, France was president of the Council. Giscard d'Estaing wanted to make France into the motor of European integration and attached much importance to women's rights. He wanted to see the directive approved under French presidency. France therefore placed the member states that still resisted the directive under heavy pressure. At the domestic level, women exerted pressure. In Germany, women from the Policies for Women section and the DGB lobbied the officials of the Ministry of Labour who were conducting the negotiations (Hoskyns 1996a). In Coreper, Germany ultimately agreed with the directive assuming that it would not have to approve new legislation. This was because its legal advisors had concluded that, even in the case of 'work of equal value', Article 3 of the Constitution provided an adequate guarantee of the right of women to equal pay (Hoskyns 1988). Britain, however, continued to resist the directive because it did not want to change the EPA and did not want to risk having to change the wage structure for men (Davies 1987). Coreper did not reach agreement.

On 17 December 1984, the Social Affairs Council discussed the directive. During the meeting, Britain acquiesced to a compromise formulation: 'equal pay for equal work or work to which equal value is attributed' after it had received the assurance that it did not have to change the EPA on this point. However, it misjudged another stipulation in the directive: the obligation to establish a system of job classification (see Chapter 4). The Council approved the directive and settled on the definitive text on 10 February 1975 (Directive 75/117). The Commission proposed a term of six months for implementation, but the member states gave themselves an entire year.

Conclusion

For the first time, the Council approved a binding instrument for the harmonization of national social legislation (*Bulletin* 3-1975, 13). Moreover, the norm was above the minimum common denominator level. This was even more surprising because without the initiative of the Commission, equal rights policy would not have been on the European agenda at all. The Commission succeeded in obtaining state approval with the directive because of its expert knowledge on equal pay, *Defrenne I*, pressure at the national level, support from pioneer state France, and the time pressure caused by the International Women's Year. The member states felt 'sandwiched' by the pressure at the national and international levels to 'do something for women'. As expected (see Table 3.1), Germany and Britain resisted the directive. Under pressure from France, they ultimately agreed assuming that they had successfully avoided the need to modify their legislation. This assumption would turn out to be incorrect (see Chapter 4).

Equal Treatment on the Negotiating Table

The Commission Gives Women a Voice

Jacqueline Nonon was a French official who had worked at the DG V since 1959. In 1973, Commissioner Hillery had given her the responsibility for the equal rights policy in the renewed DG V. Sullerot and Nonon wrote the sections in the SAP about the position of women. Against the wishes of the trade unions, 'who claimed somewhat unconvincingly to be the best spokesmen for working women' (Shanks 1977a, 86), Hillery gave Nonon permission to establish an Ad Hoc Group of experts to advise him on these matters. Nonon used her contacts to nominate feminist experts on the group, instead of waiting to see who would be appointed by the respective governments (Hoskyns 1985). The membership of the Ad Hoc Group was comprised of five men and thirteen women, including Sullerot, Du Granrut and Vogel-Polsky. Other members were Lady Nancy Seear, who had submitted a sex discrimination bill to the British House of Lords, and Elisabeth Haines from the Policies for Women section at the German Ministry.

The Ad Hoc Group met four times between February and November of 1974. Its task was to formulate proposals for measures in the areas of recruitment, women returning to work, professional training, childcare, and flexible working hours. The Group operated under time pressure because Commissioner Hillery wanted the EEC to make a contribution to the International Women's Year that involved more than just the equal pay directive (*Bulletin* S2-1974). The Group believed that women not only needed equal treatment, but also special treatment. In June 1974, Vogel-Polsky presented a text for a 'legal instrument' in which she combined equal treatment (non-discrimination) and equal opportunities (positive action) (Hoskyns 1996a). Her proposal linked up with the British draft for an anti-discrimination act and the consensus among experts that equal pay could not be achieved without measures to counteract discrimination concerning access to the labour market (see SER 1973). Hillery accepted the proposal.

The draft directive was accompanied with a memorandum which Hillery called 'Action Programme for the Woman' (*Europa van Morgen* 1975, 12 February). The Commission approved this memorandum only after it had gone through nine versions. In contrast to equal pay, the concept of equal treatment was controversial because the Commissioners disagreed on the issue of whether they could stretch EEC legislation to cover areas outside the labour market or not. Hillery was a proponent of social policy that went beyond the labour market in the strictest sense of the word. He found a treaty basis for this viewpoint by giving a broad interpretation to Article 117, arguing that 'Equal treatment for male and female workers constitutes one of the objectives of the Community in so far as the harmonization of living and working conditions, while maintaining their improvement, are to be furthered' (Foreword, Directive 76/207). In its final version, the memorandum emphasized that the Commission was not involved with family policy as such, but only with the aspects that directly affect 'women who worked outside the home' such as parental leave and childcare (Hoskyns 1996a). The memorandum summed up the actions that the Commission wanted to undertake, such as research into childcare (Agence 1975, 13 February).

On the advice of the Legal Service of the Commission, which wanted to play safe, the draft directive was more limited than the memorandum and proposals for reconciling work and family responsibilities were eliminated (Hoskyns 1985). Hillery asked the opinion of female officials at the Commission about the draft directive. Half of them responded, and of this group 88 percent welcomed it (*Europa van Morgen* 1975, 83). On 12 February 1975, the Commission sent the draft directive and the memorandum to Coreper. During the presentation, Hillery emphasized that he supported not only measures for equal access to education, the labour market and promotion, but also for childcare, parental leave and flexible working hours. The member states refused to consider the latter proposals (*Europa van Morgen* 1975, 12 February; Shanks 1977a). Hillery and Nonon were 20 years ahead of them (see Chapter 5).

Equal Treatment at the Domestic Level

In contrast to equal pay, equal treatment of women was a relatively new issue. In 1958, the ILO approved Convention 111 concerning discrimination in employment and profession. Although Germany (1961) and the Netherlands (1973) had ratified the convention, they had not taken any measure to implement it (Commission 1974, V/1110/74). In France and Britain, legislation was being prepared. The Commission's proposal was clearly ahead of national practice.

France: Equal Treatment or Special Protection Giscard wanted to keep his election promises to women and reserved space on the parliamentary agenda for equal rights legislation. Secretary of State Giroud used the opportunity to submit proposals for equal access to admission examinations for government jobs (*concours*) and a ban on sex discrimination. The act stipulated that sex discrimination regarding access to employment and working conditions would become a criminal offence equivalent to racial discrimination and could be punished with fines and imprisonment (Code penal, Articles 187 and 416). An amendment from the right wing parties weakened the act by introducing the concept of *motif légitime*: if employers had a 'legitimate motif' for treating a female applicant or employee differently than a male one, they were absolved from discrimination (Mazur 1991). In April 1975, the parliament approved both acts.

In May 1975, Giroud submitted an 'Action Programme with Hundred Measures'. It resembled the memorandum that Hillery had submitted to the Council two months earlier, as Sullerot and Du Granrut had worked on both programmes. One major difference was that the EEC memorandum was limited to the labour market, while Giroud's Programme stated that discrimination against women on the labour market was rooted in their role in the family, allowing employers to treat women as second class employees, and that it was unacceptable that the state maintained this situation (Giroud 1976). Giroud proposed to adopt a general anti-discrimination law comprised of a single article: 'Every regulation or contract that, without a legal motive, denies a product, service or right to an individual based on their sex will be declared null and void' (Giroud 1976, 188). The women's movement supported the proposal, but wanted to eliminate the stipulation 'without a legal motive' in view of the abuse that could result (Choisir 1978). However, the government assigned a low priority to Giroud's proposal and it did not table it for discussion in the parliament.

Strong pressure was lacking. The trade unions were divided about the issue of protective measures for working women. The communist CGT (*Confédération du Travail*) supported specific protection for women in the form of early retirement and leave for the mother during a child's illness. In contrast, the CFDT (*Confédération Française Démocratique du Travail*) did not want special treatment which turned women into costly and therefore unattractive employees (Callet and Du Granrut 1973). Giroud endorsed the latter point of view (Giroud 1976). In the right-wing Barre government, she was moved to the Ministry of Culture.

Germany: Article 3 Will Do In 1975, the topic of anti-discrimination legislation was not yet on the agenda. The women's movement had other priorities. The trade unions did not want equal treatment legislation because they feared the breakdown of protective legislation and interference with their autonomy. The government supported their viewpoint that gender equality had to be realized through collective labour agreements. Chancellor Helmut Schmidt declared that he wanted 'to do something for women' during the International Women's Year, but that there was no room for legal reforms (EMMA 1991). The government also believed that forbidding specific forms of discrimination would be a step backward with respect to the general ban in the Constitution (Lovenduski 1986). Haines, who was a member of the Ad Hoc Group under the leadership of Nonon, kept the section Policies for Women informed about the preparations for the EEC directive, but German officials did not involve her in the negotiations in Coreper (Hoskyns 1996a).

The Netherlands: Wait and See As in Germany, the discussion about equal treatment got started because of the EEC draft directive. During the debate on the Equal Pay Act in December 1974, leftist members of parliament had asked the government to expand the equal pay act by banning also broader forms of discrimination as in American and British sex discrimination legislation. The government should make haste with such legislation because the recession affected women more severely than men and because working married women were being blamed for taking the place of male breadwinners.

Minister Boersma stated that he was 'aware of this issue', but wanted to wait and see if events necessitated action. Liberal and leftist members of parliament referred to the draft equal treatment directive, which the European Commission had already submitted to Coreper (*Handelingen* 1974, 13031, 1722 and 1792; *Handelingen* 1974–5, 13031, 339). Boersma assured them that he was 'prepared to cooperate sincerely for the adoption of such an EEC directive', although he also had serious objections to the proposal. He believed that both the directive and the British sex discrimination act were too ambitious. Moreover, he was not convinced that legislation was the best solution (*Handelingen* 1974, 13031, 405, 1781, 1795).

Britain: Pioneer Already in 1968, in the wake of the Race Relations Act, the lobby for sex discrimination legislation began. MP Joyce Butler submitted a bill, but Minister Castle did not want to include any anti-discrimination provisions in 'her' Equal Pay Act to prevent the TUC from rejecting the legislation in its entirety (Meehan 1985). The Fawcett Society developed into an umbrella organization for all members of the women's movement, the NCCL, the parliament, the TUC and the CBI who devoted themselves to keeping sex discrimination legislation on the agenda during the conservative Heath cabinet (Meehan 1985). During the election campaign in February 1974, the Conservatives, Labour and the Liberal Democrats all promised equal employment rights legislation (Davies 1987).

In 1974, Labour returned to power. The Fawcett Society, the TUC and the NCCL immediately urged Home Secretary Roy Jenkins to introduce anti-discrimination legislation. The government promised to draft such legislation. Conservative media discounted this promise as an attempt to 'win votes for the next elections' (Meehan 1985, 51). Jenkins, however, did not view equal rights legislation only as a way to win votes. In the 1960s, he had developed a reputation as a 'promoter of liberal laws' such as the Abortion Act, the Sexual Offences Bill (which decriminalized homosexuality) and the Race Relations Act. As he had other priorities in 1975, such as counteracting terrorism, he appointed Anthony Lester, a progressive lawyer and human rights specialist, as a member of staff to supervise 'the preparation of anti-discrimination legislation, both sexual and racial' (Jenkins 1991, 376).

Despite heavy 'departmental opposition', Jenkins and Lester published in September 1974 the Sex Discrimination White Paper (Jenkins 1991, 375). At Jenkins' request, representatives of the women's movement provided extensive written and oral comments (Meehan 1985). In March 1975, Jenkins published the definitive bill. It banned discrimination in education and employment based on sex and marital status. Protective measures for women were maintained, as TUC had demanded.

The bill went further than the White Paper on three points due to the 'diffusion of innovation' from the USA and the contribution of the women's movement (Lovenduski 1986). First, during a visit of Jenkins and Lester to the US, American officials convinced them that anti-discrimination policy would be effective only if it focused on the effects of the behaviour of employers instead of on their motives. For this reason, it was crucial to include the concept of indirect discrimination (Meehan 1985). In the British act, Jenkins defined indirect discrimination as 'where a substantial number of one sex is unable, to their detriment, to comply with an apparently neutral rule, applicable to both sexes, which cannot be shown to be related to job performance'.

Another important improvement was the establishment of a powerful Equal Opportunities Commission (EOC) for enforcing the law (Davies 1987). The third improvement concerned the introduction of positive action measures. Jenkins had originally rejected the concept of 'positive action' because this could undermine the non-discrimination philosophy on which the proposals were based (Meehan 1985). Under pressure from the women's movement, he added a clause that allowed positive discrimination in the admission procedures for training and study programmes, but not in job application procedures. The CBI succeeded in gaining an exemption in the law for companies with five or fewer employees. This significantly limited the effectiveness of the legislation because many women worked for small companies (Meehan 1985).

In parliament, the Conservative and Labour parties both supported the bill, and the Sex Discrimination Act (SDA) went into force at the end of 1975. The government simultaneously established the EOC, which was given the authority to monitor the compliance with equal rights legislation, conduct investigations, provide legal assistance and submit complaints in 'victimless cases' (such as discriminatory employment advertisements).

Conclusion Coreper began addressing Hillery's draft directive on equal treatment in April 1975, virtually at the same time as the British parliament was debating the SDA. It was important to the British to ensure that the other states were also bound to a statutory ban on sex discrimination and to prevent the European directive from going further than the SDA.

As results from Table 3.2, for Germany and the Netherlands, a European equal treatment directive was unattractive because there were few benefits to balance the costs. France did not have an explicit preference except for the preservation of protective measures. Given this picture, we would expect that the member states would not reach agreement on the directive. Yet, the intensive pressure from women at the national and supranational levels and the sensitivity of the governments towards their demands made it difficult to reject the proposal completely.

The Second Directive (Equal Treatment)

From the moment that the Ad Hoc Group had completed its task, no women experts were involved with the directive anymore. During the negotiations, the Commission was represented by a male senior official, who had to be briefed by Nonon (Hoskyns, 1985). Initially, Coreper was sympathetic towards the directive, until the potential financial consequences became clear. The Commission proposal contained two very sensitive points: the elimination of protective measures and exemptions for sex-specific professions, and the elimination of unequal treatment in social security and retirement age. The national representatives heavily amended the directive on both these points.

Table 3.2 Equal treatment: domestic costs and pressure (1975)

	France	Germany	the Netherlands	Britain
1. Relative economic costs: equal treatment in social security	Low costs (1)	Low costs (1)	High costs (3)	High costs (3)
2. Ideological costs: compatibility with domestic policy frame	Low costs (1): Compatible with vanguard role, policy of Giscard and Giroud	High costs (3): Incompatible with 'free choice' and wage autonomy	Medium costs (2): Compatible with equal opportunities, incompatible with breadwinner	Low costs (1): Compatible with SDA
Relative domestic costs of equal treatment draft directive (1+2)	Low (2)	Medium (4)	High (5)	Medium (4)
3. Domestic opposition to draft equal treatment directive	Rather limited (2: Gaullists (in the government), CGT	Strong (4): SPD (in the government), employers, DGB	Rather strong (3): CDA (in the government), employers	Rather strong (3): Labour (in the government), employers
4. Domestic support for draft equal treatment directive	Strong (4): women's movement, CFDT, liberals (in the government), PS and PCF	Limited (1): women in SPD, section Policies for Women	Strong (4): women's movement, PvdA (government), VVD, leftist parties	Rather strong (3): women's movement, civil rights, Labour backbench
Saliency (3+4) and relative domestic pressure (4–3)	High saliency (6), rather limited support (2)	Medium saliency (5), strong resistance (–3)	High saliency (7), limited support (1)	High saliency (7), balance support–opposition (0)
Sensitivity	High	High	High	High
Expected preference	Rather in favour	Opposed	Opposed	Opposed

The first point concerned forms of special treatment. The draft directive did not provide the usual exemptions regarding access to training and professions, such as the military, midwives, and religious schools; it also said nothing about protective legislation such as the ban on night work for women and measures related to pregnancy and motherhood. According to Hoskyns, this showed 'how new the area was to those involved' (Hoskyns 1996a, 103). However, the Ad Hoc Group that had prepared the text was not a group of 'newcomers'. Lady Seear and Du Granrut were well acquainted with the issue. Also the Legal Service of the Commission was very familiar with the principle of equal treatment provisions, since these principles were broadly applied in the EEC concerning the free movement of goods, services, individuals and capital, including all sorts of exemptions (More 1999). The Ad Hoc Group deliberately had left out the usual exemptions as it wanted to prevent misuse of special treatment.

Under pressure from Coreper, the Commission nevertheless included the 'classical' exceptions to equal treatment for protection during pregnancy and motherhood and regarding the access to sex-specific professions. However, it did limit the allowed exemptions and provided a form of monitoring which would turn out to have far-reaching consequences in the 1980s. Member states were given four years to make an inventory of exemptions for sex-specific professions. They then had to investigate periodically whether the exemption was still justified and had to keep the Commission informed about the state of affairs. They were also required to modify protective provisions in legislation and collective labour agreements. This meant that the ban on night work for women must either be eliminated or expanded to include men.

The second sensitive point involved the provisions related to social security and retirement age. After the member states had removed social security from the first directive, this was the Commission's second attempt after *Defrenne I* to establish equal rights regarding social security. The Commission explained that a system of social security focusing on the man as breadwinner was no longer in accordance with the socio-economic reality. Germany, the Netherlands, Britain and Denmark disagreed and resisted the inclusion of social security in the directive (Agence 1975, 7 June).

A British Intervention It was planned that the Council in June 1975 would approve the directive in the presence of Hillery, who would then leave for the UN Conference in Mexico. Hillery very much wanted to announce the approval of both directives at this conference. However, in a fiery speech, British minister Castle persuaded those present that the directive was poorly thought out. Equal treatment in social security would even be disadvantageous for women because it robbed them of advantages such as early retirement (Agence 1975, 18 June).

Castle wanted to eliminate these provisions from the directive because they would otherwise conflict with the new British Pensions Act, for which she had fought for months within the British government and which some of her fellow ministers thought was already 'too generous to women' (Castle 1980, 116). The equalization of retirement age would cost £1.4 billion, 'which my country just has not got at the present time'. Moreover, in June 1975, the pound was under attack and the inflation rate of 28 percent had already forced the British government to make budget cutbacks and implement wage control measures (Castle 1980).

Castle's dissatisfaction with the directive was not only prompted by cost considerations and concern about the fate of her Pensions Act. Hillery and other proponents of the directive had the misfortune that the 'heroine' of the British Equal

Pay Act was a fierce common market opponent who had been defeated in the British referendum about the EEC one week before the Council meeting.[8] Her speech in the Council was inspired by her disappointment about the outcome of the referendum and her dislike of the EEC: 'Here am I, ready to accept that I must cooperate now with the Council of Ministers, but still nursing reticence and unhappiness about the Market' (Castle 1980, 410). She had decided to attend the Council meeting herself in order to teach 'them' a lesson (Castle 1980, 420). The draft directive on equal treatment was typically 'one of those pretentious pieces of EEC "legislation" which can be as grandiose as you like because everyone ignores them when it suits them', whereas, as she told the French Minister of Finance during lunch, 'A law is a law and should be drafted with the intention that it shall be enforced' (Castle 1980, 419).

The result of her intervention was that the Council adjourned the meeting. After bilateral negotiations, the meeting resumed, but around midnight the chair ascertained that agreement was infeasible (Agence 1975, 19 June). The draft returned to Coreper for further study. Hillery had to limit his statement in Mexico to reporting 'the efforts of the Community to bring about equal pay' (Commission 1975, 289).

Italian Intervention Another point of contention was the treaty basis of the directive (Agence 1975, 7 June). The Commission had proposed the combination of Article 100 ('the harmonization of statutory and administrative provisions that directly affect the operation of the common market') with Article 235 'for unforeseen cases'. Germany did not want a general ban on sex discrimination (Agence 1975, 13 June). It preferred to base the directive on Article 100, because in that case it would only have to deal with unequal treatment and remove discriminatory provisions from its legislation to the extent that they damaged free movement or competition. Such a minimalist interpretation was unacceptable to the Commission, Britain and France. In contrast, Article 235 called for 'appropriate measures' to achieve a specific aim, in this case the principle of equal treatment. Coreper decided to base the directive on Article 235.

Italy wanted to see the directive approved under its presidency of the EEC in the second half of 1975. In all countries, 'women' were on the agenda due to the manifestations for the International Women's Year and because women were severely affected by the economic recession. Unemployment was especially high among young women, but the Council had rejected special measures for them (Agence 1975, 18 June). With an eye on the 'political and psychological effect', Italy believed it was important to take concrete measures (Agence 1975, 5 and 18 December). The Eurobarometer opinion poll showed that the population believed that 'unemployment' and 'coordination of social policy' should be among the top priorities of the EEC (Agence 1975, 19 December).

The action group Women for Europe, which included Nonon (DG V), Fausta Deshormes La Valle (DG Information and Public Relations) and Brunfaut (Belgian

8 On 5 June 1975, 68.3 percent of British voters approved the continuation of British EEC membership.

trade unions), decided to exert extra pressure on the Council. On the day of the vote on the second directive, they organized a demonstration in Brussels in which the trade unions and more than 40 women's organizations participated. Italian Minister of Labour Toros, presiding the Council, received a delegation of Women for Europe (De Groote and Thys 1979). They protested primarily against the possible elimination of social security from the directive (Brunfaut 1979). The Commission had not given in to pressure from Britain, the Netherlands, Denmark and Germany and had not amended the draft. The Council could only depart from the Commission proposal with unanimity. With the support of Italy, the Commission was able to extract the promise that equal treatment in matters of social security would be arranged in a subsequent directive (Directive 76/207, Article 1.2; Hoskyns 1996a, 105).

The member states disagreed until the last minute about the scope of the concept of non-discrimination, judicial assistance and the deadline for implementation. Regarding the scope, the directive ultimately became stronger than the Commission's draft version; the member states gave in to the British demand to include indirect discrimination. Britain made a plausible case that avoiding the term 'indirect discrimination' would only postpone the issue; American experience had shown that the courts would honour complaints about indirect discrimination. The British also wanted the member states to create a separate commission, modelled on the EOC, to provide judicial assistance and to monitor the implementation of equal treatment, but this demand was rejected. Germany especially resisted this idea because the German trade unions and employers were opposed to such an institution (Agence 1975, 18 December). The member states decided to extend the term for implementation to thirty months so that they all would have enough time to introduce legislation. This meant that the directive would not go into force until 12 August 1978. The text was formally approved on 9 February 1976 (*Official Journal* 1976, L 39/40–42, 14 February).

Conclusion

Despite the weakening of the original proposal, the directive was a far-reaching agreement; the member states approved supranational provisions concerning matters such as direct and indirect sex discrimination, positive action measures, and elimination of protective legislation and exemptions for sex-specific jobs, even though they still had few if any rules at the national level in these areas.

As it did with the equal pay directive, Germany approved this second directive with the assumption that it would not have to modify its legislation because Article 3 in the Constitution banned unequal treatment (Hoskyns 1988). However, this assumption appeared to be based more on the experience that it had little to fear from the Court than on a careful analysis of the Constitution and the directive; Article 3 only applied to pre-existing labour relationships, while the directive also contained a ban on discrimination during recruitment and hiring (Pfarr and Bertelsmann 1985). This omission would form the basis of an infringement procedure against Germany (see Chapter 4). The Dutch government approved a costly agreement. It was too sensitive towards domestic pressure to allow itself a veto against equal treatment of women, and the position of the Netherlands was too weak to block a proposal that was ultimately supported by three of the four largest member states (France, Britain and Italy). Britain approved the directive only after it became convinced that it would not have to modify its own legislation.

The Commission exploited the short time horizon of the governments by binding them concerning social security and protective provisions. Since the member states made these promises as part of a binding directive, they ultimately had to follow through unless they wanted to risk a complaint at the Court.

Social Security on the Negotiating Table

The Commission against the Current

The tide for new supranational social policy had meanwhile turned. Until the end of 1975, the implementation of the SAP was still on schedule, although there was an increasing tendency to dismantle expensive proposals, such as poverty alleviation, and to postpone policy that was costly for employers, such as reducing the workweek (Shanks 1977a). The relationship between Hillery and the Council worsened due to the growing gap between Hillery's ambitions and the unwillingness of the member states to develop supranational social policy during a time of economic crisis.

'The debacle of the SAP came in its third year' (Shanks 1977a, 16). The Council had asked the Commission to present a successor to SAP before the end of 1976. Instead of a new SAP, the Council received a 'somewhat pathetic valedictory message' from Hillery (Shanks 1977b, 382). 'Hillery's testament', as the member states called the document 'with a certain amount of disdain,' contained no concrete proposals (Agence 1976, 9 November). The 'testament' disappeared into the drawer. There was no basis for joint social policy left. Brandt, its main proponent, resigned already in 1974 due to an espionage scandal. The recession had led to a polarization of stronger and weaker economies and to diverging opinions about the aims of joint social policy. Against the background of rapidly increasing unemployment, the improvement of the position of women was even viewed as undesirable. Former director Michael Shanks of DG V warned in 1977 that

> if one concentrates one's action completely on the so-called marginal groups, it may simply be at the expense of the adult males ... Neither socially, economically or politically is there much merit in boosting employment of youths, women or handicapped if it means proportionally fewer jobs for fully trained fathers of families (Shanks 1977a, 22).

The willingness of the member states to approve a third directive in the area of equal rights was limited. However, in the equal treatment directive they had obligated themselves to act on social security. Women's organizations and women in trade unions insisted on making rapid progress with social security (Brunfaut 1979; Hoskyns 1996a), but the representatives of employers, trade unions and governments believed it was 'too early' to establish the principle. They proposed to first conduct research into the financial consequences of the application of the principle, specifically of the equalization of retirement age (*Europa van Morgen* 1975, 10 December). The Commission mandated DG V to draft a directive on equal treatment and social security (Hoskyns and Luckhaus 1989). Nonon and the other 'equal opportunities experts' were not involved in drawing up the social security directive, which was prepared by social security experts.

Drafting the Directive The research conducted by Edward James (DG V) showed that the social security systems in the member states all led to different forms of discrimination against women and that there were 'certain anomalies that need to be corrected' (Hoskyns and Luckhaus 1989, 323). The question was whether the directive should be based on the principle of individualization of rights or that of equal treatment. The Commission rejected the idea of individualization as being too costly and controversial. To give its proposal a chance of being approved, the Commission decided to follow the model of the equal treatment directive and expand the principle of equal treatment contained in this directive to include all social security provisions related to employment, even though equal treatment would in fact have negative consequences for women in the short term.

DG V conducted discussions with trade unions, employers and national experts, but did not make formal contact with women's organizations (*Bulletin* 5–1976; Hoskyns and Luckhaus 1989). As a result of the discussions, DG V decided to remove payments for widowhood and motherhood from the directive because these only concerned women and therefore could not be a source of unequal treatment. It also removed the family supplements, which 'affected family policy more than terms of employment' (Commission 1976, COM(76)650).

On 22 December 1976, the Commission approved the revised draft directive. It banned all forms of sex discrimination in statutory regulations and occupational systems for unemployment, illness, accidents and disability. The concept of 'discrimination' comprised also indirect discrimination, 'especially by reference to marital status or family circumstances'. To further increase the chance of approval by the member states, the Commission proposed to implement the directive in three phases: two years for equal treatment in statutory regulations and social security payments, three years for all allowances for dependent persons, and four years for the regulations in occupational systems, which were most numerous. After every phase the member states were required to present a report. Only during the first phase, the member states could maintain special provisions that were to the advantage of women, such as the length of employment that gave a right to retirement pay and the assignment of pension rights for periods during which women carried out unpaid work (pregnancy, giving birth) (Commission 1976, COM(76)650).

In January 1977, the prospects for the directive initially appeared to be beneficial. The new Commission was presided over by Jenkins, the promoter of the British SDA. He gave Henk Vredeling, a Dutch Social Democrat, the social affairs portfolio. In the 1960s, as a MEP, Vredeling had frequently asked questions concerning Article

119, the protection of motherhood and other aspects concerning women workers. His cabinet chief was Nel Barendregt, who had conducted the campaign for equal pay and equal treatment in the Dutch parliament. Vredeling and Barendregt were therefore on familiar terrain.

Nonetheless, the change of guard was not only positive as Vredeling enjoyed little prestige as a Commissioner. Jenkins describes him as 'a man of warmth and courage' but 'not a Commission's success' due to his impulsive actions (Jenkins 1991, xvi). Vredeling obtained no support in the Commission for new equal rights legislation, so he focused on the draft directive that already had been approved by the preceding Commission. On 10 January 1977, Vredeling sent the document without any changes to Coreper.

Social Security at the Domestic Level

In all member states, the post-war system of social security was based on guaranteeing a minimum family income. In most cases, unequal treatment resulted from the special status of the married woman, who was assumed to be financially dependent on her husband.

France and Germany In France, equal treatment in social security was not on the national agenda. Women's organizations and women in trade unions had other priorities. They demanded that the government take measures to improve the poor conditions of employment for women and alleviate rising female unemployment (Choisir 1978). The conservative government under Raymond Barre actually wanted to make it more attractive for women to stay home in the hope that unemployed men could take their place on the labour market and they would have more children. They took measures 'for the family' and enabled retirement at the age of 60 for women in the private sector. The women's movement resisted such special rights for women because this actually weakened their position on the labour market. In parliament, the Gaullists applauded the government policy: the unemployed were given the opportunity 'to once again lead a normal life'; the state had to spend less on childcare and 'the housewife would certainly return to her true calling' (Albert Liogier (RPR) quoted in Choisir 1978, 114). The most important aim for France during the negotiations about the third directive was therefore that it should not have to eliminate regulations that assigned specific rights to women.

In Germany, equal treatment in social security was on the agenda due to several rulings of German courts on the calculation of pensions and the criteria for widowers to become eligible for certain payments (Bertelsmann and Rust, 1995). The political climate had hardened due to terrorist attacks and the way in which the state responded to the violence. The autonomous women's groups were accused of providing support to violent actions. They became socially marginalized. The reform of social security therefore took place out of sight of the German women's movement.

The Netherlands In contrast to the situation in France and Germany, the Dutch women's movement assigned a high priority to the topic of social security and pension rights (Sjerps 1988). The Dutch social security system was strongly based on family ideology and discriminated against married women regarding their right to unemployment payments, disability payments and pensions. The women's movement and the NVV wanted to eliminate all 'breadwinner provisions'.

In January 1977, Minister Boersma requested the SER for advice on the draft directive of the Commission. The SER explained that the directive would have consequences primarily for the General Pensions Act, the General Disability Act and the Unemployment Act. The required changes would cost 150 to 160 million guilders per year (*Europa van Morgen* 1978, 28 November). In view of the expected costs, the SER advised the government to plead in the Council for a long implementation period (SER 1977). The parliament approved a motion in which it requested the government to make a survey of all legislation that contained discriminatory provisions (*Handelingen* 1977, 13943, *Motie-Van Winkel*).

In December 1977 a centre-right government came into power. Its first priority was to reduce social expenditures. In September 1978, parliament again asked questions about the breadwinner concept and the unequal treatment of women in social security regulations (*Handelingen* 1978, 14496, No. 24, 919). Junior Minister of Social Affairs De Graaf acknowledged that the Netherlands clearly had to modify its system because of the coming EEC directive, but that the big issue was how this was supposed to be done: treating everyone as an individual or extending the distinction between breadwinners and non-breadwinners to women as well? The latter strategy could lead to indirect discrimination, but was far less costly than individualization. In its austerity plan *Bestek '81* the government reintroduced the breadwinner concept for financial reasons. The government felt the negotiations on the EEC directive put it under time pressure (*Handelingen* 1978, 14496, 40–50).

Britain In 1975, Home Secretary Jenkins left social security and pensions outside the SDA 'because the complexities were expected to lengthen the passage of a bill that they were anxious to pass quickly' (Meehan 1985, 213). Since her appointment in 1974, Minister of Social Affairs Castle worked to correct the unequal treatment of married women in the Social Security Act and Social Security Pensions Act. In the government, she had to fight hard to prevent her proposals from being cut down to the bone because of their financial consequences. She found it 'immensely embarrassing in the International Women's Year' that she had to depend on the amendments in parliament to be able to save her proposal for a 'disabled housewives benefit' (Castle 1980, 291). Castle warned Dennis Healey, Minister of Finance, that 'we might even find ourselves before the Equal Opportunities Board if we were to continue to give women unequal benefits for the same contributions' (Castle 1980, 489).

The new pension act gave married women the right to a pension 'in their own right', but many discriminatory provisions remained (Coussins 1977, 104). The Social Security Act even introduced new inequalities because married women were explicitly excluded from payments for the care of seriously handicapped dependents

Table 3.3 Social security: domestic costs and pressure (1977)

	France	Germany	the Netherlands	Britain
1. Relative economic costs: equal treatment in social security and pensions	Low costs (1)	Low costs (1) – but high costs if incl. occupational social security	High costs (3)	High costs (3)
2. Ideological costs: compatibility with domestic policy frame	High costs (3): incompatible with protective regulation, family policy	Medium costs (2): incompatible with family policies, political climate	High costs (3): incompatible with breadwinner and budgetary policy	High costs (3): incompatible with breadwinner and budgetary policy
Relative domestic costs (1+2)	Medium costs (4)	Medium costs (3)	High costs (6)	High costs (6)
3. Domestic opposition to draft directive on social security	Rather strong (3): CGT, Gaullists (in the government)	Rather limited (2): CDU/CSU (in the opposition)	Strong (4): CDA and VVD (in the government), employers	Strong (4): Labour (in the government), Conservatives, employers
4. Domestic support for draft directive on social security	Rather limited (2): CFDT, women's organizations	Limited (1): court cases	Strong (4): opposition parties, trade unions, women's movement	Rather strong (3): NCCL, EOC, women's movement
Saliency (3+4) and relative domestic pressure (4–3)	Medium saliency (5), limited resistance (–1)	Low saliency (3), limited resistance (–1)	High saliency (8), balance between opposition and support (0)	High saliency (6), limited opposition (–1)
Sensitivity	Low	High	Until 1978, high; after 1978, low	High
Expected preference	Rather in favour	Rather in favour	Opposed	Opposed

and for disability (Atkins and Luckhaus 1987). In spite of pressure from the NCCL and the EOC for further reforms, the British government was not in favour of an EEC directive on social security because of the high costs.

Conclusion None of these four member states was in favour of a supranational regulation for equal treatment in social security (see Table 3.3). However, there were major differences between them.

In Germany and France, there was no strong pressure concerning this issue and the governments expected they would not have to modify their legislation drastically.

In Britain and the Netherlands, the issue was very salient; there was much pressure for reform and much resistance. Both governments expected that they would have to change their legislation drastically and saw high costs looming before them at a time when the economic situation was forcing them to cut back on social expenditures. We would expect that no agreement could be reached above the minimum common denominator.

The Third Directive (Social Security)

The national representatives in the Coreper workgroup were experts in the area of social security, not in the area of equal treatment. They were very conscious of the costs of system reform and attempted to limit the scope of the directive, expand the number of exemptions and prolong the time period for implementation. They did not reach agreement, which meant that the directive had to be addressed by the Council. Yet, Vredeling experienced great difficulty in getting the topic on the agenda and even getting the Council to meet at all (*Europa van Morgen* 1977, 19 October).

Between July 1977 and July 1978, the negotiations on the directive had ceased entirely because Belgium and Denmark, who held the Presidency, did not want to make any room on their agendas for this topic (Hoskyns and Luckhaus 1989). Vredeling then began a series of visits to the member states. The Dutch government promised him that Minister of Social Affairs Albeda would discuss the directive during the next Council meeting in April 1978 (*Europa van Morgen* 1978, 8 February). However, Vredeling undercut his own initiative; he allowed the Council meeting to be postponed until June because he needed time to prepare proposals concerning youth unemployment (*Europa van Morgen* 1978, 19 April). The postponed Council meeting in June ended in failure due to French resistance to Vredeling's plans for fighting youth unemployment, after which Vredeling made insulting statements about France at a press conference, which led to tension in the Commission between Vredeling and French Commissioner Ortoli and further damaged Vredeling's credibility (Jenkins 1991).

Germany came to Vredeling's aid. It wanted the directive to be approved under the German presidency during the second half of 1978. After all, the member states had obligated themselves in the second directive to regulate equal treatment in social security. Furthermore, because of a decision of the Constitutional Court, the German government had to modify several aspects of the social security system anyway as German courts would support any further complaints from citizens about discrimination in other statutory regulations (Hoskyns and Luckhaus 1989). Therefore, Germany preferred the other member states to be required to satisfy the same norms as it did, while the directive would cost the other member states probably more than Germany.

Second Round Coreper resumed negotiations in the summer of 1978 under German presidency. At the insistence of Britain, Coreper eliminated the equalization of retirement age from the directive with the argument that the difference in retirement age benefited women (Hoskyns and Luckhaus 1989). The negotiations ran aground on the inclusion of occupational schemes (Brunfaut 1979). The Netherlands and Germany opposed the inclusion of occupational schemes because this would limit the bargaining freedom of trade unions and employers. Furthermore, equal treatment in statutory systems already required a 'considerable financial effort' (Agence 1978, 25 November). However, occupational schemes could not be simply eliminated, since these were exactly the regulations that fell under the definition of 'remuneration' in Article 119 as ruled by the Court in *Defrenne I*.

'As the negotiations came nearer to a conclusion, a certain amount of panic set in, with government representatives beginning to realize what they might be signing up to' (Hoskyns 1996a, 111). Barendregt and James (the latter the author of the draft directive) appealed to women's organizations to exert pressure on their governments (Hoskyns and Luckhaus 1989).

On 27 November 1978, the Council eliminated the final obstacles. The member states ultimately applied the same tactics as they did during the equal treatment directive: they decided to pass the issue of occupational schemes to a later directive. Once again, the Commission was given a 'follow-up mandate'. This time, it had to conduct a study into the problems regarding equal treatment in pensions. Furthermore, it had to work out proposals concerning equal treatment in occupational schemes and concerning aspects of social security that fell outside the directive, such as family benefits and survivors benefits (Directive 79/7, Article 3; *Europa van Morgen* 1978, 29 November, 6 December).

Upon German initiative, the Council eliminated the provision that collective labour agreements that were in conflict with the directive must be declared invalid. It also scrapped the commitment to encourage trade unions and employers to modify such agreements. Britain and Ireland obtained exemptions in the directive for certain supplementary benefits for the dependent spouse. As proposed by France, the directive allowed to maintain 'specific provisions for women to redress existing cases of unequal treatment' and the protection of women in connection to motherhood (Prechal and Burrows 1990).

The deadline for implementation was the final point of conflict in the Council. The Netherlands, supported by Britain and Ireland, wanted a term of eight years for implementation because of the high costs of modifying their social security systems. The Commission had proposed implementation in three phases, but Germany preferred a single deadline, reducing the opportunities for monitoring by the Commission. After extended negotiations, the German presidency set the implementation term at six years, the longest term that had ever been used for a directive, but 'This long period was welcomed by most delegations' (Agence 1978, 27–8 November). It meant that women could not make an appeal based on the directive to the national courts until December 1984: a directive had no direct effect as long as the period of implementation had not elapsed. Vredeling responded to the disappointment expressed by the EP with a laconic 'if you consider how many thousands of years women have been discriminated against, then perhaps two years more is not so bad' (*Europa van Morgen* 1978, 13 December). The Council formally enacted the directive on 18 December 1978.

In this way, the third equal rights directive (79/7) was approved. It established the principle of equal treatment in statutory social security systems, a principle that had not yet been included in the national legislation of various member states. The member states nevertheless approved the directive. Domestic judicial pressure had already forced Germany to modify its legislation. France approved the directive after it had been modified in such a way that it believed it would not be required to amend its legislation. In view of the fact that the member states had obligated themselves in the Equal Treatment Directive to regulate equal treatment in social security, so the Council had to approve a directive at some point anyway, there remained little for Britain or the Netherlands to do other than approve costly policy and extend the implementation term to a maximum.

The majority of member states did not want to include occupational schemes, but they could not simply eliminate this aspect from the directive due to resistance of some member states, which enabled the Commission to keep it in the draft, their commitment in Directive 76/207 to establish equal treatment 'in the area of social security' and the ruling of the Court in *Defrenne I.* The member states therefore promised in Directive 79/7 to regulate equal treatment in occupational schemes in a subsequent instrument. In this way, equal rights policy remained on the supranational agenda. This was even more important because the window of opportunity for new supranational social policy had closed due to the economic recession and political changes in the member states.

Conclusion: The Price of Supranational Gender Equality Policies

Between 1975 and 1978, the member states approved three directives in the area of gender equality containing norms above the minimum common denominator as a result of which the EEC could function as 'a major catalyst in the generation and extension of national sex equality laws' (Mazey 1998, 131). In view of the stagnation in the 1960s and the resistance of governments, employers and trade unions to binding supranational regulation in the area of equal rights, how can we explain this remarkable progress? We have to look at the 'pincers' of pressure at different levels of action, which made it unattractive for governments not to develop supranational equal rights policy.

At the national level, social and political changes brought governments into power that were sensitive towards the call for reform, including reforms involving the position of women. The unstable situation at the international level required new joint action to prevent the further weakening of the EEC. In combination with the unstable situation at the national level, it was essential that new European policy was well received by the population. In that light, the member states committed themselves to developing supranational social policy.

The Commission used its mandate for new social policy to develop equal rights policy. This was a strategic decision, aimed at strengthening its position vis-à-vis the Council. It was supported and given content by committed officials in DG V and experts. There was pressure on the governments from 'below' (women's movement, women in trade unions and political parties), from 'inside' (women in the government and in ministries) and from 'above' (the Commission, the Court, the UN International Women's Year).

As a result, it became less attractive for the member states to do nothing than to do something. Committed officials and experts at the national and supranational levels were able to shape the direction of policy change as long as the member states wanted 'policy for women' without yet having a clear idea about the content of such policy. The actions of the Commission, supported by pioneer states France and Britain, led to the approval of far-reaching binding directives. With all three directives, it was important whether the member state that held the rotating presidency linked its prestige to the proposal under consideration.

The equality directives are telling examples of how policy instruments in multilevel systems can diffuse high national norms and improve low national norms. In its proposals, the Commission – feminist experts, committed officials and an ambitious Commissioner – established norms that were higher than the lowest national norms. 'Pioneer states' further strengthened the directives in some respects. With equal pay, France imposed the broad definition of 'work of equal value', and in the equal treatment directives, the definition of discrimination was expanded with 'indirect discrimination' following the British example. In France and Britain, these norms had been chosen to make sure that the relevant legislation would be effective. The pioneer states did not want to be disadvantaged because of their high norms, and lowering the national norm to a lower supranational norm was not allowed according to Article 117 of the EEC Treaty, which stated that agreements in the social area must involve progress. For that reason they wanted other states to be bound by the same high norm. National prestige played a role as well. France enjoyed playing a vanguard role in the social domain, while Britain wanted to teach 'the Continent' a lesson about proper legislation.

A comparison of the preferences of the member states and the results of the negotiations shows that Britain approved costly policy as the directive on social security was more expensive than its original preference and was more expensive for Britain than it was for France and Germany. The latter countries did not approve costly policy and they believed they would not have to modify their legislation. The Netherlands accepted two costly directives. In both cases, the Netherlands did not yet have national legislation and the government was not ready for it. The Dutch government was squeezed by pressure from the women's movement and supranational pressure, and lacked a strong internal and relative power position. Accordingly, it could no veto the directives.

Between 1979 and 1991, the pressure to implement these three directives and to approve new measures increased at the national and supranational levels. All member states faced increased costs for previously approved policy. Germany and France discovered that they had also approved 'costly agreements' in the past. A boomerang effect resulted, as the member states only approved very weak new instruments in spite of strong pressure. In Chapter 4, these developments will be further analysed.

Chapter 4

The Price of More Supranational Gender Equality (1979–1991)

During the 1980s there was again stagnation regarding the development of equal rights policy. Almost all proposals submitted by the Commission were blocked by the Council or weakened to the status of non-binding 'soft law'.[1] In this light, it appears even more remarkable that the member states actually implemented the far-reaching equal rights directives from the 1970s. We will investigate the developments that explain why – despite national and supranational pressure – the member states did not approve new equal rights policy, and why they finally implemented the 'old' directives.

Domestic Change, Supranational Stagnation

Domestic Pressure for Equal Rights

At the end of the 1970s, as in 1968, the call of the population for political change became louder and louder due to its concerns about the continually rising unemployment. This time conservative governments replaced predominately social democratic governments. Only in France, the political change followed the opposite direction. The ideological and political shifts affected negatively the prospects of new supranational equal rights policy.

Germany: Family Policy The SPD-FDP government under Schmidt (1974–82) did not have any affinity with gender equality policies, but the ASF (women's groups in the SPD) kept 'women's rights' on the agenda (Lovenduski 1986). After seven years of work, the parliamentary committee Woman and Society finally submitted its report on 23 September 1980. It contained more than 100 recommendations for equal rights, but Schmidt's policy statement from November 1980 did not mention a single concrete proposal. Schmidt emphasized that 'the efforts of women in the family should be valued the same as paid work for women' (Doormann 1983, 256).

The revaluation of women as housewife and widespread criticism of two-income families formed the ideological underpinning for cutbacks in social expenditures, childcare and training programmes for women re-entering the labour market. The

1 'Soft law' concerns 'instruments which are not binding but which national courts are bound to use as aids where appropriate' (Cunningham 1992, 183).

cutbacks led to a great deal of protest from the ASF and trade unions and worked as a catalyst for a renewed élan in the women's movement (Doormann 1983).

Unemployment rose to record levels. The SPD-FDP government was increasingly divided about the measures required and on 17 September 1982, the government fell. The Christian Democrats formed a new government with the FDP, under the leadership of Helmut Kohl. They won a comfortable majority in the parliamentary elections in March 1983. Cutting social expenditures was their strategy for economic recovery. The feasibility of new equal rights policy was remote.

The concept of 'equality' and the instrument of 'equal rights legislation' were not compatible with the programme of the CDU/CSU, which called for feminization of society and the revaluation of motherhood. Conservative family policy resonated with the wishes of the majority of the population. The number of people who wanted an equal division of roles between husbands and wives was significantly lower than in other countries.[2] The number of women who believed they were disadvantaged in their careers due to their sex was twice as high in Germany as the EEC average (Commission 1984, X/220/84, 31–3).

The pressure for equal rights exerted by the women's movement and the trade unions was stronger than in previous periods, but the government was insensitive towards this pressure. This was due to the government's parliamentary strength, the broad support for the CDU/CSU family policy and the sensitivity of the FDP for the resistance of employers to any increase in labour costs.

The Netherlands: Eliminating Barriers From 1977 to 1981, a centre-right coalition of CDA and VVD governed. The government froze wages and cut back on social expenditures. These measures led to widespread resistance (Agence 1980, 7 January).

In September 1981, a government with a progressive signature came into power. The new Minister for Emancipation, Hedy d'Ancona, was one of the founding members of MVM (see p. 75). D'Ancona expanded the aims of equal rights policy to include 'fair division of labour inside and outside the home, (…) participation in decision making and economic independence' (*Handelingen* 1981–2, 17100, XV, 28). She asked a committee of experts to produce a theoretical underpinning for her policy. The resulting report, 'Analysis of the women's issue', published in May 1982, offered new concepts and a new analysis. It discussed how structurally unequal power relationships between men and women were reflected in the division of paid and unpaid work, but also in the coercive character of ways of living and sexuality (*Handelingen* 1982–3, 17100 XV). However, before D'Ancona could implement her programme, the government fell and in November 1982, a CDA-VVD coalition once again came into power.

---

2 In favour of equal division of roles between man and woman: Germany, 26 percent; The Netherlands, 43 percent; France, 45 percent and Britain, 48 percent (Commission 1988, X/24/88, 14 and 60).

D'Ancona's pioneering ideas did not fit with the ideology of the new government (Van Arnhem 1984). Cutbacks in family and health care led to declining employment for women (De Jong and Sjerps 1987). Like in Germany, the government policy led to a new upsurge of political action by the women's movement. In 1983, the Broad Platform for Economic Independence brought women's organizations, women in the trade unions and in political parties together in their resistance against new social security acts (De Jong and Sjerps 1987). Due to the insensitivity of the government, all this pressure had little effect.

Britain: 'The problem that there is not' On 28 March 1979, the Labour government lost a no-confidence motion. The Conservatives came into power under the leadership of Margaret Thatcher, the first female Prime Minister of Britain. Concerning equality policies, 'the government says there is no problem here, and "the problem that there is not" is best solved by voluntary agreement' (Vallance and Davies 1986, 116).

Thatcher said she was a proponent of equal opportunities, because 'more than ever we need to mobilise the skill and ability of all our citizens if we are to revitalise the currency and increase the prosperity in this country' (Meehan 1985, 130). However, her social policy was at odds with strengthening the position of women. It focused on the 'return of state welfare functions to the domestic arena' by reducing social provisions, limiting the right to social security and leaving care to 'the family' (Lovenduski 1997).

The critical distance of Women's Lib towards the state shifted to involvement in order to defend acquired rights. Labour women established the *Fightback for Women's Rights* organization and began a campaign to improve the parliamentary representation of women (Lovenduski 1986). The electoral appeal exerted by the new Social Democratic Party made Labour sensitive towards the demands of women (Childs 1992, 307). However, Labour lost the elections in 1983 and 1987. The Conservative government kept a strong power base in parliament and could ignore all pressure.

Women acquired more influence in the trade unions as the absolute and relative number of female members continued to rise (Chamberlayne 1993). They participated actively in strikes against government policy and organized mass demonstrations against the mine closures. However, the Conservative government approved legislation that weakened the position of the trade unions and limited the possibilities of women to influence government policy (Childs 1992).

Until 1984, Thatcher would block every EEC initiative with a reference to the 'British Budgetary Question'.[3] Following the compromise that the European Council reached at Fontainebleau in 1984, Britain approved only initiatives for the completion

3 Due to the functioning of the Common Agricultural Policy, Great Britain contributed more to the EEC than it received. In 1975, the member states therefore agreed to a correction mechanism, but the regulation expired on 1 January 1980. Thatcher used the expiration as an opportunity to strengthen her domestic position by appealing to the anti-EEC feelings in the electorate. She demanded compensation for the net shortfall in the British EEC budget with the famous slogan: 'I want my money back'.

of the internal market. It continued to block all proposals for supranational social policy, fearing that workers could win back the rights via the 'European route' that they had lost at the national level.

France: Imagination Comes into Power Only in France the prospects for equal rights policy were good. All parties 'placed women's issues centre-stage in their electoral strategies' (Chamberlayne 1993, 188). During the parliamentary election campaign in 1978, Giscard d'Estaing tried to win the women's vote by appointing a Junior Minister for Women's Affairs and a Junior Minister for Women's Employment. He called Nonon back from Brussels for the first position, and he appointed Nicole Pasquier to the latter post. Nonon left after six months, frustrated by the lack of power and means (*F-Magazine* 1981, No. 36). Pasquier, 'whose ignorance of, and insensitivity to, women's problems was embarrassingly revealed at her first press conference' (Duchen 1986, 127), submitted a bill for equal opportunities at work, but there was not enough time to submit the bill to parliament before the presidential elections (Mazur 1991).

The women's movement exerted focused pressure on the political parties. Women organized themselves within the PCF (*Elles voient rouge*) and the PS (*Courant G*). The radical MLF called for women to prevent another victory of the right and to vote for Mitterrand (Duchen 1986). During the campaign for the presidential elections in 1981, François Mitterrand (PS) promised that he would establish a strong ministry for women's rights (Choisir 1981).

'Imagination came into power' in May 1981 as Mitterrand won the presidential elections. He appointed six women to his government and, as promised, established a Ministry for Women's Rights with its own budget and a seat on the Council of Ministers. He appointed Yvette Roudy to this post, a prominent feminist and former chair of the Committee on Women's Rights in the EP (see next section).

Roudy was able to get legislation through parliament concerning equal opportunities on the labour market, marriage and family law, parental leave and a statute for working spouses (Coquillat 1988). Her proposals had to overcome a number of hurdles: the resistance of the president, the indifference of the other ministers, and the self-interest of the trade unions. Mitterrand was more concerned about the low population growth in France than about equal rights for women on the labour market: 'We do not forbid contraception, that is normal, that is freedom, but it is negative … The liberation of the woman often means having children' (Attali 1993, 316).

She created support for her policy by providing subsidies and formal recognition to women's organizations (Lovenduski 1997). Furthermore, Roudy invested many resources in the distribution of information to the larger public by means of media campaigns and by establishing 140 information centres. Her actions contributed to the success of the Ministry for Women's Rights. An opinion poll in December 1983 showed that 79 percent of the population had heard of the Ministry and that 77 percent believed it was essential (Northcutt and Flaitz 1985).

The 1981–83 years would go into history as 'the socialist experiment', where the government nationalized key businesses and banks. The experiment failed. In May 1983, France was forced to return to a more orthodox economic course. Budget cutbacks limited Roudy's range of action. The consecutive socialist governments suffered from chronic internal divisions, which dominated the political agenda:

> Wednesday 19 June 1985. The atmosphere in the Council of Ministers is extremely tense. The Ministers are thinking only about the quarrel between Fabius and Jospin. When Yvette Roudy informs us about the women's rights conference that the UN is planning in Nairobi, this seems totally surrealistic and causes suppressed chuckling around the table. Nevertheless, it is infinitely more important than the quarrels between those two gentlemen … (Attali 1993, 1254).

From 1981, France – as it did in 1957 and 1975 – could have once again played a leading role concerning the development of European equality policy. Roudy believed France was destined to take a role as a 'vanguard country' due to its leading position in equal rights (Northcutt and Flaitz 1985). During his election campaign, Mitterrand had declared that in the EEC 'legislation must always aim for the highest norm … At any rate that is the case for all social legislation, and should also be the case for equal rights legislation' (Choisir 1981, 104). However, the eccentric economic course and the weak economic and financial position of France reduced its potential influence. In the European Council, Mitterrand's proposal for a European social space was 'poorly received' (Attali 1993, 69). The domestic progress in equal rights policy therefore did not have a counterpart in progress at the European level.

Supranational Pressure for New Equal Rights Policy

At the European level, there was much pressure in favour of equal rights policy as well. Transnational networks developed. The Equal Opportunities Unit (Unit) of DG V played a key role in organizing and financing these networks. Commissioner Hillery had established the Unit in 1976, in accordance with the proposal in the SAP and following repeated urging from the EP and the women's committee of the European Trade Union Confederation (ETUC). Nonon led three women on the staff, 'a truly enthusiastic, but still not indefatigable mini-team' (Nonon 1979, 146).

One of the transnational networks came about at the initiative of the British Equal Opportunities Commission (EOC). The Equal Opportunities Unit organized a 'Conference on Equality' in Manchester in 1980 to which it invited the national equal rights commissions, trade unions and women's organizations from all member states. They discussed the effectiveness of the national measures for the implementation of the equality directives. Because of the conference, the Commission established a Standing Advisory Committee for Women's Issues; the members of the committee were representatives from the national equal rights commissions. The Commission hoped that the Advisory Committee could function as an 'effective transmission belt' between the European and national levels. This did not come about due to a lack of means and power. In particular, the Advisory Committee lacked a strategy to reach the grassroots and to mobilize women to support their demands (Hoskyns 1996a).

A second transnational network came about in 1980 when a group of women established the Centre of Research on European Women (CREW) with the support of DG V. The aim of CREW was to close the 'information gap' between the national and supranational levels. In 1983, it established the European Network of Women (ENOW), a 'loose association of grassroots, autonomous women's organisations' as a feminist counterpart to the Advisory Committee (Hoskyns 1996a, 130). It would remain a rather closed 'Brussels network' without a national basis.

The UN again became a catalyst for activities concerning women's rights. As part of its Decade for Women, the UN organized conferences in Copenhagen in 1980 and in Nairobi in 1985 where governments met to assess the results of 'Mexico' (Burrows 1980). In parallel with the official conferences, the Forum brought together thousands of women and non-governmental organizations.

The EP Enters the Arena Another catalyst for supranational activities was the first direct election for the European Parliament in June 1979. Women's organizations used the elections to focus the attention of the political parties on the position of women (Reinalda and Verhaaren 1989). The directly elected EP had a relatively large number of women: 67 of the 410 members (16.3 percent) were female. This was a significantly higher percentage than the parliaments in France, Britain and Germany.

The women members of the EP were able to acquire sufficient support to establish an Ad Hoc Committee for Women's Rights with the aim of organising a parliamentary debate about the situation of women (*Official Journal* 1979, C 289, 19 November). The Ad Hoc Committee appointed Roudy as chair and Hanja Maij-Weggen, a Dutch Christian-Democrat, as *rapporteur*.

Maij-Weggen based her report on a large number of written sources, public hearings and an opinion poll on 'European women in paid employment' (Agence 1980, 23 April). The meetings of the Ad Hoc Committee were public so that women's organizations could attend them (EP 1981). On 10 February 1981, the EP held a plenary discussion on the Maij-Weggen report. The report placed the theme 'women and work' in a broader, social framework and focused attention on matters such as women's health and the legal position of women migrants. The EP adopted the ensuing resolution about 'the position of the woman' with 174 votes in favour, 101 votes opposed and 24 abstentions.[4] The resolution had no judicial effect, but Ivor Richard, who succeeded Vredeling as Commissioner of Social Affairs in 1981, combined a large number of the proposals in the first 'Action Programme to promote equal opportunities for women' (Commission 1981, COM(81)758).

In 1981, due to the 'productive cooperation of women members of parliament and EEC bureaucrats' (Randall 1987, 243), supported by national and transnational

4 The opposition came predominately from those who disagreed with the section on abortion.

women's networks, the issue of equal rights for women was unmistakably on the European agenda.

Supranational Bargaining: Hard Vetoes, Soft Laws (1981–85)

The Action Programme comprised proposals for directives in the area of occupational social security schemes, equal treatment for self-employed women, parental leave, taxation and maternity leave. The Commission wanted the Council to approve the Action Programme, so it could submit draft directives without having to ask the Council separately for permission for every initiative (Rutherford 1989). The EP considered the Action Programme as an absolute minimum in terms of its content. However, in view of the lack of progress since 1978 and the economic recession, it would be a major step forward if the Council were to approve it at all. On the day of the Council meeting in Brussels, women's organizations, political parties and trade unions demonstrated in favour of strengthening the Action Programme (Agence 1982, 28 May).

The pressure of the EP, the demonstrations, the efforts of Commissioner Richard and Chair Hansenne (from Belgium) and the persuasive skills of Roudy (who represented France) led to the ministers approving the Action Programme (Pillinger 1992). Roudy even convinced the Council to replace the text that 'under the current conditions, the financial means of the Community and the member states are limited' with the statement that equal treatment must be realized 'regardless of the economic situation' (Agence 1982, 28 May). Against Roudy's wishes, the Council did not strengthen the role of women's organizations in national equal rights commissions, but instead strengthened the role of employers' organizations and trade unions (*Official Journal* 1982, C 186/3, 21 July).

The approval of the Action Programme meant that the member states allowed the Commission to submit a series of proposals. Moreover, in December 1979, the Council had approved a resolution on 'the reduction and adaptation of working time', aimed at reducing unemployment. With reference to the Action Programme and the working time resolution, Commissioner Richard submitted five draft directives and three recommendations to the Council.

The EP drafted a report on each proposal, submitted amendments, developed its own proposals about the rights of migrant women and other topics, and continually urged the Commission and the Council to accept its proposals. However, negotiations in the Council proceeded with great difficulty, as can be seen in Table 4.1. Until January 1985, when a new Commission under Jacques Delors took office, the ministers only approved two non-binding recommendations and a non-binding declaration. We will take a closer look at the negotiations concerning the five proposals for 'hard law' – the draft directives.

Part-time Work and Temporary Work In December 1981, the Commission presented a draft directive concerning part-time work. The directive had the aim of giving part-time workers proportionally the same rights as fulltime workers regarding pay,

Table 4.1 Commission proposals and outcome of negotiations (1979–1985)

Topic	Commission proposal (format and date)	Outcome of negotiations (until January 1985)
Part-time work	Draft Directive, December 1981	–
Temporary work	Draft Directive, April 1982	–
Flexible retirement age	Draft Recommendation, December 1981	Recommendation, May 1982
Adaptation of working time	Draft Recommendation, September 1983	Declaration, June 1984
Positive action	Draft Recommendation, April 1984	Recommendation, December 1984
Parental leave	Draft Directive, November 1983	–
Social security (occupational schemes)	Draft Directive, April 1983	–
Self-employed, including agriculture	Draft Directive, March 1984	–

vacation, pensions and social security (Agence 1981, 11 December). Commissioner Richard viewed the proposed directive as a supplement to the existing equal rights directives because women made up 90 percent of part-time workers and 25 percent of the female professional population worked part-time.

In May 1982, the ministers held a first discussion about the directive. France supported the proposal and wanted to go even further, but Germany preferred to leave the entire topic to collective agreements (Pillinger 1992). Protests from women in the SPD led to Germany agreeing with the idea of a directive on the condition that its content would be diluted (Agence 1982, 27 September). Britain believed the directive was absolutely unacceptable as it 'would introduce undesirable rigidities into the labour market and generally decrease the opportunities for part-time work' (Agence 1982, 26 May). Coreper 'reached deadlock'. In view of the resistance, the Council ascertained in October 1983 that further discussion was futile (Agence 1983, 3–4 October).

In May 1984, the Commission decided that Richard could replace the draft directive with a non-binding recommendation. When in June 1984 Britain blocked a related recommendation[5] in the Social Council, Richard informed the Council that he did not change the directive into a recommendation because this change would

5 Recommendation on the adaptation of working time.

obviously not increase the probability of approval (Agence 1984, 9 June). Coreper placed the proposal 'on ice' for an indeterminate time.[6] In spite of pressure by the EP, the draft directive on temporary work was destined for the same fate as the part-time work directive. British resistance blocked this proposal as well (Agence 1983, 5 May).

Parental Leave and Leave for Family Reasons In its resolution on the situation of women (1981), the EP requested the Commission to investigate the desirability of harmonizing national regulations in the area of parental leave. In the Action Programme, the Commission announced a directive concerning parental leave. Commissioner Richard viewed parental leave as 'an essential part of any strategy to achieve equality in the labour market' because it would reduce the career gap of mothers and would increase the number of fathers who participated in raising their children (Rutherford 1989, 302). The Equal Opportunities Unit prepared the draft directive, proposing a parental leave of three months fulltime or six months part-time for each working parent on the condition that they share the leave equally. It left the method of funding to the member states.

The proposal was very controversial. For the first time, a European proposal directly affected family responsibilities (Pillinger 1992). According to the employers, parental leave was not part of the terms of employment. UNICE warned that parental leave 'would provide for institutionalized absenteeism' (Vallance and Davies 1986, 132). The Commission was divided as well. Commissioners Davignon, Narjes and Andriessen believed the proposal was inopportune during a time of high unemployment, but they were persuaded by the argument that the Council had already approved the proposal in the Action Programme (Agence 1983, 9 October).

In November 1983, the Commission presented the draft directive to the Council (Commission 1983, COM(83)686). It 'gave rise to intense passions' (Rutherford 1989, 302). ENOW exerted pressure on the Council (Agence 1983, 9 October). As chair of the EEC, France (Ministers Pierre Bérégovoy and Roudy) staunchly supported the directive, but other member states resisted. The Netherlands called the directive 'premature'. It was preparing its own proposal and did not want any EEC interference. Initially, the British resisted primarily because of the costs. The Commission had hoped to bypass this point by leaving the method of funding up to the member states, but it held on to the principle of *paid* parental leave because it was only in this way that fathers could be motivated to take it. The British Minister of Employment made the issue a question of principle: as legislation applied only to basic labour conditions and parental leave was not part of them, it should be regulated through collective negotiations. Commissioner Richard argued in vain that sharing of family responsibilities was a precondition of equal treatment in employment and therefore a basic labour condition (Rutherford 1989).

---

6 Twelve years and a treaty change later, in December 1997, the Council would finally approve a directive on part-time work (see Chapter 5).

A preliminary ruling weakened the position of the Commission. In July 1984, the Court decided that the Equal Treatment Directive did *not* concern the redistribution of work in the family and that a government therefore had the right to assign parental leave to women only (Case 184/83, *Hofmann*). To their relief, the member states discovered that they had not yet unknowingly taken on obligations in the area of parental leave. Negotiations ran aground.

Occupational Social Security Schemes In the Social Security Directive, the member states had promised that they would settle equal treatment in occupational schemes in a later instrument (Directive 79/7, Article 3). In April 1983, the Commission submitted a draft directive which stipulated that the member states were required to take measures so that all forms of discrimination would be eliminated from collective labour agreements by 1 June 1986 (Commission 1983, COM(83)217). The proposal allowed two exceptions to the principle of equal treatment: retirement age and payments to the surviving spouse. Negotiations in Coreper ran aground.

Self-Employed In 1980, the COPA Women's Committee organized a seminar with the support of DG V about the weak legal position of women farmers (Commission 1980, COM(80)832, 220). Commissioner Vredeling established a workgroup to study the issue (Agence 1980, 21 June). In her report, MEP Maij-Weggen proposed to create a judicial statute for self-employed women and co-working spouses. In May 1983, the EP approved a report from Simone Martin, who herself was a farmer, about the uncertain financial and judicial position of married women in self-employed professions, especially in agriculture. Martin asked for a directive to recognize legally women's work in family enterprises and to establish their right to maternity leave (Agence 1983, 12 May).

The Action Programme also contained the promise to promote the equal treatment of women in self-employed professions and agriculture. In March 1984, Commissioner Richard presented a draft directive. Self-employed women and co-working spouses would be entitled to maternity leave, replacement and benefits. Co-working spouses would build up individual rights to social security. Self-employed women should have the same access to credit as men. Statutory and fiscal obstacles to equal treatment must be eliminated (Agence 1984, 9 March). In Coreper, member states filed thirty reservations. The draft directive led to 'controversial and heated discussions' in the Council. Although there was a certain amount of agreement with the idea that arranging something in this area was an essential supplementation to the social security directive from 1978, they made no progress (Pillinger 1992).

Conclusion

Pressure at the national and supranational levels led to a full European agenda, also owing to the efforts of the responsible commissioner Richard and the Equal Opportunities Unit under the leadership of Odile Quintin. In a very short time, Richard and Quintin converted an entire series of demands into proposals for

European instruments. However, the political will of the member states, with the exception of France, to approve new equal rights policy turned out to be nil (see Table 4.2).

Table 4.2 New equality policies: domestic costs and pressure (1980s)

	France	Germany	the Netherlands	Britain
1. Ideological costs: compatibility with domestic policy frame	Low costs (1): compatible with gender equality (Roudy), Keynesian policy and social role model (Mitterrand)	High costs (3): incompatible with revaluation of motherhood and budgetary policy	High costs (3): incompatible with deregulation and budgetary policy	High costs (3): incompatible with 'problem there is not', deregulation, budgetary policy
2. Domestic opposition to new supranational equality policies	Limited (1): employers, opposition	Strong (4): employers, governing parties CDU/CSU and FDP	Strong (4): employers, CDA and VVD (in the government)	Strong (4): employers, Conservatives (in the government)
3. Domestic support for supranational equality policies	Strong (4): PS and PCF (in government), trade unions, women's movement	Rather strong (3): women's movement, women in DGB, women in SPD	Strong (4): Broad Platform (women's groups, trade unions, political parties)	Strong (4): TUC, women's movement, Labour, Social Democrats
Saliency (2+3) and relative domestic pressure (3–2)	Medium saliency (5), rather strong support (3)	High saliency (7), limited resistance (–1)	High saliency (8), balance between support and opposition (0)	High saliency (8), balance between support and opposition (0)
Sensitivity	High	Low	High in 1981, low after 1981	Low
Expected preference	In favour	Opposed	Opposed	Opposed

The stagnation in the Council had two reasons. First, for the centre-right governments in Germany, the Netherlands and Britain, the ideological costs of equal rights policy were high (see Table 4.2). There was strong pressure for equal rights policy, but the sensitivity of these governments was very limited as they had a strong position in parliament and their electorate (employers, conservatives) strongly resisted gender equality policies. Therefore, they were able to ignore pressure in favour of new equal rights policy.

Secondly, there was no necessity to approve 'flanking' supranational social policy with the aim of acquiring the approval of the population for intensifying the economic integration. In fact, the stagnation in equal rights policy reflected the general stagnation in the EEC from 1979 to 1985. Despite the unattractive status quo resulting from domestic social unrest and the economic weakening of the EEC vis-à-vis Japan and the US, the member states were incapable of taking new joint initiatives. This was due to the deep differences of opinion between France and the other member states concerning economic and monetary policy and the British blockade of all decisions as long as the 'British Budgetary Question' had not been solved. Therefore, in spite of all national and supranational pressure, the governments approved no new gender equality directives for the time being. In contrast, the consequences for the implementation of the existing directives were different.

Implementation of Costly Policies: The 'Pincers'

At the end of the 1970s, the governments faced the deadlines for the implementation of the Equal Pay and Equal Treatment Directives. They discovered that they could no longer avoid implementation as easily as their predecessors in the 1960s had done. This was due to the 'pincer' mechanism of pressure from the supranational and national levels.

Implementing the Equal Pay and Equal Treatment Directives

Equal Pay In 1976, the second Court ruling in *Defrenne* gave women an instrument to exercise their rights via the national courts. Accordingly, it became less profitable for the member states to postpone implementing the Equal Pay Directive. The Belgian Labour Appeal Court had asked the Court if Article 119 had a direct effect (Case 43/75, *Defrenne II*). Britain submitted a written commentary, warning for the serious economic problems that would ensue if the Court acknowledged the direct effect. The clothing industry would be 'especially threatened' and the increase in labour costs would seriously hamper inflation control (*ECR* 1976, 464).

The Court ruled that Article 119 did have a direct effect and that this effect had been in force since 1 January 1962, the end of the first phase of the customs union. Financial objections did not alter this obligation, but the Court limited the retroactive effect to the date of its ruling (April 1976), because the member states had been able to violate Article 119 over an extended period without the Commission initiating an infringement procedure. As a result, there could have been a lack of clarity about the obligation to implement equal pay (*ECR* 1976, 481). The Court clearly wanted to strengthen the effectiveness of European law and enhance the possibilities for citizens to use their European rights against unwilling governments, thus confirming its own authority vis-à-vis governments. Yet, it did not want to push this too far. Limiting the retroactive effect, it hoped to avoid finding all governments opposing it.

The member states were required to include the provisions of the EPD in their legislation before February 1976 and to provide the Commission with the required information before February 1978. To this end, the Commission sent a questionnaire to the governments and the European employers and trade unions. Commissioner Vredeling promised the EP that the Commission would initiate infringement procedures if it turned out that the member states were in default.

In February 1978, the EP showed impatience at his 'wait-and-see attitude'. Vredeling defended himself with the argument that the member states had not yet submitted the national reports. He hoped women's organizations would exert pressure on their governments to submit the requested information to 'Brussels' (*Europa van Morgen* 1978, 22 February). In January 1979, the Commission finally submitted its report. The principle of equal pay had not been realized in any member state (Commission 1978, COM(78)711; Commission 1987, X/152/87, 6). With *Defrenne II* in mind, Vredeling immediately started infringement proceedings against seven member states.

Equal Treatment Meanwhile, the monitoring of implementing the Equal Treatment Directive (ETD) had started as well. Before August 1978, all discriminatory provisions had to be eliminated from national legislation and collective labour agreements, and all protective provisions had to be abolished. Exceptions were only permitted regarding positive action measures, professions where the sex of the employee was crucial and provisions for the protection of pregnant women.

In December 1979, the Equal Opportunities Unit sent a questionnaire to the trade unions, employers and the national equal opportunities commissions. On 15 December 1980, the Commission approved the extensive report (230 pages) that the Unit had drafted (Commission 1980, COM(80)832). It announced an investigation into 'professions for which sex was a determining factor' because the member states had forbidden a total of 26 professions for women, but not a single 'professional injunction' applied in all member states. The overview made it clear that these exclusions 'do not derive from universally accepted, unchanging criteria' (Agence 1980, 19 December; CREW 1983). The same phenomenon was seen in the protective regulations for women.

The Commission ascertained 'with pleasure' that 'at all levels remarkable progress' had been made, but that 'in fact not a single government has implemented the Directive correctly' (Commission 1984, X/220/84, 16). Vredeling sent warnings to all nine member states (Agence 1980, 26 July). The reactions differed.

France: A Pioneer Stumbles On 3 April 1979, the Commission sent France an official warning concerning equal pay. Its only criticism was that in mining companies, only heads of families were given a housing allowance, and only married men were considered heads of families. Because of the warning, Giscard d'Estaing abolished the 'head of family provision' on 2 May 1979. As a result, France satisfied the formal provisions of the Equal Pay Directive according to the Commission.

However, in 1976, the Committee on Women's Work had issued a report indicating that the enforcement of the 1972 Equal Pay Act was inadequate (Mazur 1991). Even though the wage gap was still smaller in France than in other countries, by 1977 this lead was shrinking due to the introduction of equal pay legislation in the Netherlands and Britain (see Table 4.3).

Table 4.3 Women's wages as percentage of men's wages (1972–1985)

	France	Germany	the Netherlands	Britain
1972	78.63	69.91	64.58	62.80
1977	77.43	72.81	73.48	71.60
1985	80.76	72.99	73.55	69.31

Source: Commission 1989, 60.

The number of court cases was very limited in France (Mazur 1991). The employer usually won in appeal because the court limited the concept of 'work of equal value' to 'work at the same location in the same company' (Sabourin-Ragnaud 1993). In 1979, feminist lawyer Gisèle Halimi lost an equal treatment case because the court ruled that the employer had a 'legitimate motive' to treat the female employee differently than her male colleague (Mazur 1991). Therefore, in 1982, socialist Minister of Women's Rights Roudy submitted a bill to improve enforcement of equal pay and equal treatment.

The leftist majority in parliament approved the 'Roudy Act' in July 1983 (Loi No. 83–635). It forbade discrimination based on sex or family situation. It eliminated the 'legitimate motive' clause. New collective labour agreements could no longer include protective measures. Personnel advertisements could no longer specify the sex of potential applicants (Mazur 1991). Despite the protests of the employers, the burden of proof was reversed. Employers now had to prove that unequal pay was not the result of discrimination (Sabourin-Ragnaud 1993). The Roudy Act was the most far-reaching equal rights legislation in the EEC. France therefore believed it had more than satisfied the requirements of the two directives. It was mistaken.

The First Procedure against France On 30 July 1980, the Commission had sent a first warning to France, followed on 12 May 1981 by a reasoned opinion, because women were excluded from certain training programmes and jobs in the public sector. The government thought it could solve the problem by approving a law that forbade employers from making a distinction according to sex (Act No. 82/380, Decree 82/886).

In an appendix, however, the law still contained a list of job groups for which separate admission procedures for men and women applied: job groups in the police, the prison system, the customs service, teaching, physical education and sports. According to the Commission, this list went further than the directive allowed. On 12 August 1983, it asked the French government to provide an explanation (ECR 1988, 3562). The government answered that there was only a 'formal incongruity' between the French law and the directive. The Commission sent a new warning on 7 August 1984 and a new reasoned opinion on 29 January 1986. As France did not respond, the Commission took the case to the Court.

Meanwhile, in 1986, the SP lost the parliamentary elections and Gaullist Chirac became prime minister of a right-wing government. Roudy left office. During the written Court procedure, France shortened the list of exceptions in steps: in March 1986, the government eliminated the job groups of the customs service, in February 1987, it eliminated the teachers, and after the oral presentations before the Court in March 1988, it eliminated the instructors and assistant instructors for physical education and sport. The Court ultimately had to evaluate only the jobs with the police and the prison directors. France insisted on a quota for these job groups because a high percentage of women would seriously erode the credibility of the police (ECR 1988, 3566). The Commission argued that it was not sex, but physical suitability, that should be decisive for certain police jobs. It had not been proven that women were unable to act against violent behaviour, and such a general deviation from the principle of equal treatment was not justified.

The Court ruled that the Commission was correct. Only with respect to directors of small prisons, separate male and female recruiting was acceptable (Case 318/86). In accordance with the court decree, France maintained separate male and female recruiting only in the latter category. After eight years of Commission's tenacity, the French government followed the directive.

The Second Procedure against France The Commission initiated another infringement procedure (Case 312/86) because protective measures still flourished in collective agreements. The Roudy Act required that the employers and trade unions bring these measures into accordance with the principle of equal treatment, but it did not propose a time limit for this obligation. Between 1984 and 1987, the provisions in 16 collective agreements had been amended, which was an 'extremely modest' number compared to the 3,450 collective agreements that were concluded in 1983 alone.

France defended itself with the argument that the trade unions had asked for these provisions in the interest of women to allow them to combine work and family life, and that the provisions contributed to an increasing birth rate (*ECR* 1988, 06315). The Court rejected both of these arguments because the 'special measures for women' covered an excessively broad area and it was unacceptable that, years after the deadline stipulated in the directive, there was still no time limit for trade unions and employers to comply with it.

France passed a law on 10 July 1989 requiring the trade unions and employers to adapt collective agreements within two years (*Journal Officiel* 1989, 14 July, 8872). However, as the law contained no sanctions, employers and trade unions just ignored it. The 'pincers' of simultaneous national and supranational pressure only started to work when the case of an employer, Alfred Stoeckel, came before the court.

Stoeckel was accused of violating the French Labour Code because he had employed women during night shifts. He defended himself by arguing that the

Labour Code had contravened the Equal Treatment Directive (ETD). Asked for its interpretation, the Court ruled in favour of Stoeckel (Case C-345/89). Hence, in 1992, the socialist Minister of Labour, Martine Aubry, proposed a law to harmonize labour conditions for women and men, but the parliament rejected it.

The Commission started a new infringement procedure in March 1994. Aubry was no longer in charge, as a right-wing government under Edouard Balladur had taken over. The government argued that the Labour Code article was no longer effective due to the direct effect of the ETD, so there was no need to repeal it. The Court dismissed the argument, because 'the incompatibility of national legislation with Community provisions ... can be finally remedied only by means of national provisions of a binding nature' (*ECR* 1997, I-01489). As the French government seemed to ignore this ruling, the Commission decided to use the powers it had obtained at Maastricht in December 1991 to bring proceedings before the Court for failure to comply with a Court ruling (Article 228).

On 21 April 1999, the Commission asked the Court to impose a penalty payment of 142,425 euros per day for the non-implementation of the earlier judgement (Case C-224/99). This time, the French government did not wait for the Court ruling and Minister Aubry (again) proposed a law to implement the directive. Trade unions and women's organizations were split on the issue; employers were in favour of lifting the ban on night work for women for economic reasons (Reuter and Mazur 2003). After much parliamentary debate, the ban was repealed (*Journal Officiel* 2001, 10 May) and Case C-224/99 was discreetly removed from the Court's register. France could not bear to be the first member state condemned to pay penalties due to non-compliance in the domain of social affairs. In the end, it was double judicial pressure and concern about French prestige that caused compliance, not political pressure as societal groups partly agreed with non-implementation and only partly wanted policy change.

Germany: Fundamental Rights at Stake The government had always maintained that it had implemented the equality directives thanks to Article 3 of the Constitution. The wage differences between men and women had decreased (see Table 4.3), but this decline was more modest than in the Netherlands and Britain, which had passed new legislation.

First Round On 3 April 1979, the Commission sent the government a warning concerning the Equal Pay Directive, and on 10 May 1979, a warning concerning the Equal Treatment Directive, because the government could not declare discriminatory provisions in collective labour agreements to be invalid and did not have 'effective means' to assure compliance. When there was no response, the Commission sent a 'reasoned opinion' (Agence 1980, 23 February). This time, the government promised the Commission it would modify its legislation. After twenty years, it bowed its head.

The decision to modify its legislation was the result of simultaneous pressure at the national and supranational levels. The criticism of the Commission made it plausible that the Court had sufficient cause to condemn Germany if it did not take action. The Court had made it clear in *Defrenne III* (Case 149/77) that it considered the 'abolition of discrimination based on sex' a fundamental principle of Community law (*ECR* 1978, 1365). A condemnation for violating the fundamental rights of its citizens would be especially painful for Germany since it had always claimed that German law protected fundamental rights better than Community law (Weiler 1999).

The Commission's warnings coincided with strong pressure at the national level. Equal pay was the central issue in a series of court cases on behalf of 29 women employed at the Heinze photographic laboratory. Their actions received a great deal of publicity and caused other women to file cases as a group with the courts (Hund 1983; Doormann 1983). Parliamentary elections were coming up.

The government submitted a bill to parliament to avoid condemnation by the Court and to take the wind out of the sails of women in the SPD, the DGB and the women's movement. The bill was very controversial. During a hearing in the *Bundestag*, the employers maintained that discrimination was not only forbidden in Germany, but that it simply did not exist. Under pressure from employers and with parliamentary support from the CDU/CSU, the coalition partner FDP weakened the bill by limiting the reversal of the burden of proof and the sanctions. In June 1980, parliament approved the bill, although women in the SPD feared that it would be a 'paper tiger without teeth' (Hörburger and Rath-Hörburger 1983, 28). The resulting act, titled 'EC Labour Law Adaptation Act – Act Concerning the Equal Treatment of Men and Women in the Workplace' of 13 August 1980 was, as its name indicates, intended only to satisfy the obligations of the European directives and did not aim to improve the position of working women.[7]

Second Round On 15 January 1982, the Commission sent the government a new warning in which it ascertained four shortcomings: the act did not apply to the public sector, it did not apply to the self-employed, the prohibition of discrimination in personnel advertisements was only a non-mandatory recommendation, and the exceptions to equal treatment were formulated in general terms.

Following a 'futile correspondence' with the government, the Commission sent a reasoned opinion in October 1982 (*ECR* 1985, 1462). The new government of CDU-FDP replied that Germany had fully met its obligations by amending the civil code. On 9 November 1983, the Commission brought Germany before the Court (Case 248/83). Advocate General Mancini concluded that Article 3 of the Constitution was insufficiently clear to guarantee equal treatment for civil servants and the self-employed (*ECR* 1985, 1468). However, in its ruling of 21 May 1985,

7 The act stated that lower pay for equal work or work of equal value was forbidden if this was based on the sex of the employee (§612, Civil Code). The act forbade direct and indirect discrimination regarding access to the labour process, training, promotion, firing and the terms and conditions of employment (§611a, Civil Code). If an employee could make a plausible case that there was discrimination regarding sex, the employer had to prove that this was not the case.

the Court rejected Mancini's argument. The German system appeared to work in practice because the Commission could not show that it led to discrimination. The Commission had underestimated the strength of the German system of constitutional review, and the Court did not dare to compete directly with the German Constitutional Court.

The Commission only won its case regarding the fourth point: that the civil code did not specify which professions were excluded from equal treatment. Germany believed that the directive did not obligate them to make such a list. However, in this matter the Court agreed with Mancini's argument that Germany had neglected to create 'even a minimum of clarity'; as a result, it made it impossible for the Commission to monitor compliance. Moreover, the lack of a list hampered employees in exercising their rights (*ECR* 1985, 1487). In November 1987, Germany sent the Commission the requested list of professions for which sex was the determining factor (Bertelsmann and Rust 1995).

Further progress resulted from preliminary rulings. Regarding the issue of *Leichtlohnarbeit* (the underpayment of physically 'light' work), which led to systematic and widespread discrimination of female employees, progress could finally be made thanks to the case of Gisela Rummler (Case 237/85). The Court ruled that work could not be defined as heavy or light in criteria that were based on the physical efforts that a specific sex can exert. Because of the ruling, the Federal Labour Court decided that all forms of effort must be included when classifying jobs instead of physical strength only.

Due to another preliminary decision, the 'practical importance' of the EC Labour Law Adaptation Act increased significantly. The amended Civil Code required an employer who had been convicted of discriminating a job applicant to only reimburse the expenses of the applicant, which usually amounted to 2.31 DM for the postage stamp and photocopying the letter of application. Von Colson and Kamann, two female social workers, were both turned down for a job at a prison, even though they were the best-qualified candidates. The director preferred to employ a man. The German court confirmed that there was open discrimination, but could not impose any other sanction besides the 'postage stamp reimbursement'. The Court was asked which sanction the ETD required. The Court ruled concerning this case (Case 14/83) and a similar case from Hamburg (Case 79/83, *Harz*) that compensation must be 'effective' (*ECR* 1984, 1907). Because of this decision, German courts would award compensation amounting to six months pay. Von Colson and Kamann were each awarded 21,000 DM instead of 2.31 DM.

The Netherlands: Fear of Being in Advance The Netherlands believed that it had correctly implemented the Equal Pay Directive. The last collective labour agreement – in the textile sector – with different wages for men and women doing the same work had expired and the wage gap had become smaller thanks to the Equal Pay Act (see Table 4.3).

The Commission initiated an infringement procedure because the Equal Pay Act did not cover civil servants (Commission 1978, COM(78)711, 132). During the debate on the bill, Minister Boersma had assured parliament that the Dutch government did not discriminate, but the Commission criticized the situation that civil servants could not go to court if they felt they were being discriminated against (Agence 1980, 23 February). The government did not respond to the warning. Only when the Commission sent a 'reasoned opinion', the government decided to amend the law. On 2 July 1980, the parliament approved the act ensuring equal pay for men and women in the civil service (Landau 1985).

On the approval of the ETD by the Council in December 1975, Secretary of State Mertens had stated that he would certainly need the 30-month implementation period to draw up the required legislation (*Europa van Morgen* 1975, 627). His estimate turned out to be overly optimistic.

In August 1976, the parliament approved legislation that finally forbade employees from being fired due to marriage, pregnancy and motherhood. The Emancipation Commission and the parliament asked for a more general law against sex discrimination, but Mertens replied that he could not submit any general anti-discrimination legislation in the short term (*Handelingen* 1977, 13943, 3207). However, as the Netherlands should comply with the ETD, he submitted a 'priority bill' for a limited law against sex discrimination in employment in December 1978, four months after the implementation deadline of the directive had elapsed.

On 10 May 1979, the Commission initiated an infringement procedure against the Netherlands for failure to implement the directive. On 1 March 1980, the parliament approved the limited Equal Treatment Act. A government official who was involved in drafting the Act called it 'the bare minimum required by the relevant directive' (Dijkstra and Swiebel 1982, 50). The Equal Treatment Act showed many shortcomings leading to additional pieces of legislation. The breadwinner's criterion continued to thrive in collective labour agreements, because the government had not included a provision in the act to declare agreements invalid on this basis (*Handelingen* 1987–8, 19908, 5416). Redundancy pay schemes treated non-breadwinners worse than breadwinners, but they fell outside the scope of the law. When in August 1980, hundreds of married teachers in Catholic schools were threatened with dismissal, protests by the parliament and the Emancipation Commission led to the government hastily passing an emergency law for 'Temporary provisions concerning equal treatment of men and women, and married and unmarried individuals, in case of termination of employment'.

As the Equal Treatment Act did not have any provisions for civil servants, the Commission promptly sent a warning. The Civil Service Tribunal of Rotterdam on 18 February 1980 already had accepted the direct effect of the directive for civil servants. This forced the government to make haste. The Equal Opportunities (Civil Service) Act went into force on 2 July 1980.

The Emancipation Commission found that 'the intermittent adaptation of Dutch legislation to the EC directives for equal pay and equal treatment has led to a patchwork of provisions in which holes are clearly visible' (Emancipatiekommissie 1981). The Commission had drawn this same conclusion. It began a new infringement procedure because, like in Germany, the exceptions to equal treatment were too broadly formulated and the act allowed supplementary payments for breadwinners under 23. The government defended itself with the arguments that the directive did not prescribe establishing a list and that a 'reasonable interpretation of the directive' allowed the breadwinner benefit for such a limited group. The Commission was not convinced and it sent a reasoned opinion on 20 May 1983 (*Handelingen* 1986–7, 19908, No. 3).

While decision making about the general anti-discrimination act dragged on,[8] in 1984, Secretary of State Annelien Kappeyne van de Coppello submitted an amendment bill to avoid further steps from the Commission and fill the worst holes in Dutch equal treatment legislation. Because of a preliminary decision of the Court in a German case (Case 170/84, *Bilka-Kaufhaus*), the government amended the amendment bill.

It was only in August 1988 that Minister of Social Affairs Jan de Koning offered parliament its final Act of Amendment, expressing his hope that it would finally allow the Netherlands to satisfy the requirements of the first two directives (*Handelingen* 1987–8, 19908, 5436). The government had included the list of professions for which sex would be a determining factor. The parliament criticized the fact that the government only aimed at avoiding further Court proceedings instead of realizing the intended equal treatment, as was shown by the explicit exclusion of pensions from the Act. As EEC norms only required equal treatment in the area of pensions to be achieved until 1993, the government preferred to wait instead of including any measure 'in advance' (*Handelingen* 1987–8, 19908, 5426). Parliament approved the act in 1989.

Several times already pensions had been on the Council agenda when discussing gender equality directives. Pensions also were a central issue in several court cases, to start with the *Defrenne* cases. In *Liefting* (Case 23/83), the Court ruled that pension contributions were considered pay and that the Dutch regulation of retirement premiums for civil servants was not in accordance with Article 119. The ruling caused a great deal of commotion in the government, which feared thousands of claims from female civil servants (Van Bergen 1984). The responsible minister mailed a circular to the relevant services stating that they were not required to accept such claims since the court ruling was only binding for the nine women who had submitted a complaint (Prechal and Burrows 1990). However, the court ruling was given a great deal of publicity and led to new court proceedings and questions in parliament. The civil servants union insisted on a general solution. Because the third EEC directive on social security also required changes in the pension system, the government decided at this point to abolish the discriminatory provision.

---

8 In September 1981, the government submitted a broad anti-discrimination bill. Due to enduring criticisms, primarily related to the ban on discrimination based on homosexuality, the General Equal Treatment Act would only be approved in 1994.

Britain: Thatcher or Dickens? A combination of domestic and supranational pressure would, greatly to the dismay of the British government, lead to a strengthening of British equal rights legislation.

Equal Pay In 1975, the British Equal Pay Act (EPA) came into effect and the wage gap decreased, although it remained larger than in other member states (see Table 4.3). In April 1979, the Commission sent Britain a warning because an employee only had a right to equal pay if the company had a job classification system. If the employer refused to implement such a system, employees only had the right to the same wages as their colleagues of the other sex if they did identically the same work. In practice, employers and trade unions made it difficult for women to compare their work with that of men by modifying job descriptions and reorganizing entire divisions so that men and women carried out different kinds of work (Coussins 1977; Boston 1985).

The government replied to the Commission 'that they saw no reason to change current legislation' (Agence 1980, 23 February). In May 1980, the Commission sent a reasoned opinion. The government replied that British legislation was completely in accordance with the directive (*ECR* 1982, 2604). Moreover, during the negotiations on the equal pay directive, it had been given assurance that it would not have to amend national legislation.

In the meantime, the Court made two decisions related to defining 'the equal value' of work that reduced the room of manoeuvre of the British government. The first case concerned a British company that had paid its employee Wendy Smith a wage that was 17 percent lower than the wage her male predecessor received. The British court asked the Court whether Article 119 only applied when the man and the woman are employed contemporaneously (Case 129/79, *Macarthys v. Smith*). The Court ruled that 'equal work' was not limited to situations where men and women did the same work at exactly the same moment (*ECR* 1980, 1275). Because of this decision, the number of complaints submitted under the EPA increased substantially (Randall 1987). Smith's victory strengthened the confidence of other complainants, while the decision of the Court expanded the comparability of jobs and thereby increased the probability that employees could win their cases.

A second important ruling was *Worringham and Humphreys v. Lloyds Bank* (Case 69/80). The Court confirmed that pension contributions were wages in the sense of Article 119. The ruling ended the 5 percent gross difference in wages between the 14,000 women who worked at Lloyds and their male colleagues who did the same work (Landau 1985). The Court did not accept the request of Lloyds to limit the financial consequences of the judgement (McCrudden 1994).

One week later, on 18 March 1981, the Commission brought the case against Britain concerning non-compliance with the Equal Pay Directive before the Court (Case 61/81). Britain accused the Commission of negligence because it had ascertained only now, five years after the directive had been approved, that the EPA was in conflict with it. The Court rejected the accusation. On 6 July 1982, it ruled that Britain had failed to meet its obligations because an employee had no means to exercise her right to equal pay if the employer resisted the implementation of a job classification system (*ECR* 1982, 2616). The EOC 'applauded the Court's decision' (Warner 1984, 153); the government now had to amend the EPA to prevent further court cases.

The first version of the bill resulted in an 'unworkable' mechanism for defining work of equal value. While drafting the second version, the government finally consulted the EOC, the NCCL, the trade unions and employers. The influence of the employers was apparent in the criteria for submitting a complaint, which were 'unreasonably weighted against the claimant'. The government's bill caused 'uproar in the House of Lords'. The 'Lords' believed that the amendments did not go far enough to satisfy the EEC obligations and also led to confusion because 'while the enactments of the Treaty and the directives are reasonably clear and can be understood, our own enactments are deplorable' (Pillinger 1992, 108). In the definitive version of the bill, the burden of proof was no longer born entirely by the claimant. The parliament approved the Equal Pay Amendment Regulations on 7 December 1983 (Government Order no. 1794/83 and 1807/83).

Although the improvement was minimal, the first court case under the new act proved that the amended Act was indeed able to achieve equal pay where the EPA failed. Julie Hayward, a cook in the canteen of a shipyard, demanded the same wage as skilled workers on the wharf. Under the old EPA, the court would have had to reject her complaint because there was no job classification system at the company. Now it examined her complaint. The case resulted in a 30.3 percent wage increase (Hoskyns 1985).

Equal Treatment Britain also assumed that it had correctly implemented the ETD, as the Sex Discrimination Act (SDA) was the most detailed and extensive law on equal treatment in the EEC. However, on 29 August 1980, the Commission sent a warning, as the British government was unable to abolish discriminatory collective agreements. In addition, the SDA did not cover domestic staff and companies with five or fewer employees. Finally, the Commission thought it was strange that men were excluded from the profession of midwifery 'due to its nature', even though they could practice the profession of gynaecology. On 9 October 1981, the Commission sent a reasoned opinion and on 28 May 1982, it took the matter to the Court (Case 165/82).

Britain argued that exclusion of domestic staff was justified because 'the activities defined here often involve very direct personal contact between the employer and employee, (…) for example where live-in companion ladies or maids are concerned'. It defended the exemption of small companies arguing that it is often older women who own a small shop and who would prefer to employ someone of their own sex, which led to the Commission's comment that this reminded one more of 'the England of Dickens than the European Community of 1980' (*ECR* 1983, 3439). Regarding the first criticism, the government argued that non-binding collective agreements 'are of no legal effect whether or not they are discriminatory'.

The Court did not accept 'such donnish reasoning' (Rubenstein 1987, 95). In its decision on 8 November 1983, it pointed out that the directive covered all collective agreements, because regardless of their formal status, they all had significant de facto consequences for labour relations. The Court also agreed with the Commission regarding the unacceptable exclusion of household staff and small companies. It only accepted that Britain, for the time being, could exclude men from the profession of midwifery.

The British government took no measures in response to the Court decision until a British court asked the Court for a preliminary ruling in *Marshall v. Southampton* (Case 152/84). Miss Marshall was dismissed because she had passed the retirement age for women. The Court ruled that this was a case of discrimination according to the ETD, and that the directive had direct effect; individuals could appeal to the directive against the state, both as government and as an employer (Prechal and Burrows 1990).

The combination of the infringement procedure and the *Marshall* ruling convinced the government to amend the SDA (McCrudden 1994). It eliminated the exemption for small companies and limited the exemption for domestic staff to very narrowly defined cases. The provision was added that a collective agreement became invalid when it contained discriminatory provisions and the ban on discrimination because of the lower retirement age was expanded to include the private sector (McCrudden 1994). Despite its ideological dislike of social policies and supranational legislation, the Thatcher government could not ignore the judicial pincers which forced it to amend British legislation.

Equal Treatment in Social Security

The member states had given themselves until 23 December 1984 to implement the Social Security Directive (SSD) from 1978. They were very reluctant to improve the legal position of women in a time of increasing unemployment and an increasing number of applications for social benefits while they wanted to reduce government spending (Warner 1984). As a result, they implemented the directive in a very restrictive way. The European Network of Women (ENOW) submitted a complaint to the Commission (Agence 1983, 28/29 December), but the Commission would not deal with the issue that equal treatment led to loss of benefits for all.[9]

Still, this time, the Commission did not postpone its reporting until the directive was in force. Already in June 1979, DG V reminded the governments that they had agreed to 'gradually' implement the directive. It therefore demanded detailed information about the measures the governments wanted to take. The Commission anticipated that there would be problems with social security systems based on the

9 The Commission could have considered this a breach of Article 117 (now Art. 136 EC) which called for the improvement of work and living conditions, but this article was too vague to be relied upon before the Court. Accordingly, if governments would accuse the Commission of stretching its mandate, it would lose its case.

concept of the husband as head of the family and the wife as a dependent partner (Agence 1980, 5 January).

In an interim report in 1983, DG V found that all governments had started to implement equal treatment in social security, although the differences between the member states were significant. France had informed the Commission that it already applied equal treatment and that no changes in its legislation were deemed necessary (Commission 1983, COM(83)793). Germany stated that it needed to take no further statutory measures. It had amended various laws, primarily because of decrees of the Constitutional Court that declared them incompatible with Article 3 of the Constitution (Bertelsmann and Rust 1995; Hörburger and Rath-Hörburger 1983). In the Netherlands and Britain, as expected, the directive had far-reaching consequences.

The Netherlands The regulations directly affected by the SSD were unemployment benefits, benefits pursuant to the health act, pensions and disability benefits. These regulations all discriminated against married women. Disabled men had a right to benefits regardless of whether they previously had a source of income, while disabled married women only qualified for benefits if they had previously earned an income. Married women did not have a right to unemployment benefits unless they could show that they were the breadwinner, while married men were automatically treated as the breadwinner. A married couple received pension benefits only when the husband turned 65, even if his wife was older than he was.

The government (CDA-VVD) combined the obligation to eliminate these discriminating provisions with its aim to reduce government spending. It amended the regulations by assuming for every type of benefit that there was a family income which could be supplemented with extra payments to the dependent spouse. It ignored the fact that provisions formulated in a sex-neutral fashion could lead to indirect discrimination if in practice they primarily affected employees of a specific sex (Commission 1983, COM(83)793). EP *rapporteur* Ien van den Heuvel criticized the worsening of the position of Dutch women due to the way in which the government implemented the directive (Agence 1983, 22 June). Yet, Prime Minister Ruud Lubbers maintained that the right to benefits would remain dependent on the number of incomes in a household. Preliminary rulings would force the government to revise its opinion on this matter.

Beginning with the day it went into force, 23 December 1984, the SSD was cited by Dutch courts. They asked the Court for its interpretation. The Court criticized the way in which the Dutch government had amended regulations and ruled that the directive had direct effect beginning on 23 December 1984, entitling married women to the same benefits as men from that day onwards (Case 30/85, *Teuling*; Case 71/85, *The State of the Netherlands v. FNV*; Case 80/87, *Dik et al.*). As a result, the Dutch courts rejected not only the old regulations, but also the amended acts and granted women the same benefits as men under the same conditions.

In a memorandum to parliament, 'the tone of which is mild panic', the Junior Minister of Social Affairs Lou de Graaf calculated that the *Teuling* ruling could cost the state seven billion guilders (*De Volkskrant* 1988, 23–4 February). He assumed that half of those who qualified for benefits would submit a request and that the ruling would affect other types of benefits as well. The 'blunt manner' with which he responded to the Court ruling inspired women's organizations to establish the Equal Rights Now Committee. They placed advertisements in local papers and women's magazines calling for married women to apply for benefits (*De Volkskrant* 1988, 19 April).

On 3 November 1988, the Commission sent a warning to the government. It would fail to meet its obligations if it did not take the necessary measures to implement the directive. The judicial pincers squeezed the unwilling Dutch government hard enough to repair some forms of discrimination in the social security system.

Britain The British government combined the obligation to implement equal treatment with reductions in government spending as well. In contrast to the Dutch government, it was able to eliminate most forms of direct discrimination regarding unemployment, sickness, and benefits related to pregnancy and parenthood before December 1984 (Millar 1989). To fulfil the requirements of the directive, the government eliminated the 'household criterion' from the invalidity pension. Until then, women were often refused a pension because they did not satisfy a criterion that applied only to married women, namely, that they were no longer capable of carrying out their 'normal household duties'.

However, the Commission warned Britain that there was still discrimination in a number of areas (Commission 1987, X/24/88). As in the Netherlands, direct discrimination had often been replaced primarily by indirect discrimination. Equal treatment meant that women could now apply for benefits on the same basis as men, but since the criteria themselves had not been changed, only women who had the same working pattern as most men (fulltime and without interruptions) enjoyed equal rights. Workers with part-time or flexible contracts, predominantly women, remained excluded from such benefits. Income support benefits were not based on individual income but on the family income. As a result, it was financially more beneficial for the partner with the lowest income to stop working if the partner with the highest income became unemployed, because the income earned would otherwise be subtracted from the benefits (Millar 1989).

The first British case presented to the Court concerned the allowance which was granted to individuals who provided care for an invalid. When Jacqueline Drake gave up her job to take care of her invalid mother, she was refused benefits because she was a married woman. According to the adjudication officer, the invalid care allowance was not subject to the SSD since it was intended for persons who do not belong to the working population. The Court ruled that the term 'working population' must be interpreted as including individuals who have interrupted their work in order to provide the necessary care to a disabled relative. Furthermore, there was indeed sex discrimination because the benefit was not payable to a married woman although it was paid to a married man (*Drake*, Case 150/85; *ECR* 1986, 01995).

Conclusion In its report of 18 December 1988 on the state of affairs, the Commission concluded that in the Netherlands and Britain there was still direct discrimination (Commission 1988, COM(88)769). The situation in Germany and France was slightly better, although DG V was not convinced that the special protection enjoyed by women in France was compatible with the directive (Prechal and Burrows 1990). The Commission had not yet evaluated the persistence of indirect discrimination. The British and Dutch court cases showed that it was exactly on this point that the implementation of the directive was problematic, as indirect discrimination often replaced direct discrimination. However, Commissioner Manuel Marin did not initiate any infringement procedure. Therefore, the elimination of discrimination progressed mainly thanks to judicial pressure resulting from the cases before the national courts and the interpretations by the Court.

The 'Pincers'

Between 1978 and 1991, these four member states adapted regulations or introduced new legislation in order to comply with the three gender equality directives. In virtually all cases, judicial pressure at the supranational and the domestic levels was necessary to ensure implementation.

At the supranational level, the Commission initiated several infringement procedures. In the *Defrenne II* ruling in April 1976, the Court had accused the Commission of failing to act against non-compliance, causing legal ambiguity as a result. In the 1960s, the Commission refrained from initiating infringement procedures because the member states who were formally non-compliant were not the worst violators of Article 119 in practice. The Court rejected this standpoint; the fact that the Commission could not act against all forms of non-compliance did not justify its lack of action against any of it. The credibility of the Commission as 'guardian of the treaties' was at stake. Therefore, every time the Equal Opportunities Unit of DG V acquired sufficient data, the Commission initiated an infringement procedure against a member state that formally had not correctly implemented a directive, even if the practices in other member states left much more to be desired. In the latter countries, it was the task of the trade unions and women's organizations to undertake actions (*Het Laatste Nieuws* 1979, 24 March).

DG V also received written complaints from citizens and non-state actors, which informed it of discriminatory practices. It investigated such cases and asked the relevant government for an explanation. In order to avoid an infringement procedure, this usually led the government to modify the challenged regulation (Commission 1987, X/24/88, 25 and 66).

At the national level, women's organizations and women in the trade unions, political parties and the parliament insisted that their governments implement the directives. The Netherlands and Britain had established Equal Opportunities Commissions that supported employees who felt they were being discriminated against. More and more frequently, victims of discrimination submitted complaints and brought cases to the courts; as a result, national courts were given the opportunity to cite European provisions and to ask the Court for its interpretation. This practice created a strong link between the national and supranational levels. Table 4.4 presents an overview of the cases.

In the 1960s, not a single court had used the procedure for preliminary rulings in connection with equal pay. During the 1970s, Belgian courts made three requests for interpretation of Article 119 (the *Defrenne* cases). Between 1979 and 1991, national courts submitted no less than 39 cases to the Court that concerned equal pay and equal treatment: 14 British cases, nine Dutch cases, eight German cases and a single French case.[10]

The majority of requests for interpretations came from Britain owing to the actions of the Equal Opportunities Commission, which used European legislation 'to clarify domestic law' (Meehan 1993, 196). The British government actively tracked equal rights cases. In virtually every case – also those from other member states – it submitted written opinions to the Court (Usher 1987). In the Council, Thatcher was able to thwart all supranational influence on social policy, but now it threatened to enter the country via jurisprudence. The British judge Lord Denning warned that 'the flowing tide of Community law is coming in fast' (Landau 1985, 103). Written commentary was the only means the government had to exert influence, so it did not miss any opportunity to inform the Court of its opinion.

In contrast, French courts did not ask for a single preliminary ruling on equal rights until 1989. Compared to the other member states, few cases were submitted to national courts in France because of the high threshold in the court system and, due to the resistance of the trade unions, the lack of an independent equal rights commission that could advise discrimination victims (Pettiti 1995).

Infringement procedures made it impossible for governments to hide behind ignorance concerning equal rights. The procedures increased the costs of non-compliance in those cases where national prestige was at stake. The cases before the Court resulted in the member states having to take measures that went further than they had expected when they had approved the directives. In spite of the costs, most governments ultimately accepted the judgements of the Court and adapted their legislation.

In two cases, a member state initially ignored a ruling of the Court. France did not implement the Court ruling on the equal treatment directive. As long as not only the government but also employers and trade unions resisted implementation and no cases were presented to the national courts, the 'pincers' of simultaneous national and supranational pressure could not operate. Britain, also, only complied after the infringement procedures were followed by preliminary rulings as well.

In general, preliminary rulings made it more attractive for governments to amend their legislation than to risk large numbers of expensive court cases. In many cases, such Court rulings also strengthened the actual contents and impact of the directives, confronting governments with surprises as the implementation of directives proceeded differently than they had expected when they approved them.

10 In addition, one Belgian case, two Danish and four Irish cases.

Table 4.4 Judicial pressure for equal pay and equal treatment, 1977–1991

	France	Germany	the Netherlands	Britain
Existing legislation	Equal Pay Act 1972 Sex Discrimination Act 1975 Roudy Act 1983	Constitution 1949, Articles 3.2 and 3.3	Equal Pay Act 1975	Equal Pay Act 1970 Sex Discrimination Act 1975
Infringement procedures, settled after warning or reasoned opinion	1979, Warning → Decree	1980, Reasoned opinion → EC Labour Law Adaptation Act	1979, Warning → Equal Treatment Act 1980, Reasoned Opinion → EPA civil service 1980, Warning → ETA civil service 1983, Reasoned opinion → Amendment Act	–
Infringement procedures, settled after a ruling by the Court	Case 318/86 → Amendment Case 312/86 → Amendment Case C–197/96 → – Case C–224/99 → Law 2001	Case 248/83 → Amendment on 1 point, 1987	–	Case 61/81 → EPA 1984 Case 165/82 → SDA 1986

Preliminary decisions equal pay	–	Case 170/84, *Bilka* Case 235/84, *Rummler* Case 171/88, *Rinner-Kühn* Case C–33/89, *Kowalska* Case C–184/89, *Nimz*	Case 23/83, *Liefting*	Case 129/79, *Macarthy's* Case 69/80, *Worringham* Case 96/80, *Jenkins* Case 12/81, *Garland* Case 19/81, *Burton* Case 192/85, *Newstead* Case 262/88, *Barber*
Preliminary decisions equal treatment	Case C–345/89, *Stoeckel*	Case 14/83, *Von Colson* Case 79/83, *Harz* Case 184/83, *Hofmann*	Case 262/84, *Beets-Proper* Case C–177/88, *Dekker*	Case 151/84, *Roberts* Case 152/84, *Marshall* Case 222/84, *Johnston* Case 188/89, *Foster* Case 31/90, *Johnson*
Preliminary decisions social security	–	–	Case 30/85, *Teuling* Case 80/87, *Dik* Case 71/85, *FNV* Case 48/88, 106/88, 107/88 *Achterberg-te Riele* and others Case C–102/88, *Ruzius* Case C–87/90, 88/90, 89/90 *Verholen* and others	Case 384/85, *Borrie Clarke* Case 150/85, *Drake*

Because of these costly experiences with the implementation of the first three directives, the member states were more conscious of the costs and the scope of equal rights policy in the 1980s than before. They learned that it was difficult *not* to comply with joint agreements. Social groups became more aware of the possibilities offered by the supranational level to influence government policy. These learning processes affected the negotiations about new equal rights policies, as will be discussed in the following section.

Stagnation, Progress and Decline (1985–91)

General progress again became possible in the EEC after 1984 when the member states reached agreement on a compromise for the British Budgetary Question and France had returned to a more orthodox monetary and economic policy. The appointment of former French finance minister Jacques Delors as a potentially strong president of the new Commission (1985) confirmed the transition and contributed to it (Ludlow 1991). National policies to reduce unemployment had failed and the economic position of the EEC with respect to the US and Japan had been weakening. In this light, Delors was able to create a consensus for a programme to complete 'the internal market', an area where goods, persons, services and capital would move freely (Sandholtz and Zysman 1989). In February 1986, the member states signed the Single European Act that amended the Treaty of Rome. In areas related to the completion of the internal market, they would take decisions by qualified majority.

Equal Rights Policy: Thawed Out and Watered Down

Although the passing of the Single European Act 'brought a new wave of interest to the EC's social dimension' (Pillinger 1992, 124), Commissioner Alois Pfeiffer did not formulate any new proposal on equal treatment. He concentrated on 'the matters underway' during the year (January 1985–6) that he was responsible for the social portfolio (Agence 1985, 2 March). A large number of blocked proposals (part-time work, temporary work, parental leave, self-employment, social security) had accumulated during the past five years.

Italy, taking over the EEC Presidency, placed the draft directive on occupational security schemes on the agenda of the Council in June 1985. Negotiations in Coreper had run aground. The ministers ascertained that 'the envisaged solution still needed in-depth reflection' and sent the directive back to Coreper. The main obstacle was that the member states wanted to take the longer life span of women into account when calculating premiums and payments. However, the Commission refused to weaken the directive on this point because it would actually hollow out the right to equal treatment (Agence 1986, 4 June).

Italy also submitted a severely amended version of the draft directive on parental leave for discussion. It had tried to create goodwill for the directive by eliminating the section about leave for family reasons, excluding civil servants, and limiting the maximum duration of leave to four months (Agence 1985, 12 June). The weakened version ran aground on a tentative reservation from the Netherlands and Germany and a substantive reservation from Britain, stating that the proposal was 'indecent at a time when there are 13 million unemployed' (Agence 1985, 14 June). The ministers sent the dossier back to Coreper.

When Luxembourg took over the Presidency, the negotiations on these directives lost their momentum. Minister of Labour Jean-Claude Juncker even wondered whether it was sensible to call a meeting of the Social Council (Agence 1985, 18 October). Nevertheless, in December 1985, the Council held a meeting. The Commission had authorized Pfeiffer to withdraw the draft directive on parental leave if the Council weakened it excessively. This was because Luxembourg, against the wishes of Pfeiffer, had proposed an escape clause that would allow individual employers to refuse or postpone parental leave (Rutherford 1989). The Commissioner did not have to make use of his special authority. 'Firm opposition' from Britain and a Dutch reservation even blocked the weak 'Luxembourg' proposal (Agence 1985, 7 December).

Occupational Security The Netherlands chaired the EEC during the first half of 1986. They did not place the draft parental leave directive on the agenda because, according to Minister Jan de Koning, 'no development seems to be on the horizon' (Agence 1986, 30 January). During an informal Council on Equal Opportunities in March 1986, the ministers advised the new Commissioner Marin to aim for a compromise on the directive for the self-employed and the directive on occupational social security, and to cancel the directive on parental leave. Marin told the ministers that he was prepared to give the parental leave directive 'a different form' – that is, reduce it to a non-binding instrument – on the condition that the member states approve the other two directives. Marin wanted the Council 'to state clearly its case on the package of directives still pending. Does it want it or not?' (Agence 1986, 24 May). The Council was not impressed. The Social Council of June 1986 was entirely devoted to these three directives. After a long and difficult meeting, the ministers finally approved the directive on occupational social security, and that was all.

This outcome was not so odd. After all, the member states were bound by their promise to regulate in the Social Security Directive. Moreover, the *Defrenne* rulings of the Court had made it clear that Article 119 covered premiums and benefits under occupational schemes for social security. Victims of discrimination therefore already had the right to appeal to the courts. Still, the ministers greatly weakened the draft directive. Despite protests from the Commission, they unanimously amended the Commission proposal by stipulating that the longer life span of women would be taken into account until January 1999. The member states gave themselves plenty of time (until 1 January 1993) to implement the directive. Next, the Council ascertained that there was no consensus about parental leave and put the proposal away for 'an undetermined period' (Rutherford 1989, 301). Ironically, during this same meeting the ministers approved the second Action Programme for Equal Opportunities, in which they declared that they 'must quickly move to accept the Commission proposal for a directive on parental leave' (Commission 1986, COM(86)758, 15). Despite this declaration, it would take another ten years before parental leave could be settled (see Chapter 5).

Self-Employment While chairing the EEC, the Netherlands had actually aimed to have the 'self-employment directive' approved (Agence 1985, 18 October; 1986, 30 January). During the informal Council on Equal Opportunities, the ministers extensively discussed the bottlenecks in the proposed directive. It was especially the necessary changes in taxation systems from collective to individual taxation for the spouses 'which would be the equivalent of a tax revolution', and the status of co-working spouses, requiring changes of the civil code in some member states, which encountered resistance (Agence 1986, 12 March; 17/18 March). The ministers returned the dossier to Coreper.

In June 1986, the Netherlands presented a greatly weakened draft directive. It had eliminated the equal treatment provision in taxation systems. Article 7 concerning the legal acknowledgement of the work of co-working spouses only invited member states 'to take appropriate initiatives'. This meant that co-working spouses could not claim any rights based on the directive. In an open letter to Minister De Koning, ENOW stated that it preferred to postpone the approval of the directive rather than 'to allow poor decisions that could add discredit and slow Community action in this matter' (Agence 1986, 4 June).

In spite of the non-committing character of the draft directive, Britain and Ireland continued to oppose approval due to Article 8 of the directive concerning the right to benefits and replacement during pregnancy and maternity leave. After a long discussion, the formulation 'that the member states would take initiatives' was changed into the promise that they 'would investigate if and how' women could exercise such rights. All delegations then appeared to be able to agree with the directive, but Britain and Ireland now wanted to reduce the text in Article 7 even further to the formula that the member states would 'examine what initiatives could eventually be taken'. This reduction went too far for the Netherlands, Belgium and Italy, because it emptied the provision of all content. They even expected that the directive would cause judicial problems because it did not have the mandatory content that was appropriate for a binding instrument (Agence 1986, 6 June).

The dossier once again returned to Coreper. When Britain took over the Presidency, it succeeded in formulating a compromise for Articles 7 and 8 with which all member states could agree; they 'committed themselves to study if and how' the work of spouses could be acknowledged, and 'if and how' benefits and replacement related to pregnancy and maternity leave could be granted. In December 1986, the Council approved the directive.[11]

11 Directive 86/613 on 'the application of the principle of equal treatment between men and women engaged in an activity, including agriculture, in a self-employed capacity and on the protection of self-employed women during pregnancy and motherhood'.

The directive was new, compared to previous equal rights directives, because it not only established norms for the equal treatment of men and women in a specific sector, but also assigned a legal status to co-working spouses, a category of individuals that had not previously enjoyed an acknowledged status. The directive potentially could have great effect on the condition that 'it is implemented in the spirit which is intended' (Prechal and Burrows 1990, 293). This condition was not fulfilled and the nature of the obligations was so non-specific that the member states could back out of their obligations without consequences. Later comments by legal experts would confirm the fear of ENOW that the directive was 'markedly unhelpful'. It did not lead to an improvement in the position of self-employed women and co-working spouses because, in contrast to the 'old' equality directives, it did not assign any 'specific and clear-cut rights' to the parties it was intended to help (Ellis 1998).

Stagnation After the Council meeting in June 1986, Commissioner Marin stated that he would no longer try to get the other 'frozen directives' (see Table 4.1) approved in a more or less binding form. According to Marin, 'the European Commission may abandon its effort to promote women's equality' because the member states 'do not want an EEC policy in favour of women. They are not interested in it' (Pillinger 1992, 100).

Furthermore, the victory of centre-right political parties in 1986 forced Mitterrand into a *cohabitation* with Chirac (Gaullist) as Prime Minister of a rightist government. Chirac made every effort to reverse socialist reforms. He degraded Roudy's full ministry to a Delegated Ministry for Women's Affairs under the leadership of Hélène Gisserot, a lawyer without party affiliation. She lacked the political support and the financial means to carry out any significant measures (Mazur 1991). The most important proponent of European equal rights policy was silenced.

Finally, Delors preferred to give shape to a European social dimension by means of the 'social dialogue' instead of using directives. He hoped that the trade unions and employers would integrate the promotion of equal rights into their collective agreements (Agence 1986, 17 October).

Without backing from the Commissioner of Social Affairs, the Commission President or a pioneer state, pressure by women's groups and women in trade unions and political parties for progress in the field of equality policies was ineffective, both at the national and at the supranational level.

Potential Progress: A Charter

Due to the development of the internal market and the expansion of the EEC with Spain and Portugal, the call for European social policies became louder. As in the 1950s, there was tension between liberalization and different conditions of employment. In 1956, France had feared the competition of Dutch and German companies that could produce cheaply due to the low wages of female workers. In 1986, the wealthier member states feared that companies would move to the low-wage countries of Portugal and Spain. The ETUC and the EP warned that social inequality could increase because not everyone would profit equally from the opportunities of the internal market (Pillinger 1992). Delors emphasized the importance of European social policy as an instrument to strengthen social cohesion, counteract downward harmonization ('social dumping') and convince citizens of the value of a single European market. Therefore, the Commission drafted a new Social Action Programme, this time called 'Charter of the Fundamental Social Rights of Citizens'.

The Social Charter Mitterrand wanted the member states to sign the charter while France chaired the EEC (Attali 1995). In October 1989, eleven ministers of social affairs approved the draft charter, but the British minister rejected it. On 8 December 1989, the European Council in Strasbourg would officially approve the 'Social Charter'. The member states had greatly weakened the contents of the Charter and had limited the fundamental rights of 'citizens' to those of 'workers'. Although the Charter did not even have a binding character and was nothing more than a 'solemn commitment', Britain categorically refused to approve it.

According to Thatcher, the Charter was a socialist document 'that I believe would form the basis for directives that were intended to bring the *Delors* variant of socialism in through the backdoor'. Furthermore, it was an instrument of 'German protectionism', used by Germany to reduce its competitive disadvantage by driving up the costs in the other member states (Thatcher 1993, 806). Attali reminisced about how an electricity outage in Strasbourg put the government leaders in the dark and Thatcher mischievously called out, 'This is the right moment to talk about the Social Charter!' (Attali 1995, 464). All member states except Britain signed the Charter.

Women in the European Arena The British 'opt out' led in Britain to 'increasing awareness of the Union as a potentially fruitful focus of political action' and caused women's groups to 'redouble their efforts at the Community level' and intensify transnational contacts (Mazey and Richardson 1993, 98). Women's groups in other member states also felt the need for more concerted action and information. At a seminar in Britain, they decided to set up a lobby in order to be better informed and to offer women a permanent representation at the supranational level. The Commission provided funding. The European Women's Lobby (EWL) was formally established in September 1990. Its membership was predominately 'white, professional and middle-aged' (Hoskyns 1991). The EWL would develop its capacities during the 1990s, resulting in written opinions on equality policy initiatives and treaty amendments and useful input for the EP and the Commission.

Like the SAP in 1974, the Charter called for the Commission to formulate concrete proposals. In 1989, a new Commission took office, once again chaired by Delors. For the first time, there were two women on the Commission, one of whom was Vasso Papandreou from Greece, responsible for Social Affairs. It became her task to convert the 'fundamental rights' into proposals. This resulted in no less than 47 proposals that she wanted to see approved before the completion of the internal market programme on 1 January 1993. However, unanimity was still required for the approval of joint social policy, except for measures in the area of safety and health of workers, which the ministers could approve by a qualified majority.

In the area of equal rights policy, the Council had already blocked draft directives concerning the completion of social security (COM(87)494) and the reversal of the burden of proof (COM(88)269). As a result of the Charter, the Commission presented new draft directives concerning survivor's benefits, supplementary benefits for families, retirement age, pregnancy leave and atypical employment. Eleven member states appeared to be proponents of progress in the area of social policy, but 'they were in a situation – foreknowledge of the likely British veto – that made cheap talk' (Lange 1993, 8; Egan 1993).

Progress: the Social Protocol

The European Council of Strasbourg would not go into history as the summit of the social charter, but as the summit where the member states decided to hold an Intergovernmental Conference (IGC) to amend the Treaties of Rome. Dramatic changes had occurred. The fall of the Berlin Wall in 1989 and the collapse of the Soviet Union shook the international system. Against the background of this unstable situation, Mitterrand and Kohl choose to deepen economic and political cooperation in the EEC. A monetary union should tie a unified Germany firmly to Western Europe (Lieshout 1999).

In the margin of the IGC, national and supranational pressure for a stronger social dimension increased. France, where the socialists were back in power, Germany and Delors argued that monetary integration should be accompanied by social progress. The Commission submitted draft texts for strengthening the social chapter in the Treaty. UNICE reluctantly accepted the proposal for a new procedure, 'negotiate or we'll legislate', which enabled the European organizations of employers and trade unions to conclude European collective agreements, which the member states could then confirm with a directive (Moravcsik 1998).

The British Opt-Out The Commission's proposals encountered loud British resistance and protests from other member states because they were 'too interventionist'. In October 1991, the Netherlands holding the presidency submitted a more moderate proposal. 'Quantitative' issues such as social security would continue to require unanimity, and all 'core issues of wage bargaining' remained excluded from European interference (Ross 1995). Only in some 'non-quantitative areas', decisions could be taken by a qualified majority. Yet, Britain threatened to run the entire treaty reform aground if qualified majority decision-making applied to *any* aspect of social policy.

Prime Minister John Major, like his predecessor Thatcher, was 'ideologically committed to preventing any EC regulation in a broader area of labour market and social policies' (Lange 1993, 25). As successive Conservative governments had focused on 'low-cost, low-technology production' and low expenditures for social security, Britain had much to win from non-participation in social policy that created higher costs for its competitors (Lange 1993). Major was under heavy pressure from Thatcher and Conservative backbenchers to refuse any concession on social policy. It was quite likely that the Conservative majority in parliament 'would have rejected any treaty not containing a British opt-out' (Moravcsik 1998, 453).

When it became clear that Britain would not sign the treaty if it contained a social section while Germany would not sign a treaty without one, Dutch Prime Minister Lubbers, after consulting with Mitterrand, submitted a last minute compromise to prevent the monetary union from running aground on social issues. Britain obtained an 'opt-out' for social policy and Lubbers moved the entire social section to a separate Protocol that was signed by eleven member states. Various member states had previously assumed that Britain would dilute the social section 'to insignificance' instead of 'opting out'. The result of the British opt-out was that the eleven member states approved a social protocol that was closer to the original Commission proposal than the weakened version that the Netherlands had proposed to obtain British approval (Moravcsik 1998).

From now on, gender equality directives no longer needed unanimous approval but only a qualified majority. The protocol contained the new 'negotiate or legislate' procedure. Article 6.3 created a clear statutory basis for positive action measures. This article was a step forward with respect to the equal treatment directive because it allowed measures to improve the position of women in a general sense, whereas the directive only allowed positive discrimination if the measures were intended 'to eliminate or reduce actual instances of inequality' (Case 312/86, *Commission v. France*; *ECR* 1988, 6315).

Decline: The Barber Protocol

Besides the potential progress in the area of equal rights for eleven of the twelve member states, there was also decline. In the margins of the IGC negotiations, the Dutch presidency took the initiative to limit the effect of Article 119. The reason for this was the preliminary decision of the Court in *Barber v. Guardian Royal Exchange* (Case 262/88). The Court ruled on 17 May 1990 that pensions must be considered as wages as defined in Article 119. Based on the decision, innumerable female employees could qualify for pension benefits retroactively. 'The ruling created an uproar in Britain' because many businesses had different regulations for men and women (Egan 1993, 37). Britain calculated that this ruling would cost 40 billion pounds, Germany figured the cost at 35 billion DM, and the Dutch retirement funds estimated the costs at 70 to 120 billion guilders (Leibfried and Pierson 1995, 47; *NRC-Handelsblad* 1991, 18 April). *Barber* 'provoked what is probably the most costly and intense lobbying campaign yet seen in Brussels' (Mazey and Richardson 1993, 15).

The Netherlands was extremely motivated to intervene. In October 1988, Junior Minister De Graaf had submitted a bill to implement equal treatment in pension regulations beginning on 1 January 1993, so that the Netherlands would satisfy the provisions of the EEC directive concerning occupational social security schemes

(1986). Members of parliament had already warned that pension funds would be confronted with 'unexpected demands for pension benefits' if women were able to appeal to the direct effect of Article 119 (*Handelingen* 1988–89, 20890, No. 4, 10).

Because of the ruling, the First Chamber of the parliament suspended the debate until there was more clarity about the retroactive effect (*Handelingen* 1991–2, 22300, XV, No. 2). Based on *Barber*, women appeared to be able to claim equal treatment with retroactive effect until April 1976 (*Defrenne II*), while the Dutch government wanted to implement it as of January 1993. In view of the magnitude of the discrimination against women in Dutch pension schemes, the right to equal treatment from 1976 would lead to enormous additional payments (Emancipatieraad 1991). Many pension funds, because of *Barber*, had started amending discriminatory regulations out of fear that women would otherwise attempt to exercise their rights via the courts and that they would face even higher claims (*NRC-Handelsblad* 1991, 2 November).

Because of the commotion in the member states, in April 1991 the Commission established a workgroup of legal experts to study the consequences of *Barber*. The Netherlands believed it was too risky to wait for the outcome of the study or for other preliminary rulings that could clarify the retroactive effect of the judgement. It decided to use its position as President and to try, in the margin of the treaty reform, altering Article 119. In September 1991, it mentioned *Barber* in its 'Draft Treaty': 'The question arises whether this judgement will lead the Conference to make amendments to the wording of Article 119. The Presidency reserves to itself the possibility of drawing up proposals on this matter' (*Europe Documents* 1991, No. 1733/1734).

In October, the ministers of social affairs held a 'very informal' discussion about *Barber* (Agence 1991, 15 October). The Dutch Minister of Social Affairs Bert de Vries submitted a proposal to change Article 119 by excluding pension schemes from equal pay. In this way, he hoped to 'keep the effect of Article 119 within reasonable financial limits'. During the Social Affairs Council on 3 December 1991, a majority of the member states supported the proposal (*NRC-Handelsblad* 1991, 4 December).

Women's organizations and Dutch MPs protested against the proposal because it meant that women would continue to be discriminated for a long time. They called it 'simply scandalous' that the minister wanted to implement this far-reaching treaty change 'secretly' without having consulted parliament (*NRC-Handelsblad* 1991, 4 December). At the request of Christine Crawley, who chaired the EP Committee for Women's Rights, Enrique Baron – the chair of the EP – wrote a letter to the Dutch Minister of Foreign Affairs and Chair of the Council, Hans van den Broek. The EP was 'very concerned' about the Dutch proposal to weaken Article 119 (Agence 1991, 9/10 December). However, not only employers but also the trade unions supported De Vries (*NRC-Handelsblad* 1991, 24 October). Pressure by EP and women's organizations therefore was not effective enough.

In its decision, the Court had already taken account of the 'serious financial consequences' which *Barber* could cause. Accordingly, it had limited the retroactive effect of 'entitlement to a pension' to the date of the ruling: 17 May 1990 (*ECR* 1990, 1889ff). However, this formulation left various interpretations open. Did it concern all pension payments after 17 May 1990, only the pensions paid beginning on 17 May 1990, only the pensions of employees whose contract ended after this date, or only pension entitlements accrued after 17 May 1990 (EP 1998, PE 167.336)?

In Maastricht, the member states chose the latter, most restrictive, interpretation. They agreed to add the following protocol to the Treaty:

> For the purposes of Article 119 of this Treaty, benefits under occupational social security schemes shall not be considered as remuneration if and in so far as they are attributable to periods of employment prior to 17 May 1990.

This construction showed a great deal of inventiveness, although the provision that pension rights were not considered wages until 17 May 1990 but they were considered wages afterwards, goes against every form of logic. The Netherlands maintained the 'honourable' tradition that it had established in 1957 in Rome, when it gave an interpretive explanation to Article 119: if the costs of equal rights for women threatened to become too high, every judicial trick in the book to avoid implementation was permissible.

Conclusion: The High Price of More Gender Equality Policies

This chapter addressed the questions, why in spite of all pressure no new 'costly' equal rights policy was established during the 1980s, and why the member states implemented the costly policy that they had agreed to previously.

To answer the latter question first, the costly directives from the 1970s were implemented thanks to simultaneous pressure at the national and supranational levels. This resulted in an effective 'pincer' mechanism of national and supranational jurisprudence that increased the costs of non-compliance. Additionally, the Court affirmed the direct effect of provisions in the directives (*Defrenne II*, *Marshall* and *FNV*). As a result, disadvantaged parties could take their cases to the national courts, even if their government had not yet transposed the directive in national legislation. Furthermore, due to the Court, the directives were more expensive than the member states had calculated when they approved them. The rulings increased the costs of equal treatment for the state (*Teuling*, *FNV* and *Dik*) and the employer (*Worringham*, *Von Colson* and *Harz*). They were a breakthrough in the endless struggles concerning 'work of equal value' (*Macarthys*), the classification of jobs (*Rummler*) and the rights of married women (*Liefting, Teuling, FNV, Dik, Drake* and *Clarke*). However, when a Court ruling (*Barber*) increased the costs of implementing Article 119 too much, the member states quickly agreed to an amendment of the Treaty to limit these costs.

The experiences with costly implementation resulted in a 'boomerang effect', making member states more reluctant regarding the approval of new equal rights policy. Between 1979 and 1992, the member states approved two new directives in the area of equal rights: one on self-employed and one on occupational social security schemes. The latter could be traced back to Court rulings and the promises made in the social security directive from 1978. The former directive was so severely weakened by the member states that it did not provide any new rights. British vetoes blocked all other proposals in the field of gender equality.

Political and societal pressure at the domestic and the supranational levels was strong. The now directly elected EP and the Equal Opportunities Unit of the Commission offered access and resources to women's groups. Active transnational networks developed between equal opportunities committees, feminist experts, women's groups, officials in the Commission and members of the EP. However, elections brought governments into power that were less sensitive to pressure for the redistribution of rights and means than were their predecessors. Equal rights policy was not compatible with their aims regarding deregulation and reducing government expenditures, nor was it compatible with the conservative ideology that focused on restoring 'law and order' where the 'classic family' with a clear role division between man and woman was the ideal model. When governments began cutting back on social provisions, the women's movement focused more strongly on influencing government policy than during the 1970s and formed alliances with political parties and trade unions to prevent the erosion of rights. However, their pressure had little effect due to the low sensitivity of the governments.

For Germany, Britain and the Netherlands, the expected costs of new supranational equal rights policies were higher than the benefits. France was the exception where the expected costs of supranational equal rights policy were low. At the European level, France attempted to play a leading role in the social area, but it did not gain any support. The ideological differences with the other large member states prevented agreement on European socio-economic policy.

In Maastricht in 1991, against the background of an unstable international situation, the member states reached agreement about deepening the integration process. In order to win the approval of the population for new steps forward in the area of economic and monetary cooperation, they also agreed to progress in the social domain. The Social Protocol added to the Treaty improved the prospects for new equal rights policy by allowing decision making in the Council by QMV. Whether new procedures indeed would lead to stronger outcomes will be discussed in Chapter 5.

Chapter 5

Shifting Costs and Concepts of Gender Equality (1992–2005)

In the 1980s, no costly, far-reaching new policies were developed in the field of gender equality. Governments complied reluctantly with the costly policies already approved in the 1970s. Compared to the stagnation of the 1980s, the 1990s appear to be a period of remarkable progress: the Treaties of Rome were revised, not just once but three times, in Maastricht, Amsterdam and Nice and, in addition, monetary union was implemented, culminating in the replacement of national currencies by the euro in twelve member states. Last but not least, the EU more than doubled its membership from 12 members in 1991 to 25 in 2004. Arguably, the member states had already succeeded in breathing new life into the process of European integration in 1986 with the signing of the Single European Act (SEA), which enabled progress towards a single European market. In December 1991 in Maastricht, a general reform of the Treaties of Rome was agreed upon, and the European Community became the European Union.

Post-'Maastricht' attitudes towards new supranational social policies became more equivocal. On the one hand, in the aftermath of the very narrow 'yes' and the decisive 'no' in the respective French and Danish referenda on the Maastricht Treaty, governments saw the implementation of new social policies as a way of building support for European integration and the single currency. Sharply rising unemployment also emphasized the fact that the single European market had generated fewer jobs than hoped. On the other hand, the Commission and liberal governments feared that new social policies would further increase labour costs, hamper job creation and make European firms still less competitive than their US and Japanese counterparts.

In 1994, the European Council selected 'fighting unemployment' as the key issue in the field of social policy. Commission President Jacques Delors stressed the role of women as a labour market resource, the utilization of which could enhance European economic competitiveness and labour flexibility, while promoting a more rational division of professional and family responsibilities (Rossilli 2000).

Such a climate offered mixed prospects for new, costly gender equality policies. At the supranational level, pressure for action on gender equality from the European Women's Lobby (EWL) and the Committee for Women's Rights of the EP was strong. Although governments were not willing to approve policies that would increase labour costs, they were prepared to accept measures to increase the number of working women and to facilitate the combination of work and care, such measures being seen as helpful to reducing unemployment and enhancing competitiveness. 'Maastricht' introduced new provisions concerning social policy and opened up the policy making arena for new actors, new procedures and new instruments. The central question of this chapter is whether these changes resulted in new costly gender equality policies.

Table 5.1 Overview actors and procedures

Directive	Treaty Base	Labour and Management	Vote Council	Role and influence EP
Parental leave 1996	Treaty of Maastricht, Social Protocol	Involved, agreement	QMV	–
Part-time work, 1997	Treaty of Maastricht, Social Protocol	Involved, agreement	QMV	–
Pregnant workers, 1992	Single European Act, Art. 118A (new Art. 138 EC)	–	QMV	Cooperation, limited influence
Burden of proof, 1997	Treaty of Maastricht, Social Protocol	Not interested	QMV	Cooperation, limited influence
Equal treatment, 2002 (revision 76/207)	Treaty of Amsterdam, Art. 141.3 EC (ex Art. 119)	–	QMV	Co-decision, influence
Race discrimination (also outside the workplace) 2000	Treaty of Amsterdam, Art. 13 EC	–	unanimity	Consultation, very limited influence
Discrimination on multiple grounds (work), 2000	Treaty of Amsterdam, Art. 13 EC	–	unanimity	Consultation, very limited influence
Equal treatment, goods and services, 2004	Treaty of Amsterdam, Art. 13 EC	–	unanimity	Consultation, very limited influence

'New' Actors on the Supranational Scene

A procedure introduced by the Social Protocol offered employers and trade unions a role in supranational policymaking. Under this procedure, the Commission sends its proposal to representatives of employers and trade unions at EU level (primarily UNICE, CEEP and ETUC) who decide whether they want to regulate on the matter. The agreement resulting from these negotiations goes to the Council, which approves it by either QMV or unanimity, depending on the subject matter.

For Delors, the procedure finally gave employers and trade unions a stronger role in the development of supranational social legislation. Those in favour of supranational social legislation hoped that the procedure would make the use of the veto in the Council less likely because it was assumed that the Council would not dare to vote down an agreement reached between management and labour. Others were of the opinion that the procedure would not result in bold decision making because trade unions and employers would never be able to find enough common ground to reach any 'costly' agreement on important matters.

In the field of gender equality, between 1991 and 2005, employers and trade unions reached two agreements that were subsequently approved by the Council: the agreement on parental leave and the agreement on part-time work. Did these directives represent 'minimum common denominator' outcomes, laying down standards at a level already realized in (almost) all member states? Or did they require member states to introduce costly policy changes? In other words, have women benefited from the presence of these new actors in the supranational arena?

Parental Leave

In 1982, Commissioner Richard had put the issue of parental leave on the agenda as one of the proposals in the Action Programme (Commission 1983, COM(1983)686). He viewed it as a crucial instrument for minimizing the career gap of working mothers and encouraging fathers to accept family responsibilities. British resistance blocked adoption (see Chapter 4).

In 1993, the Belgian Council Presidency put the issue back on the agenda. The delegations discussed the Belgian compromise proposal several times, but Britain wanted to limit parental leave to mothers and Luxembourg also had reservations (Commission 1994, No. 40). The draft was discussed again in September 1994, under the German Council Presidency. As Britain 'stressed its opposition in principle to the proposal and the fact that this would not change in future', Commissioner Pádraig Flynn decided to reintroduce the proposal under the Social Protocol procedure (EIRR 1994, 249:2).

The Commission initiated consultations between the supranational representatives of employers and trade unions in February 1995. On 6 November 1995, UNICE, CEEP and ETUC reached an agreement on parental leave, which they signed on 14 December. The Commission proposed the draft directive to the Council, where 'it was a matter of controversy' because some delegations thought that the content of the directive left too much room for interpretation (Falkner et al. 2005, 144).

In March 1996, the Council reached a political consensus and in June 1996, it formally adopted the directive on parental leave (Directive 96/34/EC) which implemented the agreement. It provides parents with a minimum of three months' leave before a child's eighth birthday, entitles them to leave no matter what type of employment contract they have, and guarantees them the right to return to work following this leave. It also introduced binding legal rules on force majeure leave, absence from work for urgent family reasons.

A comparison of the directive with the existing national standards shows that the directive reflected the minimum common denominator. It left all contentious and potentially costly issues, such as pay and the right to social security benefits during leave, to be decided at national level. Experts concluded that 'For the majority of countries, the Directive is unlikely to entail major changes to existing parental leave arrangements' (EIRonline 1998, 10). In most countries, entitlement to leave was already at a standard superior to that envisioned in the EC directive. The minimum length of leave (three months) represented the lowest amount granted in any of the member states that had already legislated on a statutory right to parental leave. Furthermore, the potential for transforming gender roles, and for pushing men to take up an equal share of family responsibilities, was not realized either. First, the directive did not clearly prohibit the transfer of the individual right to leave to the female partner, and second, there was no compulsory provision for a minimum allowance or pay.

Three countries had to take costly measures, as they did not have a statutory right to parental leave yet. Why had they approved the directive? Ireland and Luxembourg could not block it, as they had only five of the 16 votes needed to form a blocking minority under the 11-state Social Agreement procedure. The UK had vetoed the parental leave directive several times between 1983 and 1986, but due to its 'opt-out' concerning social policy, it could no longer veto the directive. In 1997 new Prime Minister Tony Blair ended the British opt-out.

The British government adopted the Employment Relations Act implementing the Parental Leave Directive in 1999. Because the British act excluded parents of children born before 1999, the TUC initiated proceedings in the British court, which referred the case to the Court. The Commission put simultaneous pressure on the government and started an infringement procedure because of the limited scope of the British act. The British government, sandwiched, did not await Court rulings and removed the 1999 cut-off date with the Maternity and Parental Leave (Amendment) Regulation in 2001 (Sifft 2003). The directive therefore proved costly for the British government as it had led to a more far-reaching improvement in the rights of working parents than the government had intended.

For the other member states, the directive was not costly, although Falkner points to minor improvements in several countries (Falkner et al. 2005, 156). In particular, the lack of any obligation to provide paid leave significantly reduced the costs and limited the impact of the directive in practice because for parents on low wages, unpaid parental leave is no viable option and it discourages the parent with the highest income, mostly fathers, from taking any leave.

Explaining the Low Price of the Directive The interests and motivations of the actors involved explain this modest outcome. Pressure to tackle the issue of parental leave came from the European Council, the Commission, employers and trade unions, for different reasons. None of them, however, was primarily motivated by a desire to change gender roles or concern about the rights of working parents.

The European Council was worried about the credibility of its efforts in the field of employment. It repeatedly insisted, therefore, that full use be made of the Social Protocol procedure (European Council 1993 and 1994). The Commission seized the opportunity to achieve progress on parental leave at last. To this end it reframed the issue in terms of increased labour market flexibility rather than in terms of gender equality (Stratigaki 2000).

Employers and trade unions were anxious to negotiate an agreement, as 'this would prove the social partners' ability to be key players in the process of European integration' (EIRR 1995, 261:3). Until that point, the 'social dialogue procedure' had produced no results, the parties involved being deadlocked on the proposal for the creation of a European Works Council. As the Social Protocol was on the agenda of the looming IGC on treaty reform ('Amsterdam'), the social partners wanted to avoid seeing the procedure redrafted and the reduction of their 'co-regulatory power' due to their inability to produce results (Falkner 1998). They considered the issue of parental leave as a relatively easy subject, as for employers and trade unions alike, no crucial interests were at stake as long as the costs could be limited; the issue seemed 'a suitable "guinea pig" for Euro-level collective negotiations' (Falkner 1998, 114). Employers preferred to participate in negotiations rather than leaving the matter to legislation – as the Commission would legislate anyway if management and labour did not come to an agreement.

So it clearly was not the desire to encourage women and men to share family responsibilities which was central to the negotiations, but rather the prestige of the European Council, the Commission and the supranational corporatist actors. The directive was not a breakthrough after many years of stagnation, but 'rather more significant for the fact that it has been concluded, than for its content' (EIRR 1995, 263, 3; Geyer and Springer 1998).

Part-time Work

Part-time work was the second issue for which the supranational representatives of employers and trade unions managed to negotiate an agreement. Given the high number of women working part-time and the extent of the discrimination they suffered as compared to full-time workers, the directive would improve the position of many women workers. Ensuring part-time workers similar conditions to full-time workers for social security and career development also offered the advantage of making part-time work more attractive for highly skilled workers and male workers in general, thus enabling families to share household duties and care more equally.

Draft directives on 'atypical work' had been awaiting approval by the Council since 1981. They were shelved in 1985, as Britain, supported by Greece and Denmark blocked all supranational action concerning working time (see Chapter 4). The EP pushed for regulation of atypical work as a means of combating indirect discrimination against women who choose part-time jobs to combine household tasks and work (Bleijenbergh 2004).

In 1991, within the framework of the action programme implementing the 1989 Social Charter, Commissioner Vasso Papandreou came up with new proposals. Her predecessors considered work without a standard full-time contract as exceptional and sought to restrict such work as much as possible. Papandreou strategically reframed the issue, following the line of reasoning of the EP. She based her draft directives on the ideas that atypical work satisfied workers' needs to reconcile work and family, and national differences in the costs of employing 'atypical workers' might lead to the distortion of competition. As was the case with parental leave, both the Belgian and the German Presidencies made efforts in 1993–4 to gain approval for a watered-down draft on 'part-time and fixed-term contracts'. These hopes were dashed when Britain cast an outright veto (Falkner 1998).

The Commission reframed the issue once again. It replaced the notion of 'atypical' work with 'flexible' work, arguing that the promotion of flexible forms of work was necessary for job creation. In September 1995, the Commission reintroduced the draft directive under the 'social dialogue' procedure, encouraged by the concern of the European Council to promote new forms of work and combat unemployment.

The negotiations were tough. Employers and trade unions struggled over the right balance between flexibility for management and protection for workers. Moreover, trade unions were split about the desirability of part-time work. Representatives from southern low-wage countries considered part-time work a precarious form of employment and preferred to promote the combination of work and family life through a general reduction of working hours. Representatives from northern countries, meanwhile, wanted to promote part-time work (Falkner et al. 2005). Employers wanted to restrict the scope of the agreement to part-time workers, demanding and obtaining – after tough negotiations – the exclusion of fixed-term work, temporary work and casual work (Bleijenbergh 2004).[1] Employers also insisted that care remain a strictly private responsibility and refused any measure to encourage men's involvement in care giving (Bleijenbergh 2004). Despite considerable criticism of the weak results from representatives of some trade unions and the Women's Committee of the ETUC, the European representatives of employers and trade unions adopted the framework agreement on part-time work in May 1997 (Falkner et al. 2005). In December 1997, the Council decided to approve the agreement without change (Directive 97/81/EC).

After such fierce opposition in the 1980s and 1990s to the draft directives, one wonders why this time member states agreed. Crucial to this were various restrictions on the original Commission proposal, which reduced potential costs for most member states to a minimum. In fact, the directive did not go beyond what was already covered by non-discrimination laws in member states with many part-time workers (the Netherlands, Britain). First, divergent social security provisions for part-time and full-time workers and for part-timers in different member states constituted the major source of discrimination, and it was measures to tackle these disparities that had motivated previous opposition from Germany and Britain. Due to employers' opposition, statutory social security matters had been eliminated from the proposal, which was a step back even from the level of protection afforded by previous Court rulings on part-time work (Bergamaschi 2000).[2] Secondly, the directive also limited the scope of the Commission proposal in that it excluded other flexible forms of

1 The protection of fixed-term workers would be dealt with later in Directive 1999/70/EC of 28 June 1999.

2 In several preliminary rulings (*Bilka Kaufhaus* Case 170/84, *Rinner-Kühn* Case 171/88) the Court had ruled that unequal treatment of part-timers was a source of indirect discrimination.

work and allowed exceptions to the principle of non-discrimination in the case of part-time workers who had a limited period of service with a company, who worked below a certain number of hours, or who earned below a specified amount. Finally, the vague terms of the directive left considerable room for flexibility when it came to implementation at national level. Falkner et al. count no fewer than eleven non-binding provisions (2005, 160), for instance the recommendation that part-time work be facilitated for employees in skilled and managerial positions, which has the potential to encourage change in gender roles but in fact provides little leverage for women and men who want to claim this right against the wishes of their employer.

For British part-time workers, the directive was not very helpful as a 'comparable full-time worker' was needed to prove discrimination, which was often impossible in the decentralized British industrial relations system (Falkner et al. 2005, 166). Germany even 'over-implemented' the directive, because the centre-left government conceived of part-time work as a useful instrument to reduce unemployment. The 'job creation' argument also convinced southern member states to approve the directive. The directive could have been of great interest to women, but it fell short of expectations.

Conclusion

Since these two directives were adopted after a blockade of some 15 years in the Council, at first glance Rossilli seems to be right when she argues that 'the approval of these directives is primarily due to the emergence of a European corporatist polity' (Rossilli 2000, 9). However, the shift from blockade to approval was enabled not only by the new 'corporatist' procedure involving employers and trade unions, but also by the British opt-out and the watering-down of the Commission proposals.

When we look at the content of the directives, the shift from bargaining between Commission and Council to bargaining between employers and trade unions does not improve prospects of strong gender equality policies. The 'corporatist' procedure has resulted in two directives which, compared to other social policy directives, stand out because of the high number of non-binding provisions they contain (Falkner et al. 2005, 142). Where employers and trade unions were not able to reach agreement, they left decisions on important aspects of the policies to be decided at the national implementation stage.

Futhermore, 'corporatist' interests often differ from women's interests. Employers prefer voluntary agreements to legislation, whereas women generally benefit more from legislation, which covers all groups in the labour market. Employers also oppose all measures that increase labour costs, whereas the goal of gender equality often necessitates increased costs.

Trade union involvement does not lead to high standards on gender issues either (Van der Vleuten 2004). The under-representation of women in trade union decision-making bodies is reflected in a male-oriented bargaining agenda.[3] Gender equality seldom has priority. Trade unions are often opposed to regulating on gender equality, as they are afraid of losing autonomy and bargaining power. As Bergamaschi argues, the model of collective bargaining seems to be a barrier to 'the full recognition of the principles of equal treatment and equal opportunity' (Bergamaschi 2000, 172).

Unfortunately, the 'social dialogue' procedure undermines the influence of actors in favour of supranational gender equality legislation. As in the 'normal' procedure for the elaboration of directives, the Commission sets the agenda. However, the rule that the Council can deviate from the Commission proposal only by unanimity, which applies in the 'normal' procedure, has been lost in the 'social dialogue procedure'. Bargaining is done in 'secret discussions' between representatives of European organizations of employers and trade unions, without Commission control (Stratigaki 2000, 42).

The EP 'is merely an onlooker', similar to its passive role in the 'old' legislative consultation procedure, and as such it cannot influence the content of the agreement (Glase 1996). In its report on parental leave and its debate on part-time work, the EP voiced its disappointment, aptly criticizing the crucial gaps in the agreements – but procedures required only that Parliament be 'informed'; it had no influence whatsoever on the outcome. Thus the introduction of the social dialogue procedure does not contribute positively to gender equality policies, as actors that have little interest in strong gender equality provisions dominate the procedure.

The modest success of the agreements concerning parental leave and part-time work are thrown into even sharper relief by the fact that management and labour were not able to reach agreement on other Commission proposals on gender equality. Employers refused to negotiate on sexual harassment (Gregory 2000). They declared that 'the issue was not the domain of agreements involving them' (Commission 1997, 15). Concerning the reversal of the burden of proof in sex discrimination cases, UNICE first had argued that the directive would burden the employers with new costs and responsibilities. After a first round of consultations, the Commission therefore drafted a new proposal that moderated the burden of proof so that the employer and the employee concerned would share the responsibility (Geyer and Springer 1998). The second round of consultations made it clear to Commissioner Flynn that employers and trade unions did not want to start negotiations at all, so he put the proposal before the Council.

Despite its limited success in producing meaningful policy outcomes – or perhaps precisely because of it – the social dialogue procedure survived the treaty reform in 1997 and was included in the Treaty of Amsterdam (Art. 139 EC).

3 Women make up half of the population, 40 percent of the trade union membership, 5–20 percent of the delegations of management and labour, and their representation decreases dramatically towards the top levels (Ghilardotti 1996).

New Procedures

At Maastricht, Germany and the Netherlands successfully insisted on a certain 'democratization' of the European decision-making process. The single market programme had led to a significant increase in the amount of European regulation, the legitimacy of which was being questioned in some quarters. To tackle this, alongside Delors' social dialogue procedure, the EP was given a more prominent role. Member states agreed to extend the use of the cooperation procedure (introduced by the SEA in 1987), under which the EP can propose amendments which Council can only overturn by unanimity. Member states also introduced a new procedure for decision making in certain areas: the co-decision procedure. As the name indicates, the EP and the Council decide together, on equal terms, because a proposal has to be approved by QMV in the Council and by an absolute majority of the European Parliament.

In the field of gender equality, social security matters continue to be covered by the consultation procedure, meaning unanimous voting in the Council and a limited, advisory role for the EP. As a result, sex discrimination in social security remains difficult to tackle. Proposals based on Article 118A (now Art. 138 EC) – improvement of the working environment, working conditions, equality between women and men with regard to labour market conditions and treatment at work – and Article 119 (now Art. 141 EC) – equal pay and equal treatment – came under the cooperation procedure and were after the Amsterdam treaty reform placed under the co-decision procedure.

This change pleased advocates of gender equality legislation. As the Committee of Women's Rights in the EP had acquired a reputation for successful advocacy of gender equality and support for the Commission's proposals in this field, the increased involvement of EP in the decision making process offered a greater prospect of far-reaching gender equality policies. The EP now had the power to block legislation which it did not approve of. This blocking power would cast its shadow onto the bargaining process, proving useful in cases where the Council is keen to legislate. It is less useful, however, where the EP is keen to legislate but the Council is unwilling to do so. In that situation, consensus between Council and EP might arise when the status quo is unattractive, the Commission comes up with an innovative proposal and the state holding the Presidency or a pioneer state actively supports the EP's position. Finally, when voting on the Council takes place by QMV, a country wanting to block new legislation must build a coalition strong enough to constitute a blocking minority.

Since the Maastricht treaty reform, some new gender equality directives have been approved. Have new procedures indeed resulted in higher norms, requiring member states to introduce costly changes? And if so, why have such norms been approved?

Pregnant Workers

In spite of the neutral designation 'pregnant workers and workers who have recently given birth or are breastfeeding', for obvious biological reasons this directive only applies to women. It does not cover all pregnant women but only women workers. Commissioner Papandreou did not present the directive as one of the gender equality directives, but linked it to a set of directives on health and safety at work so that it would only require a qualified majority in the Council (Commission 1990, COM(90)406). Moreover, Court rulings had shown that pregnancy and equal treatment are a difficult couple, precisely because there can be no comparison between a pregnant women and a man (*Boyle*, Case C-411/96). So the Court argued that discrimination on grounds of pregnancy is always direct discrimination because it is based on a uniquely female biological characteristic (*Dekker*, Case C-177/88; *Webb*, Case C-32/93).

Papandreou had obtained Commission approval for her proposal by framing it in the context of concern about population decline in Europe and a deficit of skilled workers, a situation requiring a higher level of female participation in the labour market whilst simultaneously ensuring that this would not negatively influence their decision to have children (Commission 1990, No. 12).

Britain opposed the Commission proposal, not because of the safety standards (for instance, prevention of pregnant women from being exposed to hazardous agents) but because of the employment rights (no dismissal) and the level of pay. The Commission proposed maternity leave on full pay for women with at least nine months of prior employment. British women were entitled to take maternity leave only if they had been employed with the same employer for two years (part-time workers for five years) and if they worked more than eight hours a week (Falkner et al. 2005, 80). British maternity benefits were very low and as such the directive would be very costly for Britain.

Several countries criticized the legal basis of the directive; these provisions seemed properly to concern labour conditions rather than health and safety. All reference to paternity leave was eliminated. As with all protective legislation (see the case of night work in Chapter 4), tension existed between those aiming at the maximum protection of pregnant and breastfeeding women workers (France, Germany) and those who wanted to avoid making women expensive, unattractive workers (the Netherlands) (Falkner et al. 2005).

The Dutch presidency reached a compromise which substantially lowered the costs, meaning payments would only be set at the level of sickness benefits and the eligibility threshold was raised to 12 months. The Council approved this compromise; Britain and Italy abstained (Commission 1991, No. 22). Both Commissioner Papandreou and the EP were dissatisfied with the compromise; 'pregnancy is not a sickness' but a normal biological condition and women should not be penalized for becoming mothers by linking pay during maternity leave to sickness benefits (Commission 1992, No. 27).

The EP proposed raising maternity benefits to 80 percent of previous pay and Papandreou inserted this amendment into her revised proposal. The Council could accept the amended proposal by qualified majority or stick to its previous compromise with unanimity. Eleven member states preferred to stick to the compromise, showing that they felt comfortable with the watered-down text. Only Italy preferred the stronger amended proposal. The directive remained blocked until the British presidency convinced Italy to abstain from the vote. On 19 October 1992, the weak Dutch compromise text was accepted with abstentions from Italy and Britain, who remained opposed to the directive in principle.

The Directive (92/85/EEC) set only minimum requirements, including fourteen weeks of maternity leave and the provision of pay or an allowance at least equivalent to sickness benefits. It contained a provision protecting pregnant workers against dismissal, but the provision was weaker than that afforded by the 'old' gender equality directives, so unfair dismissal cases would continue to be dealt with under the 1976 Equal Treatment Directive. The directive remained silent on the right of a woman to return to her job or an equivalent job at the end of her maternity leave nor did it cover employees on short-term and temporary contracts.

Although the directive was watered down, it still required reforms in all member states except Denmark. Some countries had to extend the length of maternity leave or the entitlement to benefits; others had to improve their schemes for protection against dismissal or legislate to protect pregnant women from unhealthy night work. As the 1976 Equal Treatment Directive did not allow a general night work ban for women, such a ban had to be introduced in a specific provision allowing pregnant women to refuse night work. The Directorate Gender Equality started an infringement procedure against the general night work ban in France. It was dismissed when France repealed the ban in order to implement the 1976 Equal Treatment Directive (see Chapter 4, *Stoeckel*). Germany has still not repealed its general night work ban for pregnant women; the Commission (the Directorate Health and Safety) had informally assured German negotiators that their ban was in line with the directive and Germany perceived its own system as superior to the EU norm (Falkner et al. 2005, 82–3).

Burden of Proof

The reversal of the burden of proof is yet another example of an instrument which had already been drafted by the Commission in the 1980s and blocked several times by opposition within the Council. In September 1994, the proposal was once more blocked in the Council by British opposition (EIRR 1994, 249:2).

The Commission decided to resort to the social dialogue procedure. On 5 July 1995, the supranational representatives of employers and trade unions were consulted. After their refusal to deal with the issue, Commissioner Pádraig Flynn sent the proposal to the EP and the Council on 20 September 1996. He argued that 'it has been shown in practice that it is difficult and sometimes impossible for complainants to prove that differences in pay or treatment amount to discrimination' (EIRR 1995, 259:30).

In cases before the national courts and in preliminary rulings by the Court, it had become clear that effective enforcement of the principle of equal treatment was often difficult, especially when someone had to bring evidence of indirect discrimination.[4] Seven member states had therefore already introduced legislation shifting the burden of proof to the employer when there was prima facie evidence of discrimination based on gender. In those cases the employer had to prove that his or her practice was not in fact discriminatory. The Commission wanted the other member states[5] to introduce such a mechanism as well in order to improve protection against discrimination and to ensure consistency in the operation of procedural rules in national courts. It based its proposal on the Court rulings (Weatherill and Beaumont 1999).

The EP welcomed the fact that finally a definition of indirect discrimination and of the burden of proof appeared in a directive, as both concepts had been interpreted in different ways in different member states. It proposed 20 amendments, which aimed primarily to clarify the definition of 'indirect discrimination', extend the scope of the directive to include parental leave and social protection, and shorten the time limit for implementation: 1 January 2000 instead of 2001 (EP 1997, A4–0115/97). The Commission accepted most of these amendments (Bulletin 1997, 5:1.3.174; Commission 1997, SYN/1996/0196).

The Council adopted a common position on 27 June. It differed significantly from the Commission proposal and took on few of the EP's amendments. In order to satisfy Britain,[6] a derogation was included to take account of certain special features of national legal systems. The Council weakened the definition of indirect discrimination, deleted all references to marital or family status as a basis for discrimination, limited the scope of the directive even further than the Commission's original proposal and excluded social security. It did not accept that the plaintiff would benefit if any doubt subsisted and retained the initial deadline for implementation (Commission 1997, SYN/1996/0196).

In its second reading, the EP again tabled the amendments to the first reading on definition and scope. Council stuck to its previous position, ignoring the amendments of the Commission and EP, and approved the directive with unanimity on 15 December 1997 (Directive 97/80/EC, Official Journal 1998, OJ L 14/6–8).

The outcome was a directive that mainly confirmed what had already been laid down by the Court. Member states clearly did not see the interests of victims of discrimination as their priority, being primarily concerned about the costs that

4 *Commission v. France* C-318/86; *Danfoss* C-109/88, *Enderby* C-127/92 and *Royal Copenhagen* C-400/93.

5 Belgium, Denmark, Greece, Ireland, Luxembourg, the Netherlands, Britain and Portugal did not have explicit legislation shifting the burden of proof in sex discrimination cases (EIRR 1995, 259:30).

6 Since the conclusion of the Treaty of Amsterdam, Britain had taken part in discussions on social policy again.

any shift in the burden of proof in social security cases would involve. As with the pregnant workers directive, all costly elements were eliminated from the draft and the cooperation procedure left the EP powerless before a unanimous Council.

Equal Treatment

Several preliminary rulings of the Court had upset governments and companies because of their far-reaching financial impact, but pleased women's groups, the Commission and others who favoured strong gender equality policies. In October 1995, however, the Court (11 judges!) delivered a ruling that upset the latter: *Eckhard Kalanke v. Freie Hansestadt Bremen* (Case C-450/93). It caused the Commission to submit a proposal amending the famous 1976 Equal Treatment Directive.

Kalanke, a German official, was refused a promotion. A female candidate, having the same qualifications, was to be given priority under the *Landesgleichstellungsgesetz* (Law on Equal Treatment for Men and Women), because women were under-represented in this sector. The implication of the ruling was that positive action measures were incompatible with the Equal Treatment Directive when the measures automatically and unconditionally gave priority to women (*ECR* 1995, I–03051).

Many were unhappy with the ruling. It seemed to conflict with the intentions of those who had drafted the Directive in the 1970s. Therefore, in March 1996, DG Employment and Social Affairs proposed a modification of Article 2(4) of the 1976 Directive in order to clarify the concepts of discrimination and determine which forms of positive action and quotas would be allowed by the Court (Commission 1996, COM(96)93). The Commission proposed 'the most neutral text possible', giving employers the possibility of choosing someone not belonging to the under-represented sex, because unanimous approval was required from all fifteen member states.[7] Even this 'neutral' proposal encountered resistance in the Council and was shelved.

The EP's Committees on Women's Rights and Legal Affairs held a joint hearing on 25 April 1996 to examine the consequences of the *Kalanke* ruling. They concluded that the IGC preparing the Amsterdam treaty reform should handle the issue. The principle of and the right to equality should be written into the Treaty. Moreover, the legal basis of Article 119 was too limited and 'poorly situated in the Treaty'; the Commission therefore had no alternative but to base its amendment on Article 235 (EWL 1996, 9–10). Another Court ruling in November 1997 had led to further confusion. In *Marschall*, Advocate General Francis Jacobs had declared the positive action policy in Nordrhein-Westfalen in breach of the Directive, in line with *Kalanke*, but the Court disagreed as the policy gave no automatic priority to women (Case C-409/95; *ECR* 1997, I-6363).

The revised treaty did indeed realize the wishes of the parliamentary committees, as Article 119 on equal pay was extended to read:

7 The Commission had to base its proposal on Art. 235, which prescribed the consultation procedure (with only an advisory role for the EP) and required unanimity in the Council.

> The Council (…) shall adopt measures to ensure the application of the principle of equal opportunities and equal treatment of men and women in matters of employment and occupation (…)'(renumbered Art. 141(4)).

In June 2000, after the treaty came into force, Commissioner Anna Diamantopoulou submitted a reframed proposal for the revision of the 1976 Directive, basing it on the extended Article 141 (Commission 2000, COM(2000)334). In this way, the codecision procedure would apply, requiring only a qualified majority in the Council.

The EP seized the occasion to pronounce on the issue. The Committee on Women's Rights advocated a fundamental rethink of the directive. It disagreed with Diamantopoulou that only limited revision was needed, codifying the existing case law of the Court (Sjerps 2000). The Committee organized expert meetings and a hearing, and in May 2001 issued its opinion (first reading), adopting the Commission proposal with 46 amendments. The amendments aimed at strengthening the directive, lifting it to the level of the Race Discrimination Directive (see next section), enabling stronger action on sexual harassment, widening the sanctions available, improving the definitions of indirect discrimination and positive action, and improving the protection against discrimination linked to pregnancy and maternity. The Commission fully or partially accepted 38 amendments and transmitted the amended proposal to the Council (Commission 2001, COM(2001)321final/2).

The Council adopted its common position on 23 July 2001. It accepted 18 amendments, and refused 17 others. It eliminated the obligations on employers to promote equality, to produce a yearly report and to nominate confidential counsellors, one of the proposed measures to tackle harassment and sexual harassment. The Council justified this refusal by referring to the 'autonomy of management and labour'. Council rejected the idea of entitling groups or organizations to submit complaints to equal opportunities commissions. It also refused to give a 'legal role' to equal opportunities commissions: they could assist victims of discrimination in starting legal proceedings, but they should have no role in examining complaints (Council 2001, 9848/01 ADD 1).

The Commission found that the common position went further than the initial proposal but regretted that the Council had not shown more ambition (Commission 2001, SEC(2001)1332). In October 2001, the EP approved the common position of the Council with 15 amendments, reintroducing the elements which the Council had eliminated (EP 2001, A5-0358/2001). The Commission accepted seven amendments (Commission 2001, COM(2001)689). As the Council disagreed with some amendments, in February 2002, a conciliation committee was convened. Four 'trialogues' between 15 MEPs and 15 representatives of the Council were necessary to reach agreement.

The problematic issues were the definition of sexual harassment, the obligation on employers to take preventive measures, the role of equal opportunity bodies, and protection in case of pregnancy and maternity leave (EP 2002, PE 287.611). The committee agreed on a joint text on 17 April 2002 which was approved by the

EP and Council on its third reading in June 2002. After twenty-five years, Directive 76/207/EEC was replaced by Directive 2002/73/EC.

In three readings, the EP managed to include new elements that considerably increased the costs of the amended directive for member states, requiring more legislative changes in more member states. The directive now contains a clear definition of the different types of discrimination, including for the first time an explicit recognition of harassment and sexual harassment[8] as a form of sex discrimination (Gregory 2000). It has strengthened the protection of women in case of pregnancy and maternity, including the right to return to the same job after maternity leave. It provides for sanctions, and obliges member states to create specific bodies to ensure compliance with equality legislation, and to issue follow-up reports every four years.

The involvement of Parliament lifted the directive to a level above the minimum common denominator. The co-decision procedure indeed seems to create a window of opportunity for costly gender equality policies, when compared to the consultation and cooperation procedures, as member states can no longer adopt a directive against the will of the EP, one of the actors in favour of strong gender equality legislation.[9]

New Issues

The scope of supranational legislation on gender equality has recently been extended to include other grounds of discrimination, to promote equality outside the workplace and tackle violence against women.

Multiple Discriminations

As enlargement with Central and Eastern European countries drew closer and with it the prospect of new member states with less experience of democracy, member states wanted to confirm their commitment to the principles of liberty, democracy, respect for human rights and fundamental freedoms, as well as to have the power to suspend member states' privileges should any breach of these principles take place (Art. 6 and 7 TEU).

---

8 Sexual harassment is 'any form of unwanted verbal, non-verbal or physical conduct of a sexual nature that occurs with the purpose or effect of violating the dignity of a person, in particular when creating an intimidating, hostile, degrading, humiliating or offensive environment' (Directive 2002/73/EC).

9 The proliferation of equality directives and Court rulings has inspired the Commission to propose a Recast Directive, which aims to 'simplify, modernise and improve EC law on equal treatment between women and men in matters of employment and occupation' by amalgamating the relevant gender equality directives and case law into one single text (COM(2004)279 final). Parliament has tried to use the opportunity to extend the scope of existing legislation, but in vain (COM(2005)380final). The Recast Directive 2006/54/EC was approved by the EP at its second reading on 1 June 2006.

Article 13 of the Treaty of Amsterdam provides a general legal basis for legislation to address discrimination beyond employment and also on grounds other than sex such as racial or ethnic origin, religion, belief, disability, age, or sexual orientation. The Council adopts directives based on this article by unanimity, with the EP playing only an advisory role (consultation procedure). Due to rising levels of xenophobia and racism, there was strong political pressure for action in this field. In December 1999, the Commission presented two draft directives based on Article 13, which were both approved in 2000. Neither covers sex discrimination because of the already existing directives in this field. The EP formulated its criticisms and suggestions, but use of the consultation procedure meant the Council could ignore them.

The first directive prohibits discrimination on the grounds of race or ethnic origin (Directive 2000/43/EC). For the first time, women belonging to an ethnic minority could go to court in the case of perceived discrimination on grounds of ethnic origin. In several respects, the race discrimination directive is stronger than the sex discrimination *acquis*. It covers discrimination outside the world of work in education, access to and supply of goods and social protection; it opens up the possibility of group legal action; it clearly prohibits harassment; it provides for the establishment of an independent equality agency; it contains more explicit provisions for sanctions, and plaintiffs are allowed to produce a hypothetical 'comparator', which is not accepted in sex discrimination cases.

As a result, it was feared that differences might arise between the level of protection offered to women and men from ethnic minorities and white women and men, creating an 'equality hierarchy' (EP 2004, A5-0155/2004, 28). This motivated the Commission and the EP to modify the 'old' 76/207 Equal Treatment Directive more thoroughly than had initially been planned (see previous section).

The second directive establishes a general framework for equal treatment in employment and occupation (Directive 2000/78/EC). It prohibits discrimination based on religion or belief, disability, age or sexual orientation. It forbids direct and indirect discrimination, and it deems harassment a form of discrimination. Despite criticisms from employers, the burden of proof was shifted in accordance with the burden of proof directive (1997).

The directive was important for women who are often the victims of multiple forms of discrimination, because they are overrepresented among unemployed, religious minorities, disabled and elderly people. Women's organizations and other non-governmental organizations were therefore concerned that the scope of the directive was limited to employment and that it failed to address the fight against sex discrimination. To counteract these shortcomings, legal experts asked for a link between this directive and the 76/207 Directive in order to combat multiple discrimination and realize equal opportunities for women (Holtmaat et al. 2000). This request was taken up by Parliament when it formulated amendments to the 76/207 Directive.

Equal Treatment in the Access to and the Supply of Goods and Services

On 5 November 2003, Commissioner Diamantopoulou submitted a proposal for a directive to ban gender discrimination in the access to and supply of goods and services. Already in its Social Policy Agenda of June 2000, the Commission had announced its intention to promote gender equality in areas other than employment and professional life and in December 2000, the European Council in Nice had approved the initiative of the Commission to submit a proposal for a directive to this end (Commission 2003, COM(2003)657).

After the approval of the directive combating race discrimination outside the workplace, there was considerable pressure from the EP and women's organizations to extend the scope of the fight against sex-based discrimination in the same sense. Due to strong opposition from the insurance and media industries and from the British and German governments, and also to divergent opinions within the Commission, it took the Commission a further three years to submit a proposal. Diamantopoulou had to eliminate advertising, media,[10] and taxation (EP 2004, PE 337.825, 23).

The proposal explicitly prohibits the consideration of gender as a factor in calculating premiums and benefits for insurance and related financial services (pensions, life insurance, health insurance, motor insurance). Diamantopoulou deemed the provision important because increasingly, state social insurance schemes are being replaced by private ones which often disadvantage women (Commission 2003, SEC(2003)1213).

The proposal was immediately 'greeted with pessimism from some parts of industry' (Commission 2003, Press Release IP/03/1501). The *Comité Européen des Assurances* (CEA) and national insurance associations feared serious repercussions in their sector and threatened to raise all premiums (Buddingh and de Waard 2003). Interestingly, a comparison of insurers' practices showed that the 'objective' life expectancy tables used vary by over 100% between the member states. France and Portugal use a single, though different, rate for men and women (Commission 2003, SEC(2003)1213). Women often pay higher premiums for pensions on the grounds that they live longer, and men pay higher premiums in motor insurance on the grounds that they cause more accidents, whereas the Commission argued that in both cases a number of factors other than sex play an equally important role.

The proposal was based on Article 13, which meant that the EP only could give advice and unanimity was required in the Council. This was a potentially costly proposal: for the first time unequal treatment of women and men outside the workplace was tackled and European citizens – as opposed to 'workers' – would be able to claim their rights before the courts. The Advisory Committee on Equal Opportunities for Women and Men and the European Women's Lobby would have preferred a broader directive including equal treatment in education, media, advertising and taxation (Commission 2003, SEC(2003)1213). The EP's Committee on Women's Rights also

10 German tabloid '*Bild*' warned its readers that 'EU-feminists want to forbid sexy cover girls' who 'sweeten our sad daily office life' (Ceiber Weiber 2003).

expressed regret that the scope of the directive had been limited to goods and services. The EP proposed 34 amendments, aimed at strengthening the directive and ensuring consistency with the other Article 13-directives (EP 2004, A5–0155/2004).

Member state representatives were not concerned about gender equality but mainly about the potential impact on the insurance sector and expressed many reservations (Council 2004, Doc. 9263/04; Doc. 9426/1/04). Ireland, holding the Presidency, tried to clarify the discussion on the use of gender as an actuarial factor in the Social Affairs Council (Council 2004, Press release 9507/04). In October, Council was able to reach political agreement on the directive; Germany disagreed but did not want to block the draft directive 'given the importance which all the other delegations attach to the directive' and abstained (Council 2004, Doc. 13137/04 ADD 1).

The compromise restricted the use of gender-based data and enabled member states to derogate from the principle. The Council gave its formal approval on 14 December 2004. The watering-down of the ban on the use of gender as an actuarial factor meant that the directive was warmly welcomed by the European insurers (CEA) and met with heavy criticism from the EWL and consumer groups (Commission 2004, COM(2004)115).

A divided Commission, intense lobbying by strong interest groups and a legislative procedure which limited the EP's role to a purely consultative one all go to explain this modest outcome. In this case, the use of QMV instead of unanimity would not have changed the outcome, since most member states preferred the minimum common denominator. Still, the directive finally opens up some possibilities for tackling sex discrimination outside the workplace and gives the Court a role in this process.

Sexual Harassment and Violence against Women

As the ambition of European legislation is no longer restricted to the realization of equal pay, as it was in 1957, but has been extended to include the promotion of equal treatment and the fight against discrimination, it becomes difficult to exclude the issue of violence against women.

Already in 1984, in a report by Dutch MEP D'Ancona, the EP had argued that sexual violence was a barrier to the social and economic integration of women. It had adopted a resolution calling for action against sexual harassment in the workplace, sexual violence, trafficking, prostitution and pornography (*Official Journal* 1986, OJ C 176/73). The Council saw no reason to undertake action on most of the topics, as they were still too far removed from the workplace. The issue of sexual harassment, however, had a clear link with employment and equal treatment. In the case of a young woman apprentice motor mechanic in 1983, a British court had ruled that sexual harassment constituted unlawful discrimination (Collins 1996).

In 1986, at the informal meeting under the Dutch presidency (p. 138), the Ministers for Women's Issues discussed the issue and asked the Commission to undertake an enquiry. The resulting report concluded that a directive was needed to offer adequate protection for those suffering sexual harassment, but Commissioner Manuel Marin did not want to add another draft directive to the list of directives already being blocked by the Council (see Chapter 4).

His successor Papandreou was determined to use her mandate for social policy to make progress on the issue of sexual harassment. She framed sexual harassment as an obstacle to the proper integration of women into the labour market and protection from harassment as a precondition for equal treatment. The Irish Presidency supported her initiative and during the first half of 1990 she submitted a draft resolution. The Council approved the non-binding resolution to show that it took the issue seriously, although its recommendations constituted symbolic rather than effective action.

Women's groups (AVFT in France, *Handen Thuis* [Hands Off] in the Netherlands and WASH in Britain) exerted strong pressure on national governments and on the Commission to develop a more effective instrument. The Commission adopted a non-binding 'Recommendation on the protection of the dignity of women and men at work' and a 'Code of Practice on Measures to Combat Sexual Harassment' (*Official Journal* 1992, OJ L 49/4).

The recommendation had many weaknesses: the issue was not framed as 'sex-based discrimination' but in a gender-neutral way as 'protection of dignity'; it required the victim to complain about the behaviour before it may be considered harassment; the list enumerating offensive types of behaviour was eliminated from the recommendation; the recommendation was not binding. However, despite these weaknesses, it was expected to strengthen the rights of employees who brought their cases to court because national courts and the Court would, where relevant, take the contents of the recommendation into account. Several member states even introduced national legislation, although this was not always deemed effective because sexual harassment was only recognized as such if it was 'intentional behaviour', which is hard to prove (Baer 1996).

In 1996, the Commission decided to consult the European organizations of employers and trade unions on a text outlining proposals for the prevention of sexual harassment at work. They confirmed the importance of the problem, but after two rounds of consultation they were not able to agree on the need to negotiate a collective agreement on sexual harassment. In 1999, the Commission undertook an enquiry and concluded that between 40 and 50 percent of female employees had experienced some form of sexual harassment; that awareness of the phenomenon was very poor, and that proper legislation was lacking in most member states. In the Explanatory Memorandum for the revised 76/207 Equal Treatment Directive, the Commission simply stated that 'a very important and sensitive issue like sexual harassment could no longer be ignored and had to be addressed at Community level' (Commission 2000, COM(2000)334, 4).

Finally, as part of the new Equal Treatment Directive, the Council approved a fuller definition of sexual harassment in a binding instrument which required action on the part of member states, management and labour, and allowed recourse to national courts and the Court (see previous section).

The larger issue of violence against women entered the European arena through pressure from women's organizations, the EWL and the EP (Hanmer 1996). Several international instruments had already addressed this issue,[11] culminating in the approval in 1993 of the UN Declaration on the Elimination of Violence against Women. During regional preparatory meetings for the Fourth World Conference on Women (Beijing 1995), the issue of violence against women was on the agenda. Nonetheless, pressure on EU member states to deal with this issue failed to produce any strong supranational legal framework. Member states have not been willing to give up national competence in this area.

A window of opportunity for addressing the issue of violence against women was opened up by the aim of completing the internal market and the eastern enlargement. The establishment of an internal market where capital, goods, services and persons could freely circulate required the transfer of border controls to the external borders of the EU. This in turn required the application of common, uniform standards on the admission of persons such as asylum seekers, immigrants and refugees into the Union. It also required measures to deal with cross-border crime, including the trafficking of women and children. The enlargement of the EU to eastern and central European countries increased the urgency of such requirements as it was feared that enlargement would increase the potential for trafficking and sexual exploitation. Although the criminal law aspects of violence remain a matter for member states, this extension of the supranational domain of action has opened up opportunities for supranational measures to tackle sexual exploitation and sexual violence.

As a legal basis for dealing with the issue, the Commission chose not the equality article but the only article in the whole treaty concerning public health, which had been inserted into the treaty in Maastricht (now Art. 152 EC). The advantage of this article was that the codecision procedure applied, involving the EP and requiring only a qualified majority in the Council. The Commission sought to extend the definition of public health beyond the 'absence of disease and infirmity' to include physical, mental and social well-being. In this way, the consequences of sexual violence could be presented as a public health problem, requiring action by the EU. The disadvantage was that in the domain of public health, the Commission was permitted only to propose 'incentive measures' and 'specific action' that would support and supplement national policies. The member states had excluded legal action.

After a series of EP resolutions, the Council and EP adopted a programme on preventive measures to fight violence towards children, young persons and women (Daphne I, 2000–2003, *Official Journal* 2000, OJ L 34; Daphne II, 2004–2008). The programme is limited to supportive measures in the domain of prevention and the funding of activities to support victims of violence. It has not yet been possible to develop binding legislative instruments to tackle sexual violence. This remains an area of member state competence.

---

11 Several UN conventions; the Resolution on Violence in the Family of the Council of Europe (1985).

Conclusion

The scope of gender equality has been widened thanks to extension of European competences into fields like race discrimination and public health. The potential of Treaty Article 13 is huge as it transcends the work/non-work division and concerns not only workers but all citizens. Article 13 has no direct effect, so citizens can only invoke the rights they derive from it before the court in as far as their rights have been codified by directives. However, as long as the Council dominates decision making (unanimity, consultation), which seeks to avoid costly policies in new domains, the potential of the article will not be fully realized.

New Instruments

Gender Mainstreaming

In the Treaty of Rome, equal pay was about preventing the distortion of competition. In the Treaty of Amsterdam, equality between women and men became an explicit objective in Article 2, complemented by Article 3(2) which assigns to the EU the task of eliminating inequalities and promoting equality between men and women in all its activities. These treaty articles embody the principle of 'gender mainstreaming', which means 'integration of gender equality considerations in all activities and policies at all levels' (CEC 1998a, 22). Why did the member states approve such a far-reaching strategy, and does it give rise to costly policies in same way that 'old strategies' such as the development of binding legal instruments have done?

Mainstreaming in the Treaty A general commitment binding member states to promote gender equality had already been formulated as early as 1977 in *Defrenne III* (Case 149/77). The Court stated that the freedom from discrimination based on gender constitutes a part of fundamental rights, and that the economic aim pursued by Article 141 is secondary to the social aim which constitutes the expression of a fundamental right (*ECR* 1977, 1365). The concept of gender mainstreaming first appeared in Commission documents in 1989, in a working paper by Helle Jacobsen, a Danish expert on equal opportunities. It was also mentioned in the 3rd Medium Term Action Programme for Equal Opportunities (1991–5) of the Commission and it was discussed at seminars organized by the Commission and the Portuguese and Danish Presidencies, respectively, in 1992 and 1993.

Nevertheless, the concept remained imprecise and its results invisible. It became effective only after 'Beijing'. This time lag can be explained by a lack of expertise, plus the fact that the concept first met with scepticism among 'women's advocates' in the Commission and the European Parliament. They feared that such a vague and general strategy would lead to the abandonment of specific actions on behalf of women (Stratigaki 2000). Following the very limited success of the efforts made to develop further gender equality legislation during the first half of the 1990s, and the evident limitations of formal equality and women's rights within the workplace, they were ready to support mainstreaming as a complementary strategy.

Simultaneous triple pressure helped mainstreaming to put down constitutional 'roots'. There was strong pressure at the global level at the World Conference on Women in Beijing (1995), where women's rights were defined as human rights and therefore not limited to sectoral policies but part of general policy guidelines. The strategy of gender mainstreaming fitted this concept. Furthermore, domestic pressure was increasing from women's organizations that brought the idea of gender mainstreaming home from Beijing, pushing it onto national agendas. Their pressure was effectively coordinated by the EWL. They benefited from the fact that during the IGC charged with preparing the Amsterdam treaty revision, non-governmental organizations were for the first time informed and heard by the responsible Commissioner Marcellino Oreja.

The EWL submitted a coherent set of proposals to the IGC, including the demand for the introduction of a new title 'to provide a legal base for equality between women and men in all areas of life' (EWL 1996). The EP, which for the first time was represented during the deliberations by two observers, also supported the strengthening of women's rights as human rights (EP 1995, A4–0102/95/DEEL II/VROU). There was also pressure to come up with a new strategy for equality from pioneer states, especially the newcomers Sweden and Finland,[12] and from the Nordic Commissioners and the female members of the new European Commission.[13] In March 1996, the Commissioners' Group on Equal Opportunities[14] declared that mainstreaming was the new official policy.

The main aim of the Amsterdam treaty reform was to adapt the institutions and procedures to the forthcoming 'Eastern enlargement', which would enlarge EU membership to include at least 25 members, in order to ensure the functioning of the EU. A secondary aim was to increase the legitimacy of EU policies, which was seen to be lacking after the ratification problems surrounding 'Maastricht'.[15] The EU was to be associated with solidarity and democracy, tackling the problem of ever increasing unemployment, which had crossed the psychological barrier of 10 percent (women:

12 In 1995, the EU was enlarged with Austria, Finland and Sweden.

13 The Commission under the presidency of Jacques Santer (1995–99) counted no less than five women (25 percent): Monika Wulf-Matthies, Emma Bonino, Anita Gradin, Edith Cresson and Ritt Bjerregaard.

14 During the hearings of the candidate Commissioners, the EP had not been very happy with the renewal of the conservative Irish Commissioner Pádraig Flynn for Employment and Social Affairs, including Equal Opportunities. Thereafter, Commission President Santer created a Group on Equal Opportunities, composed of four Commissioners and chaired by the President, in order to convince the Parliament of the importance attached to gender equality and to obtain their support for Flynn.

15 In June 1992, the Danish people rejected the treaty reform (Danish women represented 60 percent of the no-votes); in September 1992 followed an extremely narrow French 'yes'; there were difficulties in the British parliament and a critical ruling of the Federal Constitutional Court in Germany.

12.6 percent) in 1994, and addressing the lack of popular support for EMU which would start its third stage in 1999. However, the crucial member states – France, Germany and Britain – were not able to reach agreement on institutional reform and the solution of all key issues (the number of Commissioners, voting weights in the Council) had to be put off to yet another treaty revision track which later resulted in the Treaty of Nice.

These apparent failures were offset by some incremental reforms strengthening the notions of European citizenship, human rights and democratic values (see also previous section on Article 13 and discrimination), transparency (including the renumbering of all treaty articles and simplifying of procedures), a new title on employment which owed its inclusion to strong pressure from the French socialist Prime Minister Lionel Jospin, and the addition of a new clause to Article 3, providing that 'In all the activities referred to in this Article, the Community shall aim to eliminate inequalities, and to promote equality, between men and women' (Art. 3(2) EC). Already feeling bound to act by the promises made in Beijing and not fully aware of the 'revolutionary potential' of the concept, governments approved what would become known among gender experts as 'The Mainstreaming Article'.

Monitoring Mainstreaming Gender mainstreaming is a strategy with an ambiguous profile, as the reluctant reactions from women's advocates and the relatively easy approval given by member states testify (Beveridge and Nott 2002; Stratigaki 2004). On the one hand, it is a 'demanding strategy' (Bretherton 2001 61), as successful implementation requires that 'a gender equality perspective is incorporated into all policies at all levels and at all stages, by the actors normally involved in policymaking' (Council of Europe 1998, 7). But mainstreaming goes further than the promotion of equality: it is not about 'balancing the statistics', but about stimulating lasting change in the roles and behaviour of both women and men. It widens the scope for agenda setting because it allows the Commission to introduce gender concerns into all policy domains. It gives women's organizations a tool to put 'gender' on every agenda.

On the other hand, mainstreaming is a strategy, and not an instrument that is legally binding upon all actors concerned. It relies upon 'soft' policy instruments, including guidelines, codes of practice, targets, benchmarking, and the exchange of good practice between member states (Mazey 2002). This raises the question of whether the strategy leads to the inclusion of gender in binding instruments, resulting in costly policies.[16]

Mainstreaming means that Commission officials who are involved in policy making in many different areas have to be convinced of the importance of gender equality. The chances of adopting 'their' policy may be reduced when a gender

---

16 Lately, strategies have proliferated: the European Employment Strategy (a voluntary process of peer review) aims to make labour markets more flexible and to boost employment (1997), and the Lisbon Strategy (2000) aims to give the EU 'the most dynamic economy in the world' by 2010. The results have been modest (Bomberg and Stubb 2003).

impact assessment reveals that an apparently gender-neutral policy will have unintended gender-specific negative consequences. Officials have to be 'seduced' into implementing gender mainstreaming by strategic framing – which Verloo refers to for this reason as a 'velvet revolution' (Verloo 2001). It is to be expected that member states will mainstream a policy when mainstreaming leads only to marginal changes in the distribution of costs and benefits between and within states. They will ignore it when mainstreaming would substantially increase costs or lead to a redistribution of benefits between and within states. Still, member states are concerned about their prestige. If refusal to apply gender mainstreaming damages their prestige, the costs of non-mainstreaming may tip the balance towards implementation of the strategy. So the effectiveness of mainstreaming as a strategy depends on the extent to which implementation is controlled and enforced.

The Commission monitors progress in an annual report to the Spring Summit of the European Council.[17] The Commission does not apply a coherent set of criteria for assessing gender mainstreaming[18] but rather assesses the position of women and the actions undertaken. The reports do not identify specific shortcomings or violations: there is no blaming – and no shaming. The monitoring procedure does not therefore provide sufficient pressure to increase the cost of non-mainstreaming for unwilling governments. The most tangible results of ten years of mainstreaming are the increased availability of gender-desegregated data, the development of gender-sensitive indicators and the inclusion of gender equality in Structural Funds projects (Braithwaite 2000).

The 'Gender Scoreboard' shows mixed results regarding the implementation of gender mainstreaming by the Commission services (Commission 2001, COM(2001)119). There are positive results in 'traditionally gender sensitive policy domains' like education and development cooperation. Moreover, some previously 'gender-blind' services, namely Trade, Environment, Internal Market and EcoFin, have 'for the first time ever' taken gender equality initiatives. Optimism is tempered, however, by the fact that some services continue 'to do practically nothing (…) apart from paying lip service' (Commission 2001, COM(2001)119). The assessment of the gender balance within committees and expert groups shows that the target of 40 percent minimum participation of women has only been attained in the fields of Education & Culture and Employment.

Pollack and Hafner-Burton (2000) cite two main factors to explain the uneven implementation of gender mainstreaming across Commission services. The first factor is the resonance between the proposed frame (mainstreaming being interventionist, solidarity-oriented) and the dominant frame of the directorate-general (interventionist

17 Commission 2004, COM(2004)115; Commission 2005, COM(2005)44 and Commission 2006, COM(2006)71.

18 Lombardo shows how the application of a consistent set of criteria for recognizing gender mainstreaming to the European Convention and the Constitutional Treaty leads to a more sophisticated and insightful assessment (Lombardo 2005).

or non-interventionist, solidarity-oriented or neo-liberal, etc.). This factor can also be 'translated' as the ideological costs attached to a proposal of policy mainstreaming.

The second factor is the openness or the political opportunities offered by the EU institutions involved (the extent to which the institution is open to non-state actors). This factor can be 'translated' as the political costs attached to a proposal. The ideological and political costs vary between Commission services. A policy field will be more 'gender mainstreamed' if the ideological and political costs are low.

Bretherton, who investigated the implementation of mainstreaming in the accession process of the Central and East European countries (CEEC),[19] confirms the findings of Pollack and Hafner-Burton. Because the CEEC had to absorb the full *acquis*, the accession process offered an occasion to apply mainstreaming transversally to all 'chapters'. However, there was no substantial pressure within the Commission to apply gender mainstreaming to the accession process. It was even argued that social policy aspects of the *acquis* should be set aside to facilitate accession (Bretherton 2001).

The Commission did not apply gender mainstreaming in the individual country reports undertaken to assess the measures necessary in each country to satisfy the requirements of the *acquis*. The coordinating service during enlargement negotiations was DG Relex (External Relations), where a lack of awareness and expertise limited the introduction of gender mainstreaming (Bretherton 2001, 75). It is telling that the service did not reply at all to the 'Scoreboard survey' on mainstreaming (Commission 2001, COM(2001)119). Pressure in favour of gender mainstreaming came only from DG Employment, Commissioner Diamantopoulou, and the EP. The ideological and political benefits of mainstreaming were minimal. The fact that the Commission made no gender impact assessments in the framework of the accession negotiations is even more unfortunate as the status of women in CEEC has deteriorated during the transition period.

In order to tackle the gender gap, targets have been set in the Employment Guidelines (adopted in September 2001), asking member states to raise the female employment rate from 53 to 60 percent in 2010. However, no guidelines have been provided on how to reach this target and there is no method of imposing sanctions on those member states who do not reach it.

It is not only at the supranational level that the prospects for 'mainstreaming' are mixed, but also at the national level (Liebert 2002). The ambiguity of mainstreaming provisions means that their effectiveness is dependent on the national context (Verloo 2001; Walby 2005). As Stratigaki aptly summarizes, only in Scandinavian countries has the balance between paid work and family life meant that 'more men take care of their children' rather than 'fewer women are in full-time employment' (Stratigaki 2000, 47). As the 'mainstreaming article' does not require legal guarantees, domestic implementation of the principle is left to non-binding instruments. This deprives

19 On 1 May 2004, eight CEEC became member of the EU (as well as the island states Cyprus and Malta): Czech Republic, Estonia, Hungary, Latvia, Lithuania, Poland, Slovakia, and Slovenia.

women of the possibility to claim their rights and 'sandwich' the government through the judicial pincer mechanism, as the Commission and the Court cannot play their monitoring and enforcing roles.

Summarizing the argument, gender mainstreaming aims to widen the scope of gender equality policies, and to change the contents of supranational policies, for instance in the fields of transport, health, immigration, agriculture, the single market, cohesion and the environment. The procedures by which the strategy is implemented, however, mean that those actors unwilling to support progress in the field of gender equality can get away with lip service, while advocates of gender mainstreaming have no means of putting effective pressure on member states or to 'sandwich' them.

A Mainstreamed Constitution?

After the limited success of the Amsterdam and Nice treaty reforms, the European Council decided to tackle the unfinished business and push for a new founding document for the EU, a Constitutional Treaty. From February 2002 to July 2003 a Constitutional Convention was held, involving representatives of national parliaments, civil society and EP, followed by the 2004 IGC. The 'European Constitution' was signed in Rome on 29 October 2004 by the heads of state and government. However, the ratification process went less smoothly than in 1957 (see p. 51–2). In France and the Netherlands, a majority of the population voted 'no'. Since then, a prolonged phase of 'reflection' has set in.

Does the Constitution, if the text will be ratified as it is, present new opportunities for the development of strong gender equality instruments? Lombardo shows that progress in the field of gender equality is limited. The concept of gender equality has not been extended beyond the workplace and the legal basis of gender policy has not been strengthened (Lombardo 2005, 420–22). This might be explained by the under-representation of women in the constitution-making process (León et al. 2003), the dominant neoliberal identity of the EU and unwillingness of member states to get caught another time in costly measures precisely in this field: the 'boomerang effect' (p. 27).

Yet, the present deadlock offers also opportunities for strengthening the gender dimension of the treaty. If governments feel forced to convince European citizens of the importance of further integration, this always has increased their sensitivity to citizens' demands, resulting in a stronger 'social dimension' than they initially intended. In the past, women have each time benefited from such an 'unattractive status quo' (see Chapters 3–4). Still, two conditions have to be fulfilled: the commitment of pioneer states, the Presidency of the Council, the president of the Commission and the Commissioner in charge of social affairs; and pressure by women at national and European levels.

Implementation: Change or Continuity?

During the 1990s, how well did France, Germany, the Netherlands and Britain fare when it came to implementing costly equality directives? The number of infringement procedures has remained limited to on average less than one per year (see Table 5.2). Nonetheless, since the *Defrenne* cases in the 1970s, the number of preliminary rulings on gender equality has continued to increase, creating an impressive collection of case law (see Table 5.2). The Court has given its interpretation on aspects of the Equal Treatment Directive (76/207) in over 40 cases. The number of rulings varies considerably between member states. When we look at the four member states from our sample, German and British courts have been very active, whereas French courts have been reluctant to ask for Court interpretations and the Netherlands occupies a middle position. However, few preliminary rulings do not necessarily indicate that implementation has been successful but rather that the national legal system is not easily accessible. We will discuss some interesting cases where member states had to pay a higher price than they initially were willing to do.

Table 5.2 Gender equality rulings of the Court (1957–2005), EU-15

	Preliminary Rulings			Infringement Procedures		
	1957–1991	1992–2005	Total	1957–1991	1992–2005	Total
Austria	–	8	8	–	1	1
Belgium	4	6	10	1	1	2
Denmark	2	5	7	1	–	1
Finland	–	1	1	–	–	–
France	1	7	8	2	2	4
Germany	8	38	46	1	–	1
Greece	–	2	2	–	2	2
Ireland	4	1	5	–	–	–
Italy	–	1	1	1	1	2
Luxembourg	–	–	0	1	1	2
the Netherlands	9	13	22	–	–	–
Portugal	–	–	0	–	–	–
Spain	–	2	2	–	–	–
Sweden	–	2	2	–	–	–
UK	14	35	49	2	–	2
Total	42	121	163	9	8	17

Source: http://ec.europa.eu/employment_social/gender_equality/legislation/case_law_en.html. Compiled by the author.

France

Concerning the implementation of the set of directives which were approved between 1986 and 1997, France did not encounter major problems. In all cases, French legislation contained norms that were superior to the provisions contained in the directives (Reuter and Mazur 2003). The fact that directives concerning the combination of work and care (parental leave, pregnancy) created less problems in France than in some other states is not explained by the 'equality ideology' in state regulations of the labour market, however. It is rather the result of long-term French preoccupation with birth rates and family policy, resulting in generous provisions for leave. For this reason, implementation was not costly at all.

Infringement Procedures The major issue during the 1990s was the lifting of protectionist measures for women, in particular the ban on night work, as required by the 1976 Equal Treatment Directive. There was little support for the lifting of such measures. This was seen not only as hurting the interests of women and violating the French tradition of protecting the family, but also as an example of neoliberal market-oriented ideology. Only the heaviest instrument of supranational pressure, the threat of a 142,425 Euros per day penalty for non-compliance, pushed France to introduce new legislation (see p. 122).

The same law dealt with the issue of night work for pregnant women where changes were necessary to comply with the Pregnancy and Maternity Directive (92/85/EEC). This directive also required France to introduce specific leave for health and safety reasons connected with pregnancy. The French government stated that French regulation 'provided sufficient or even better protection' (Falkner et al. 2005, 84). As with the ban on night work, implementation was controversial because doctors, trade unions, feminist experts and politicians all thought that amending the existing law would lead to a less favourable situation (CNLE, 2001, 1:17). Double judicial pressure was necessary before the government gave in. After a Letter of Formal Notice, in August 2000, the Commission sent a Reasoned Opinion. Almost simultaneously, the French Court of Cassation ruled on a case concerning pregnant stewardesses employed by Air France, upon which the government implemented the directive by *Ordonnance* No. 2001/173 (*Journal Officiel* 2001, 3018).

As far back as 1983, France had dealt with the issue of the burden of proof in the Roudy Act, which shifted the burden of proof to the employer (see Chapter 4). One of the reasons that litigation on the grounds of (in-)equality remained very limited was the fact that the concept of indirect discrimination was not understood and there was no protection for the complainants against victimization (CNLE 1998, 12). France therefore had to change the Roudy Act. The Directive on the burden of proof had to be implemented by 20 January 2001, but due to parliamentary elections the law was not adopted on time. In addition, parliamentary discussions showed considerable divergence between the two chambers, as the Senate required that the worker who felt victim of discrimination should 'establish the facts' whereas in the bill of law, the worker should only 'present factual elements' (CNLE 2001, 2:19). Only in

November 2001 was a new law passed (*Loi* No. 2001-1066) which implemented the reversal of the burden of proof in the Labour Code (CNLE 2002, 1:18).

Correct implementation of the Social Security Directive (86/378, amended by Directive 96/97 in order to integrate the *Barber* ruling) also necessitated an infringement procedure. The French Social Security Code implemented Directive 86/378, but made some exceptions relating to the pension age and the conditions of entitlement to a 'reversion pension' (a pension after the death of a partner). As a result, widowers were not treated equally to widows. These exceptions were rejected by the *Barber* judgment. After condemnation by the Court (C-354/98), *Ordonnance* 2001/178 abrogated the paragraph that provided for these exceptions (*Journal Officiel* 2001, 3018).

Preliminary Rulings In 2001, two preliminary rulings upset France. Both concerned pensions and, once again, special provisions for women. *Mouflin* (Case C-206/00) concerned the French provision which granted female civil servants the right to take early retirement in order to care for their disabled or terminally ill husband, but granted no equivalent right to male workers. In December 2001, the Court concluded that the provision infringed the equal pay principle.

Under the French Civil and Military Pensions Code, the retirement pension of civil servant mothers (and not fathers) was calculated according to the number of years worked plus one year per child born. This rule was challenged in *Griesmar* (Case C-366/99). Following the reasoning of the French government, Advocate General Albert concluded that there was no breach of the principle of equal pay because the provision was designed to offset the professional disadvantages which result from raising children. The Court, however, disagreed since this reasoning equated maternity with the raising of children. In November 2001, it ruled that pensions were to be considered wages and that the provision (one year extra per child) infringed the principle of equal pay as it excluded male civil servants (CNLE 2001 and 2002). The French *Conseil d'état* followed the Court ruling. In December 2004, the law on pensions was amended, extending the rights to male civil servants (CNLE 2005).

Paradoxically, European equal rights legislation has benefited French men more than French women as some protective measures have been extended to the former whereas other protective measures have been lifted for the latter. The issue of protective measures for women and their 'European' prohibition is the only issue where France was confronted with ideologically and politically costly measures. In those cases, strong double pressure was necessary to obtain implementation.

Germany

Correct implementation of the Pregnancy and Maternity Directive required the government to amend the Maternity Protection Act in order to guarantee full maternity leave of 14 weeks in cases of early birth and 3 weeks post-birth leave for mothers of stillborn children (CNLE 2001, 3:20). However, this was a minor amendment. Preliminary rulings asking for interpretation of the 'old' Equal Pay Article (Art. 141) and the 'old' directives, especially the 1976 Equal Treatment Directive had more far-reaching consequences.

Based on Article 141, in the joint cases *Sievers* and *Schrage* (C–270/97 and C–271/97), the Court ruled that *Deutsche Post* had discriminated against part-time workers and had to extend its occupational pension scheme to include them. Following the ruling, *Deutsche Post* announced plans to raise the postage for standard letters from 1.10 to 1.20 DM because it would cost them more than one million DM in retrospective pension contributions for its 30,000 part-time workers. After strong public opposition, the company dropped the plan to raise prices, but it could not escape implementation of the ruling as both the German Federal Labour Court and the Federal Constitutional Court confirmed the ruling (CNLE 2000, 1:59).

Even more far-reaching was *Kreil* (Case C-285/98). In July 1998, the Administrative Court Hannover asked the Court for a preliminary ruling on the interpretation of the Equal Treatment Directive. Tanja Kreil had applied for work in the maintenance (weapon electronics) branch of the *Bundeswehr* [army]. Her application was rejected on the grounds that Article 12A of the Constitution excludes women from the armed services. Women can enlist only in the medical and the military-music services.

The German government argued that Community law does not govern matters of defence, 'which remain within member states' sphere of sovereignty' (*ECR* 2000, 144). Even if the Directive could apply to the armed forces, the exclusion of women from certain posts was justifiable under Article 2 of the 1976 Directive concerning the protection of women, particularly as regards pregnancy and maternity. In January 2000, the Court, composed of no less than nine judges, ruled that the complaint of Kreil was valid.

The ruling caused quite a political stir. 'Soon the equality directive will force upon us that the next Chancellor is a woman', Edmund Stoiber, Prime Minister of Bavaria, quipped (Weinlein 2000, 7). Over 2,000 women immediately applied for jobs in the *Bundeswehr* (Hühn 2000, 9). Of course, this was not the first time that the issue of the position of women in the army had surfaced in political debate, but Christian-Democrats had always resisted any change because of the need to respect 'the nature and destiny of women' and Greens feared the 'militarization of society' (BT PlPr, 27 October, 12341–5).

Due to the *Kreil* ruling, the German Ministry of Defence decided to lift the limitations in the Soldiers Law concerning the employment of women in the army (BT Drs 2000, 14/3072, 2). The Court ruling also clearly required the amendment of Article 12A of the Constitution if the government was to avoid further cases before the German courts. In October 2000, the German parliament approved the bill amending the Constitution by a large majority, and on December 1st, the *Bundesrat* (Senate) confirmed the amendment. Compliance was not easy. Members of parliament and legal experts alike accused the Court of an illegal extension of its competences into security issues, which disqualified the *Kreil* ruling as a legal basis for the amendment to the Constitution. It was argued, therefore, that it was not the European ruling that had required the sudden revision of the German constitution, but 'a changed attitude in German society concerning voluntary service for women in the army', and it was denied that parliament had bowed to the Court ruling (BT PlPr 2000, 27 October, 12339–43; BT Drs 2000, 24 October, 14/4380).

United Kingdom

The poor implementation of the parental leave directive caused rapid double pressure because the TUC started judicial proceedings (Case C-243/00) and the Commission started an infringement ruling (see p. 150). The government adapted its legislation.

The proposed regulations to implement the part-time work directive also received 'sustained criticism' from the EOC and trade unions. They warned the government that it did not meet European requirements and they would start legal proceedings as had happened with the parental leave case. The main complaints were that the regulation would benefit very few part-time workers and that the definition of the 'comparator' was too narrow (CNLE 2000, 1:108). Several cases before the Court concerned precisely such comparisons between part-time and full-time workers (*Lawrence*, Case C-320/00; *Allonby*, Case C-256/01).

In 2001, the British government agreed to change the Sex Discrimination Act to comply with the Burden of Proof Directive. It amended the definition of indirect discrimination to include the ability to challenge a practice; furthermore, as regards direct discrimination, it provides that in cases where the claimant establishes a prima facie case of discrimination which satisfies their part of the burden of proof, it will then be the respondent's responsibility (usually the employer) to disprove the claims (CNLE 2002, 1:40).

Conclusion: Mixed Results

Two treaty revisions ('Maastricht' and 'Amsterdam') changed the institutional outlook of the gender equality policy arena. New procedures were introduced. They shifted the action in this domain from state actors to transnational non-state actors (management and labour) and to the European Parliament. As a result, they enhanced the supranational character of decision making and limited the dominance of intergovernmental decision making. They extended the scope of EU policy making.

These institutional changes have not resulted in a clear-cut set of strong, costly gender equality policies. The procedure involving employers and trade unions has resulted in minimum common denominator outcomes, which have not required expensive policy adaptation. The removal of the unanimity rule has promoted progress on a number of files that had been on ice since the 1980s due to British opposition. However, the involvement of the EP as co-legislator has been a crucial element in the strengthening of the contents of these instruments to a level above the minimum common denominator.

The new procedures, as well as the extension of the scope of EU policies in general, have enabled interesting trends of 'thematic spill over' to occur in the field of gender equality. In 1957, the objective of gender equality was linked to the prevention of distortions in competition in the single market. In the 1990s, gender equality became an aspect of fighting unemployment and achieving greater competitiveness, stressing women's role in revitalising the economy. After 1995 ('Beijing'), it was further connected to human rights and democracy. Concern with fighting race discrimination opened up possibilities to combat sex discrimination outside the workplace. The enlargement of the EU and the establishment of an internal market with open borders have stimulated policy making on sexual violence. Demographical concerns mobilize broad support for policies on the combination of work and care. Member states are being pushed to act by their own ambitions and by Commissioners who are willing to exploit their mandate, as well as being pushed by non-state actors (EWL) who creatively reframe issues to fit changing objectives.

The supranational institutions have played a key role in ensuring lasting progress. Court rulings have shaped the directives on the reversal of the burden of proof and on pregnancy, and provoked the revision of the 1976 Equal Treatment Directive (*Kalanke*) and the 1986 Occupational Security Directive (*Barber*). The Commission has functioned as the institutional memory, reviving the same issues time after time and adapting their wording to reflect current preoccupations (parental leave, part-time work, sexual violence). It is expected that this institutional continuity in the field of gender equality will further be strengthened by the setting up of a European Institute for Gender Equality.[20]

20 The institute will be a centre of excellence for gender equality issues, providing expertise and improving knowledge. Its tasks will include raising awareness among EU citizens, gathering and analyzing reliable data and developing new methodological tools (Commission 2005, COM(2005)81).

Chapter 6

Costly Women and Contrary States

In general, women are inexpensive. They are not costly citizens. They provide an enormous quantity of unpaid work, more so than men. They provide paid work at lower rates than men. But as soon as they claim the right to be treated on equal footing with male citizens, they become 'costly'. Companies panic. They are ready to raise the price of postage (p. 176) and to reorganize entire divisions (p. 127) in order to avoid having to bear the costs of paying female employees the same as male employees. States panic. Despite the lip service paid to equal rights, they revise treaty articles (p. 144) and circumvent the law (p. 126) to avoid having to pay women what they are entitled to. When women become costly, states become contrary.

Yet, states have on occasion approved and implemented costly policies. Why would states approve supranational agreements introducing ideas that clash with domestic frames, producing political resistance and economic costs? Why does a neo–liberal project conceived to eliminate barriers to the free movement of goods, services, capital, and workers, develop policies that introduce new regulation? If women inside and outside the institutions are the main actors pushing for supranational gender equality policies, how do we explain their varying degrees of success? Why are the Commission and the Court often supportive of women's interests? In this chapter, we will first explain why EU member states have accepted and even implemented costly binding policies in the field of gender equality, summarizing the results of the previous chapters. Then we will investigate the issue of women's representation in the EU and the varying success of their actions. We will investigate the issue of actors' preferences, and conclude with a look at gender in the multi-tiered European system.

How to 'Sandwich' Contrary States

We have offered a theoretically guided empirical analysis of the formation and implementation of gender equality policies by the EU, 1955–2005. EU gender equality policies are defined here as the set of legal instruments to which two criteria apply. These instruments have the aim of promoting equal rights, equal treatment, and equal opportunities for women and men and of fighting discrimination, and they define standards and open up opportunities for women (and men) to denounce discrimination and claim equal treatment before the court.

Focus

Our focus has excluded many activities at the EU level, led mainly by the European Parliament and the Commission, which concern the position of women. The EP resolutions concerning black and migrant women, sexual violence, women in agriculture, and many more, contain valuable information and important recommendations but are not binding and therefore cannot compel contrary states to change their policies. The Commission Action Programmes on Equal Opportunities have raised awareness and contributed to putting their issues on the agenda, but they did not directly result in enforceable rights for women. Financial support for projects in the framework of NOW (New Opportunities for Women) and EQUAL have contributed to the development of pilot projects and transnational cooperation, but they do not change national budgetary politics in a structural way.

We wanted to know whether states, the stronghold of sovereign power, could be forced to change their behaviour. The answer is 'yes'. Despite the economic and ideological costs, costly binding regulation has been approved. In 1957, the Dutch government approved the costly 'equal pay' provision in the Treaty of Rome, because it needed to participate in the common market and was too weak to block the approval of the costly provision. In the 1970s, the UK and the Netherlands approved costly directives on equal treatment and social security. France and Germany would discover to their dismay that these same directives also required costly legislative changes. They tried in vain to escape implementation. Double judicial pressure would force them to revise domestic law and in Germany's case the Constitution itself. Hence, the neo-liberal project of the creation of an internal market with free movement of goods, capital, service and workers has also resulted in binding regulations whose aim is equal rights and opportunities for women and men. We have identified three complementary explanations.

Explaining Costly Gender Equality Policies

Some member states are more sensitive to criticisms of undemocratic policy making than others. Germany, for instance, has a high sensitivity to such accusations. This sensitivity depends on the internal power position of the government and state identity. In order to obtain the necessary popular support for the implementation of measures pertaining to the internal market, these 'sensitive' states have successfully insisted upon strengthening the social dimension of EU policies. This has created a window of opportunity for committed officials to put gender equality on the agenda.

Pioneer states in the field of gender equality have pushed for binding instruments instead of symbolic recommendations, because they have feared that their expensive social lead would mean suffering a competitive disadvantage in the internal market. Furthermore, in an internal market, regulation must be binding on all participants, regardless of their power, because only binding rules and matching sanctions can create a 'level playing field'. The market only functions well when all parties respect the rules – so binding regulation is less of a *Fremdkörper* in neo-liberal thinking than certain actors (political leaders, transnational business) often like to suggest.

The supranational institutions – the European Commission, Court and Parliament – have exploited their mandate to strengthen the contents and format of gender equality policies. They have skilfully managed to link equality with various key concepts, depending on the dominant preoccupations of the day. In 1957, the gender pay gap was defined as a source of distortion – an alarming situation for neo-liberals. In the 1970s, equal opportunities for women in the labour market were reframed within the fight against unemployment. In the 1990s, gender equality became part of the aim to transform the European economy into the most competitive in the world (the Lisbon strategy). And in 2000, sex discrimination became connected with the fight against discrimination on other grounds, most importantly race and ethnicity. These changing policy contexts have at times enabled an extension of the scope of gender equality policies, for instance to include parental leave or discrimination outside the workplace. But they have also, at times, had a negative influence on the quality of the outcome, limiting the regulation on temporary work to part-time work and excluding those most in need of better protection.

Any explanation for the outcome of EU negotiations needs to combine the factors of pressure, prestige (linked to identity) and power. The preferences that a state takes into international negotiations vary in their intensity depending on the anticipated extent of economic and ideological costs and the degree of pressure from non-state actors for or against the proposal. Depending on its identity and internal power position, a state will be more or less sensitive to such pressure. The ideological costs are related to the degree to which the proposal coincides with existing government policy; the economic costs depend on the consequences of the proposed measure on the relevant aspects of the economy.

Negotiations

The state negotiates at the supranational level with other states within a framework of formal and informal rules and practices. During this process, the Commission acts as agenda-setter and broker. At certain moments, costly gender equality policies appeared on the agenda and a window of opportunity opened because new European initiatives with the potential for finding broad popular support were being sought. Such opportunities could be skilfully used by a strong Commission president or Commissioner of Social Affairs to table strong, innovative proposals. Such proposals would be approved when the Commission received support from a pioneer state or the state holding the presidency. Concerned about their prestige and sensitive to pressure, certain states used their presidencies to make progress on difficult issues concerning gender equality.

Whether a member state approves costly gender equality policies also depends on its prestige, its power position and the intensity of its preferences. On several occasions, a state well aware of the costs attached to a proposal has been convinced that it did not have to adapt its own legislation – until some years later actions by the Commission and the Court would show that this was not the case. States simply did not always 'calculate' well and sometimes underestimated the power of 'double' legal proceedings.

Implementation: Pincers

Whether or not a state implements a costly joint policy depends on the economic and ideological costs of policy change, the actions of the Commission and the Court, pressure at the national level, and the sensitivity of the government to this pressure. Where relative domestic costs were higher, governments chose not to implement the policy (Germany and the Netherlands, 1960s). They were forced to change their minds when they were 'sandwiched' by double political and judicial pressure at the domestic and supranational levels. Supranational pressure is only effective when there is simultaneous domestic pressure, political or judicial. The former refers to actions by women's groups, trade unions and members of national parliaments, which demand policy change. The latter refers to the mechanism of preliminary rulings, where domestic courts request an interpretation of Community law by the Court and governments are thus compelled to respect European rules by their own courts. In several cases governments have opposed implementation while a majority of social actors favoured the reform of domestic legislation: in the Netherlands, equal pay in the 1970s and social security in the 1980s; in Germany and Britain, equal treatment in the 1980s.

Implementation was only achieved when national pressure coincided with strong pressure from the supranational institutions. Most notably, in the 1980s the judicial pressure that resulted from infringement procedures and preliminary rulings amplified political pressure from political parties, the women's movement, and trade unions. Governments found it more attractive to comply than be confronted with a large number of court cases. Even the Conservative British government under Thatcher revised national legislation. Domestic pressure is not effective without supranational pressure – and when supranational pressure is not backed up by domestic pressure, governments do not go beyond 'rhetorical implementation'. This explains non-compliance in France in the 1980s, because societal pressure in favour of implementation was lacking. The Commission and the Court are well aware of the crucial importance of this 'pincer' mechanism. They both actively supported the establishment of transnational judicial and political networks.

The decision of whether to implement is also influenced by the importance which a state attaches to its prestige. Depending on its identity, a state may value its prestige in a specific domain to a greater or lesser extent. Analysis of state behaviour reveals that states attach much value to their prestige. They have attempted to 'immunize' their prestige and justified their non-compliance with the argument that no reliable data was available (the Netherlands, 1960s), that the Commission had assured them that their legislation did not require adaptation (the UK in the 1980s, France and Germany recently), that the intervention requested was outside their authority (Germany 1960s and 1970s; France 1980s) or that the intervention damaged the rights of women (France 1990s). These tactics were successful as long as the Court was not involved. When condemnation by the Court became imminent or even real, governments usually considered this to be so damaging to their prestige that it caused them to 'surrender' and modify their legislation. They were sensitive to such condemnation when their reputation as a 'progressive government' was at stake (the Netherlands, 1973), as the 'guardian of fundamental rights' (Germany, 1980 and 2000), or as the 'role model for social policy' (France).

Unfortunately, the implementation of costly policy can cause a 'boomerang' effect. During subsequent negotiations, states will be less willing to approve new policies. In the 1980s, governments were much more aware of the potential costs of gender equality legislation. Their experiences in implementing the Equal Pay and Equal Treatment Directives, which turned out to be more costly than they had calculated, made them more cautious concerning the approval of new binding measures. They showed a net preference for non-binding symbolic measures. So we see that it is not only 'spill-over' which is a common feature of multi-tiered politics, but also 'spill-back'. Both phenomena are typical of multi-tiered systems as they concern the shifting of issues and the authority to regulate this issue from one level to another. There is a tendency to renationalize certain issues; to refer to the concept of 'subsidiarity' and prevent the Commission from developing proposals in certain areas; to use non-binding instruments like strategies, leaving member states room to avoid costly implementation and prestige-damaging Court rulings and to deprive non-state actors of the means to claim their rights. No wonder feminist experts are sceptical about the effectiveness of the gender mainstreaming strategy, despite its revolutionary potential. It has to be fitted with the tools to 'sandwich' contrary governments if the strategy is to become effective beyond pasting '... and women' in policy proposals in all domains.

Women in the Multi-Tiered Machine

Many authors credit the presence of women in the EU arena with the success of EU policies (Elman 1996; Hoskyns 1996a; Mazey 2002; Reinalda 1997). We asked in Chapter 1 what, then, enabled women to succeed, at times, on a European level where they had suffered defeat domestically, and why their activism met with such varying degrees of success. Intense pressure has not always resulted in progress, and progress has not always been the result of intensive pressure. In the preceding section we have largely answered the question of the varying success of pressure from women's advocacy groups. Pressure is more effective when the internal power position of a government is weaker and its sensitivity is higher. Still, how important was it that women entered the European arena?

Looking at the development of gender equality policies, we have seen that committed individuals sometimes made a difference. They seized opportunities which others would have let go. Still, to make the difference, one needs ideas as well as the power to realize them. In the period 1958-68, several officials in DG

V were committed to gender equality. They honestly tried to make progress with the implementation of equal pay; they established networks with committed experts and representatives of trade unions. However, they received no support from the Commission whenever they tried to start legal proceedings against a government or whenever COREPER asked them to tone down their reports (see Chapter 2). They had to wait for a 'changing of the guards' before seeing their ideas realized.

One needs committed individuals with power and ideas. To exclude the ideas of women – more than half of the population – from the political process hinders the realization of gender equality. As Mrs Ledru, surrounded by male experts and officials, observed in October 1958, 'I believe that it would be useful that in discussions on equal pay women should be represented with a much more comfortable majority' (see p. 55). Her remark still rings true today. We have seen that the ideas of expert Evelyne Sullerot changed attitudes regarding the position of women in the labour market; the ideas of lawyer Eliane Vogel-Polsky made the Commission and member states aware of the potential of Article 119; the ideas of Jacqueline Nonon set the agenda for European gender equality policies for the next 20 years; the ideas of Yvette Roudy influenced policy making in the European Parliament and in France (see Chapters 3–4). In addition, these individuals were backed by strong pressure from women's groups, women in political parties and parliament, women in trade unions and in ministries, who all contributed the necessary 'power' to back up their ideas. Of course this is a mutually strengthening mechanism. Strong pressure legitimized the institutionalization of gender interests in an Equal Opportunities Unit (DG V) and a Committee for Women's Rights (EP). These 'institutions' in turn strengthened women's advocacy groups as these groups did not have to lobby for access and information and could concentrate their scarce resources on these openings in the supranational organization, providing expertise and 'grass roots' information.

When we look at the representation of women at the European level, it is striking that until 1989 there was not one woman Commissioner (see Table 6.1) and there has never been a female Commission president. In the European Parliament, the representation of women increased strongly after the first direct elections in 1979 from 8 to 16 percent and increased over the years further to 30 percent. Women are thus represented in substantially higher numbers in the EP than in many national parliaments (Leyenaar 2004, 50). This strong representation of women has served to keep women's issues on the agenda, to make Commissioner candidates take equal opportunities seriously and to save the Committee on Women's Rights from being disbanded.

The issue of the 'empowerment' of women in European policy making was raised during election campaigns for the EP and in its own resolutions. The Commission created an expert network – 'Women in Decision-making' – in 1992 to investigate obstacles in national political systems and formulate recommendations. Only recently has the strategy of gender mainstreaming raised awareness of the problem of the representation of women in the Commission bureaucracy, agencies and committees. Targets have been formulated, but, particularly in policy domains that are typically 'male strongholds', the situation will take time to change (Commission 2001, COM(2001)119).

Table 6.1 Gender composition of the Commission

	President of the Commission	Number of male commmissioners	Number of female commissioners	Percentage of female commissioners
1958–61	Hallstein	9 men	0 women	0
1962–67	Hallstein	9 men	0 women	0
1967–70	Rey	12 men	0 women	0
1970–72	Malfatti	9 men	0 women	0
1972	Mansholt	9 men	0 women	0
1973–76	Ortoli	13 men	0 women	0
1977–80	Jenkins	13 men	0 women	0
1981–84	Thorn	14 men	0 women	0
1985–88	Delors-I	17 men	0 women	0
1989–92	Delors-II	15 men	2 women	12
1993–94	Delors-III	16 men	1 woman	6
1995–99	Santer	15 men	5 women	25
1999–04	Prodi	15 men	5 women	25
2005–09	Barroso	18 men	7 women	28
Number of male/female presidents of the Commission	11 men, 0 women			0

Strong pressure, even double pressure from both domestic and supranational levels has not always been enough to bring about progress. The strength of the women's movement in the 1970s partially explains why strong equality directives were approved. In the 1980s, pressure was even stronger because autonomous women's groups joined the larger movement to influence the political agenda and supranationally, the EP also joined in. Still, no strong directives were approved. We have seen that the sensitivity of governments was much lower in the 1980s than in the previous decade. They could ignore pressure without concern for their prestige or their electoral success. Furthermore, due to the general stagnation of the integration process there were no major projects that needed popular support. In such circumstances, pressure from women's advocacy groups remained largely ineffective.

Power and Preferences – The Commission and the Court

Where do the preferences of the Commission and the Court come from?

The Commission

The Commission is and defines itself as the EU agenda-setter and the guardian of the treaties. Linked to its first role is its ambition to expand supranational regulation. This often coincides with the interest of those who promote supranational gender equality policies to improve national legislation. Moreover, the Commission needs innovative ideas in order to convince reluctant governments ‘to upgrade the common interest’ and go further than some compromise between the existing national positions. We have seen how crucial the framing of an issue can be for its acceptance by member states, but also for the (sometimes even negative) consequences it may have for women.

As the size of the Commission staff is limited, the Commission has always actively sought input from experts and societal groups. Because of the asymmetrical power relation between the Commission and the Council, which leaves the Commission ultimately dependent on the cooperation of the Council to see its proposals realized, the Commission must constantly look for support. It often finds such support among pioneer states and smaller member states, which generally benefit most from supranational regulation, but it also actively creates networks with non-state actors that can lobby the respective governments from ‘below’. In the field of gender equality, the Advisory Committee on Equal Opportunities, the European Women’s Lobby, the expert networks on Women in Decision-making and on Childcare, and the European Women’s Lawyers Association are some examples. Commission preferences thus strongly depend on input from the domestic and transnational levels, which in turn vary according to the sub-groups and individuals that dominate such networks.

The Court

The Court is not a feminist court. Its first concern is to strengthen its position and its reputation *vis-à-vis* member state governments and domestic courts, especially constitutional courts. Accordingly, it has affirmed the position of European law with regard to national law by the judgment on the supremacy of European law (*Costa v. ENEL,* Case 6/64) and the direct effect of European law (*Van Gend & Loos,* Case 26/62), both of which established a legal hierarchy. Next, it has interpreted its mandate as contributing to European integration through the promotion of peace and progress for all citizens (see p. 12 on identity). It aims at protecting the rights of citizens and companies against unwilling governments. This has benefited women in many cases.

However, the Court had to convince the constitutional courts of member states that the protection of citizens could and should be entrusted to it – though only as far as this was part of EU business, leaving other issues to the national judicial community. The most important addressee of this unspoken message was the German Federal Constitutional Court in Karlsruhe, which only accepts Court rulings if they do not transgress certain limits (Weatherill and Beaumont 1999). Therefore, we see two trends in Court rulings.

In preliminary rulings concerning German cases (and in the field of gender equality there are many of them, see Table 5.2), the Court has acted prudently and often chosen a large number of judges to decide them (*Kalanke, Kreil*). In addition, the Court has shown a tendency to expand the implications of treaty articles and directives, but has done this by 'delving deeper'. It has, for instance, opened up the concept of pay to show that it also includes certain social security benefits and pensions. No government had 'read' this in the concept when formulating Treaty Article 119 in 1957, but every judge would accept it as a legitimate interpretation. However, the Court does not expand the implications of treaty articles and directives by going beyond the concepts embedded in them as this might provoke negative reactions from national courts, undermining its reputation and reducing the legitimacy of its rulings particularly by courts sensitive to 'border-transgressing'.

This trend has resulted in rulings which have turned out to be less positive for women than hoped, concerning, for instance, maternity leave (p. 116) and discrimination against lesbians (Case C-249/96, *Grant*). In general, the Court has displayed caution in social security cases since the EU has only limited competencies in this field and member states have repeatedly made clear that this is a matter for national governments. Accordingly, the Court has been able to prohibit unequal treatment in social security, but not been able to prevent governments from realizing equal treatment simply by reducing benefits for women and men alike.

Where courts have reacted vehemently against the 'supremacy' ruling, which is an exception to the 'no border-transgressing rule', governments have often strongly opposed 'delving deeper' rules (Chapters 4–5). In January 2006, Austrian chancellor Wolfgang Schüssel began his country's presidency of the EU with an interview saying that

> the ECJ had in the last couple of years systematically expanded European competencies, even in areas, where there is decidedly no [European] community law ... Suddenly, judgements emerge on the role of women in the German federal army, or on access of foreign students to Austrian universities – that is clearly national law (EUobserver 2006, 3 January).

However, the Court did not in fact extend the scope of its competencies in the *Kreil* ruling on women in the German army to which Schüssel refers (p. 176). It applied the Equal Treatment Directive from 1976, 'delving deeper' into the notion of non-discrimination regarding access to employment than Schüssel or German politicians liked, but was never contested by any court.

The Composition of the Court Thus, the Court is not feminist but follows two trends, of which the second one – 'delving deeper' – has been to some extent beneficial for women. Still, one may wonder why the Court has not given more consistently gender-sensitive interpretations. Part of the explanation may lie in the fact that only men worked at the Court. In 1981, for the first time, a woman made her appearance at the Court; Simone Rozès from France, as Advocate-General. Not until 1999 were the first female judges nominated; Fidelma O'Kelly Macken from Ireland and Ninon Colneric from Germany. Even though male judges have shown themselves able to make gender-sensitive judgements, there are two reasons why an 'all-male bench' is a problem (Kennedy 2002). First, balanced participation is necessary for the legitimacy of all representative bodies. Public confidence in the law and, more specifically, in the rulings of the Court on gender equality cases, is strengthened when both genders are represented on the bench. This legitimacy argument is accepted reasoning where the representation of member states is concerned: the number of judges has been extended to 25 and every country has one representative. The second argument is that all judges bring their specific experiences to bear on their interpretations. Again, Irish, Greek, German and Polish judges each bring the traditions and culture of their country to Luxembourg and infuse rulings with their knowledge of European law as well as with their knowledge of language, culture and society. The same argument is valid for the representation of both sexes, as including women means including their experiences. Note, however, that we are not claiming these constitute the experiences of a minority group: women constitute a very heterogeneous half of the population. It is therefore a negative development that, of the current 25 judges (increased from 15 in 2004), only two are women (Ninon Colneric and Rosario Silva de Lapuerta). Fortunately, three women now sit on the bench of the Advocates–General, with five male colleagues.

What Makes Gender Different?

In spite of all the criticism concerning the limited scope and the narrow definition of its key concepts, EU gender equality policies continue to stand out in the social domain as a well-developed set of policies. We have already raised the question and shown in previous chapters that we must reject the idea that governments approve such policies because the ideological benefits of 'promoting equal rights for women' offset the economic costs. The image of women as the 'baby seals' of social policy completely overlooks the high ideological costs that are attached to equal rights in most countries.

Nonetheless, there is something specific about women. In the first place, their non-specificity – wine growers or fishermen specialized in offshore fishing are not to be found in every member state, but of course women are. Behind the men negotiating treaties and directives stand women as mothers, secretaries, or partners. They themselves are men because they are not perceived as women. This 'familiarity' with the notion of 'gender', although seldom conceived in a sophisticated way, implies a certain innate sensitivity that makes it hard to completely ignore demands for equal rights of women and men.

Second, the notion of the defence of citizens' rights or the defence of human rights is part of most EU member states' identities. Women make up more than half of their population. Proposals which promote the rights of women cannot simply be refused without damaging the prestige of the state. This implies that costs are incurred for *not* undertaking action when a strong proposal on equal rights is on the agenda. Third, there are structural differences between the interests of actors defending women's interests and actors defending workers' interests. Many supranational proposals concerning social policy have been removed from the agenda or reduced to non-binding instruments because labour and management prefer to keep these issues as bargaining chips within collective negotiation processes between them. They lose influence when an issue is transferred from the corporatist domain to the domain of state intervention. By contrast, as long as women's advocacy groups have no vested interests in the regulation of women's rights, they will support binding measures rather than softer instruments, in order to have a tool to influence policy change. Gender equality therefore has been more successfully regulated at the EU level than other social policy issues.

The EU system at times offers women opportunities to improve their position, because its multi-tiered structure empowers non-state actors and 'sandwiches' state governments. It does not radically transform gender relations, because the underlying power relations are not altered to such an extent that the system becomes an 'open' system with non-hierarchal tiers. The EU remains a political system characterized by power asymmetries, where state and non-state actors pursuing power, ideas and interests interact and produce outcomes that generally reflect a mixture of conflicting ideas and unintended consequences.

Bibliography

Agence (several years), *Europe: Bulletin quotidien* (Luxembourg: Agence International d'Information pour la Presse).

Albistur, M. and Armogathe, D. (1977), *Histoire du féminisme français, Vol. II* (Paris: Éditions des Femmes).

Alter, K.J. (1998), 'Who Are the "Masters of the Treaty"?: European Governments and the European Court of Justice', *International Organization* 52:1, 121–47.

Asscher-Vonk, I. (1995), *Equality in Law between Men and Women in the European Community. The Netherlands* (Dordrecht/Luxemburg: Martinus Nijhoff Publishers, Office for Official Publications of the EC).

Atkins, S. and Luckhaus, L. (1987), 'The Social Security Directive and U.K. Law', in McCrudden (ed.).

Attali, J. (1993), *Verbatim I* (Paris: Fayard).

— (1995), *Verbatim III* (Paris: Fayard).

BAC 008/1966, Documents from the European Community Archives, Florence.

BAC 006/1977, Documents from the European Community Archives, Florence.

Baer, S. (1996), 'Pornography and Sexual Harassment in the EU', in Elman (ed.)

Behrendt, A. et al. (1968), *Die westdeutschen Gewerkschaften und das staatsmonopolistische Herrschaftssystem 1945–1966* (Berlin: Dietz Verlag).

Bergamaschi, M. (2000), 'The Gender Perspective in the Policies on European Trade Unions', in Rossilli.

Bertelsmann, K. and Rust, U. (1995), *Equality in Law between Men and Women in the European Community. Germany* (Dordrecht/Luxemburg: Martinus Nijhoff Publishers, Office for Official Publications of the EC).

Beveridge, F. and Nott, S. (2002), 'Mainstreaming: a case for optimism and cynicism', *Feminist Legal Studies* 10, 299-311.

Beyen, J. W. (1968), *Het spel en de knikkers. Een kroniek van vijftig jaren* (Rotterdam: Ad. Donker).

Bleijenbergh, I. (2004), *Citizens who care: European social citizenship in EU debates on childcare and part-time work* (Amsterdam: Dutch University Press).

Blok, E. (1978), *Loonarbeid van vrouwen 1945–1955* (Nijmegen: SUN).

Bomberg, E. and A. C-G. Stubb (2003), *The European Union: How does it work?* (Oxford: Oxford University Press).

Boston, S. (1985), *Women Workers and the Trade Union Movement* (London: Davis-Poynter).

Braithwaite, M. (2000), 'Mainstreaming Gender in the European Structural Funds', http://eucenter.wisc.edu/Conferences/Gender/braith.htm.

Brandt, W. (1977), *Ontmoetingen en gedachten, Vols I and II* (Baarn: In den Toren).

Bretherton, C. (2001), 'Gender mainstreaming and EU enlargement: swimming against the tide?', *Journal of European Public Policy* 8:1, 60–81.

Brunfaut, E. (1979), 'De gelijkheid van man en vrouw inzake sociale zekerheid', in *Europese vrouwen over Europa* (Brussel: Ministerie van Buitenlandse Zaken).

Buckley, M. and Anderson, M. (eds) (1988), *Women, Equality and Europe* (Houndmills: Macmillan Press).

Buddingh', H. and De Waard, M. (2003), 'Gelijke zorg mannen en vrouwen. Verzekeraars dreigen met hogere premies', *NRC-Handelsblad*, 6 November.

Bueno de Mesquita, B. and Stokman, F. N. (1994), 'The Models', in B. Bueno de Mesquita and F.N. Stokman (eds), *European Community Decision Making. Models, Applications, and Comparisons* (New Haven and London: Yale University Press).

Bulletin (several years), *Bulletin of the European Communities* (Brussel: Office for Official Publications of the European Communities).

Bundesministerium für Frauen und Jugend (1992), *Frauen in der Bundesrepublik Deutschland* (Bonn: Dt. Bundestag, Referat Öffentlichkeitsarbeit).

Bundestag Drs (several years), *Drucksache* (German Parliamentary Documents) (Bonn).

Bundestag Pl Pr (several years), *Plenar Protokol* (German Parliamentary Documents) (Bonn).

Bundestag (1988), *Fragen an die deutsche Geschichte* (Bonn: Dt. Bundestag, Referat Öffentlichkeitsarbeit).

Burley, A. M. and Mattli, W. (1993), 'Europe before the Court: A Political Theory of Legal Integration', *International Organization* 47:1, 41–77.

Burrows, N. (1980), 'The Promotion of Women's Rights by the European Economic Community', *Common Market Law Review* 17, 191–209.

Byrne, P. (1997), *Social Movements in Britain* (London: Routledge).

Callet, C. and du Granrut, C. (1973), *Place aux femmes* (Paris: Stock).

Caporaso, J. and Keeler, J.T.S. (1995), 'The European Union and Regional Integration Theory', in C. Rhodes and S. Mazey (eds), *The State of the European Union, Vol. 3. Building a European Polity* (Boulder, CO: Lynne Rienner).

Carstens, K. (1976), 'Das Eingreifen Adenauers in die Europa-Verhandlungen im November 1956', in D. Blumenwitz et al., *Konrad Adenauer und seine Zeit* (Stuttgart: Deutsche Verlags Anstalt).

Castle, B. (1980), *The Castle Diaries 1974–76* (London: Weidenfeld and Nicolson).

— (1984), *The Castle Diaries 1964–70* (London: Weidenfeld and Nicolson).

CeiberWeiber (2003), 'Sexismus in den Medien', http://ceiberweiber.at/euphorum/parlament/euinfo/aktuell/aktuell24.html

Chamberlayne, P. (1993), 'Women and the state: Changes in roles and rights in France, West Germany, Italy and Britain, 1970–1990', in Lewis (ed.).

Childs, D. (1992), *Britain Since 1945. A Political History* (London: Routledge).

Choisir (1978), *Le Programme commun des femmes* (Paris: Grasset).
— (1981), *Quel Président pour les Femmes? Réponses de François Mitterrand. Préface de Gisèle Halimi* (Paris: Gallimard).
Christiansen, T. et al. (2001), *The social construction of Europe* (London: Sage).
CM 2/1958, Documents from the European Community Archives, Florence.
CM 3/NEGO, Documents from the European Community Archives, Florence.
CNLE (several years), *Bulletin – Legal Issues in Equality* (Brussels: Commission Network of Legal Experts in the fields of employment, social affairs and equality between men and women), http://ec.europa.eu/employment_social/gender_equality/legislation/bulletin_en.html
Collins, D. (1975), *The European Communities. The Social Policy of the First Phase. Volume II. The European Economic Community 1958–72* (London: Robertson).
Collins, E. (1996), 'European Union Sexual Harassment Policy' in Elman (ed.).
Commission (several years), COM(…), European Commission documents (Brussels: Commission of the European Communities).
— (several years), SEC(…), European Commission documents (Brussels: Commission of the European Communities).
— (several years), V/…, European Commission documents (Brussels: Commission of the European Communities).
— (1990), *Women of Europe Newsletter*, No. 12 (Brussels: Commission of the European Communities).
— (1991), *Women of Europe Newsletter*, No. 22 (Brussels: Commission of the European Communities).
— (1992), *Women of Europe Newsletter*, No. 27 (Brussels: Commission of the European Communities).
— (1994), *Women of Europe Newsletter*, No. 40 (Brussels: Commission of the European Communities).
— (1997), *Equal Opportunities. The Magazine*, No. 1 (Brussels: Commission of the European Communities).
— (2004), *Employment in Europe 2003*, <http://europa.eu.int/comm/employment_social/employment_analysis/employ_2003_en.htm>
Coquillat, M. (1988), 'The Achievements of the French Ministry of Women's Rights: 1981–86', in Buckley and Anderson (eds).
Council (several years), Documents of the Council <http://ec.europa.eu/prelex/>
Council of Europe (1998), *Gender Mainstreaming. Conceptual framework, methodology and presentation of good practices: final report of activities of the group of specialists on mainstreaming* (Strasbourg: Council of Europe).
Coussins, J. (1977), *The Equality Report* (London: NCCL Rights for Women Unit).
Cox, R.W. and Jacobson, H.K. (eds) (1973), *The Anatomy of Influence. Decision-making in International Organizations* (New Haven: Yale University Press).
Cram, L. (2001), 'Whither the Commission? Reform, renewal and the issue-attention cycle', *Journal of European Public Policy* 8:5, 770–86.
CREW (1993), *Crew Reports* (Brussels: CREW).

Crossman, R. (1977), *The Diaries of a Cabinet Minister. Vol. 3. Secretary of State for Social Services* (London: Hamilton and Cape).

Cunningham, S. (1992), 'The development of equal opportunities theory and practice in the European Community', *Policy and Politics* 20:3, 177–89.

Davies, P. L. (1987), 'European Equality Legislation, U.K. Legislative Policy and Industrial Relations', in McCrudden.

Degraef, V. (1988), 'Feminismus in Belgien', in Autonome Frauenredaktion (eds), *Frauenbewegungen der Welt, Band 1. Westeuropa* (Berlin/Hamburg: Argument-Verlag).

De Groote, J. and Thys (1979), 'Verkiezingsstrategie en –taktiek', in *Europese vrouwen over Europa* (Brussel: Ministerie van Buitenlandse Zaken).

De Jong, B. and Sjerps, I. (1987), 'Zweven in de breedte. Vier jaar Breed Platform Vrouwen voor Ekonomische Zelfstandigheid', *Socialisties-Feministiese Teksten 10* (Baarn: Ambo).

Deshormes La Valle, F. (1979), 'De dienst Voorlichting van de pers en de vrouwenorganisaties', in *Europese vrouwen over Europa* (Brussel: Ministerie van Buitenlandse Zaken).

Diez, T. (1999), 'Speaking "Europe": the politics of integration discourse', *Journal of European Public Policy* 6:4, 598–613.

Dijkstra, T. and Swiebel, J. (1982), 'De overheid en het vrouwenvraagstuk: emancipatiebeleid als mode en taboe', in *Socialisties-Feministiese Teksten 7* (Amsterdam: Feministische Uitgeverij Sara).

Doormann, L. (1983), 'Die neue Frauenbewegung: Zur Entwicklung seit 1968', in Hervé.

Duchen, C. (1986), *Feminism in France. From May '68 to Mitterrand* (London: Routledge).

ECR (several years), *European Court Reports*, <http://europa.eu.int/eur-lex/>

Egan, M. (1993), 'Gendered Integration: Social Policies and the European Market', *Women and Politics*, 19:4, 23–52.

Eijl, C. van (1997), *Maandag tolereren we niets meer. Vrouwen, arbeid en vakbeweging 1945–1990* (Amsterdam: Stichting FNV-Pers).

EIRonline (1998), 'The EU Parental Leave Agreement and Directive: Implications for national law and practice' <http://www.eiro.eurofound.eu.int/1998/01/study>.

EIRR (several years), *European Industrial Relations Review*, several issues.

Ellis, E. (1998), *EC Sex Equality Law* (Oxford: Clarendon Press).

Elman, R. A. (ed.) (1996), *Sexual Politics and the European Union* (Providence and Oxford: Berghahn).

— (1998), 'The EU and Women: The Virtual Equality', in P-H. Laurent and M. Maresceau (eds), *The State of the European Union, Vol. 4. Deepening and Widening* (Boulder CO: Lynne Rienner).

Emancipatiekommissie (1979), *Commentaar op het wetsontwerp gelijke behandeling van mannen en vrouwen* (Rijswijk: Emancipatiekommissie).

Emancipatieraad (1991), *Gelijke behandeling naar geslacht in aanvullende pensioenregelingen* ('s-Gravenhage: Emancipatieraad).

EMMA (1991), *Sonderband: Schwesternlust und Schwesternfrust* (Köln: Emma Frauenverlag).

Esping-Andersen, G. (ed.) (1996), *Welfare States in Transition. National Adaptations in Global Economies* (London: Sage).

EUObserver (2006), <http://euobserver.com/>

EURONAT (2005), *Final Report. Representations of Europe and the Nationa in Current and Prospective Member-States: Media, Elites and Civil Society*, <http://www.iue.it/RSCAS/Rsearch/EURONAT/>

Europa van Morgen (several years), weekly bulletin (Den Haag: Europese Voorlichtingsdienst).

European Council (1993), Brussels – Presidency Conclusions <hhtp://ue.eu.int/cms3_applications/>

— (1994), Corfu – Presidency Conclusions <http://ue.eu.int/cms3_applications/>

Europe Documents (1973), No. 771 (Luxembourg: Agence International d'Information pour la Presse).

EP (1981), *De positie van de vrouw in de Europese Gemeenschap* (Luxembourg: Bureau voor Officiële Publikaties van de Europese Gemeenschap).

— (several years), A/…, Documents EP, <http://ec.europa.eu/prelex/>

EWL (1996), 'Contribution to the Intergovernmental Conference 1996' (Brussels: European Women's Lobby).

Falkner, G. (1998), *EU Social Policy in the 1990s. Towards a corporatist policy community* (London: Routledge).

— et al. (2005), *Complying with Europe. EU Harmonisation and Soft Law in the Member States* (Cambridge: Cambridge University Press).

F-Magazine (1981), several issues.

Gardiner, F. (ed.) (1997), *Sex Equality Policy in Western Europe* (London: Routledge).

Garrett, G. (1995), 'The politics of legal integration in the European Union', *International Organization* 49:1, 171–81.

Geyer, R. and Springer, B. (1998), 'EU Social policy after Maastricht: The Works Council Directive and the British Opt-Out', in P.-H. Laurent and M. Maresceau (eds), *The State of the European Union. Deepenign and Widening, Vol. 4* (Boulder/London: Lynne Rienner Publishers).

Ghilardotti, F. (1996), 'Opinion of the Committee on Women's Rights on the Commission proposal for a Council directive on the framework agreement concluded by UNICE, CEEP and ETUC on parental leave', A4-0064/96 <http://ec.europa.eu/prelex/>.

Girault, R. (1989), 'La France entre l'Europe et l'Afrique', in Serra.

Giroud, F. (1976), *Cent Mesures pour les Femmes* (Paris: La Documentation Française).

— (1977), *La Comédie du Pouvoir* (Paris: Fayard).

Glase, A. (1996), 'Report on the Commission proposal for a Council directive on the framework agreement concluded by UNICE, CEEP and ETUC on parental leave', A4-0064/96 <http://ec.europa.eu/prelex/>

Gregory, J. (2000), 'Sexual Harassment: The Impact of EU Law in the Member States', in Rossilli.

Griffiths, R. and Asbeek-Brusse, W. (1989), 'The Dutch Cabinet and the Rome Treaties', in Serra.

Haas, E. B. (1964), *Beyond the Nation-State. Functionalism and International Organization* (Stanford: Stanford University Press).

Handelingen (several years), *Handelingen der Staten-Generaal* (Dutch Parliamentary Documents) (The Hague: SDU).

Hanmer, J. (1996), 'The Common Market of Violence', in R.A. Elman (ed.).

Hansen, L. (2000), 'Gendered Communities', in M. Kelstrup and M.C. Williams (eds), *International Relations Theory and the Politics of European Integration. Power, Security and Community* (London: Routledge).

Hantrais, L. (1993), 'Women, work and welfare in France', in Lewis.

— (1995), *Social Policy in the European Union* (Houndmills: Macmillan).

— (2000), 'From equal pay to reconciliation of employment and family life', in L. Hantrais (ed.), *Gendered Policies in Europe. Reconciling Employment and Family Life* (Houndmills: Macmillan).

Hayes-Renshaw, F. and Wallace, H. (1997), *The Council of Ministers* (Houndmills: Macmillan Press).

Hentschel, V. (1998), *Ludwig Erhard. Ein Politikerleben* (Berlin: Ullstein).

Hervé, F. (ed.) (1983), *Geschichte der deutschen Frauenbewegung* (Köln: Pahl-Rugenstein).

Hix, S. (2005), *The Political System of the European Union*, 2nd edition (Houndsmill: Palgrave Macmillan).

Holtmaat, R. et al. (2000), *Research project on the proposed legal instruments base don Art. 13 EC treaty and the acquis communautaire in the field of EC law on equality of treatment for women and men* (…) (Amsterdam: PvdA).

Hörburger, H. and Rath-Hörburger, F. (1983), *Europas Frauen – gleichberechtigt? Die Politik der EG-Länder zur Gleichberechtigung der Frau im Arbeitsleben* (Düsseldorf: WI-Verlag).

Hoskyns, C. (1985), 'Women's equality and the European Community', *Feminist Review* 20, 70–88.

— (1988), "Give us equal pay and we'll open our doors" - A Study of the Impact in the Federal Republic of Germany and the Republic of Ireland of the European Community's Policy on Women's Rights, in Buckley and Anderson.

— (1991), 'The European Women's Lobby', *Feminist Review* 38, 67–70.

— (1996a), *Integrating Gender. Women, Law and Politics in the European Union* (London/New York: Verso).

— (1996b), 'The European Union and the Women Within: An Overview of Women's Rights Policy', in R.A. Elman.

— (2004), 'Gender perspectives', in A. Wiener and T. Diez.

— and Luckhaus, L. (1989), 'The European Community Directive on Equal Treatment in Social Security', *Policy and Politics* 17:4, 321–35.

Hühn, U. (2000) 'Die Waffen der Frauen: Der Fall Kreil – erneuter Anlass zum Konflikt zwischen europäischer und deutscher Gerichtsbarkeit?' (Basel: Europainstitut der Universität Basel).

Hund, J. (1983), 'Das Recht auf Arbeit und gleichen Lohn: Zur gewerkschaftlichen Frauenarbeit in der Bundesrepublik', in Hervé.

ILO (1956), *Social Aspects of European Economic Cooperation* (Genève: ILO).

Jenkins, R. (1991), *A Life at the Centre* (London: Macmillan).

Journal Officiel (several issues), Journal Officiel de la République Française (Paris).

Kapteyn, P. J. G. and VerLoren van Themaat, P. (1995), *Inleiding tot het recht van de Europese Gemeenschappen. Na Maastricht* (Deventer: Kluwer).

Keck, M. E. and K. Sikkink (1998), *Activists beyond borders. Advocacy networks in international politics* (Ithaca: Cornell University Press).

Kennedy, S. J. (2002), 'Breaking the Silence: Gender Mainstreaming and the Composition of the European Court of Justice', *Feminist Legal Studies* 10:3, 257–70.

Keohane, R. O. (1984), *After Hegemony. Cooperation and Discord in the World Political Economy* (Princeton: Princeton University Press).

Kerremans, B. (1996), 'Do Institutions Make a Difference? Non-Institutionalism, Neo-Institutionalism, and the Logic of Common Decision-Making in the European Union', *Governance* 9, 217–40.

Kessler, M.-C. (1999), *La Politique Etrangère de la France. Acteurs et processus* (Paris, Presses de Sciences Po).

Knill, C. (2001), *The Europeanisation of National Administrations* (Cambridge: Cambridge University Press).

Köpper, E. -D. (1982), *Gewerkschaften und Außenpolitik* (Frankfurt: Campus Verlag).

Krasnogolovy, H. (1968), 'Der Kampf der Westdeutschen Gewerkschaften um die Rechte der Frau', in Behrendt.

Kronsell, A. (2005), 'Gender, power and European integration theory', *Journal of European Public Policy* 12:6, 1022–40.

Laatste Nieuws (several years), Belgian daily.

Landau, E. C. (1985), *The rights of working women in the European Community* (Luxemburg: Office for Official Publications of the EC).

Lange, P. (1992), 'The Politics of the Social Dimension', in A. Sbragia (ed.), *Euro-Politics. Institutions and Policymaking in the 'New' European Community* (Washington DC: The Brookings Institution).

— (1993), 'Maastricht and the Social Protocol: Why Did They Do It?', *Politics & Society* 21:1, 5–36.

Leibfried, S. and Pierson, P. (1995), 'Semi-sovereign Welfare States: Social Policy in a Multitiered Europe', in Leibfried and Pierson.

— (eds) (1995), *European Social Policy. Between Fragmentation and Integration* (Washington DC: Brookings Institute).

— (1996), 'Social Policy', in Wallace, H. en Wallace, W., *Policy-Making in the European Union* (Oxford: Oxford University Press).

Le Monde (several years), French daily.

León, M., Mateo Diaz, M. and Mills, S. (2003), 'Engendering the Convention: Women and the Future of the European Union', <http://www.fedtrust.co.uk/constituionalpapers>

Lewis, J. (ed.) (1993), *Women and Social Policies in Europe. Work, Family and the State* (Aldershot: Edward Elgar).

Leyenaar, M. (1989), *De geschade heerlijkheid. Politiek gedrag van vrouwen en mannen in Nederland, 1918–1988* ('s-Gravenhage: SDU).

— (2004), *Political Empowerment of Women. The Netherlands and Other Countries* (Dordrecht: Martinus Nijhoff Publishers).

Liebert, U. (ed.) (2003), *Gendering Europeanisation* (Brussels: Peter Lang).

— (2002), 'Europeanising Gender Mainstreaming: Constraints and Opportunities in the Multilevel Euro-Polity', *Feminist Legal Studies* 10:3, 241–56.

Lieshout, R. H. (1995), *Anarchy and hierarchy. A theory of international politics and foreign policy* (Aldershot: Edward Elgar).

— (1999), *The Struggle for the Organization of Europe. The Foundations of the European Union* (Cheltenham: Edward Elgar).

Lombardo, E. (2005), 'Integrating or Setting the Agenda? Gender Mainstreaming in the European Constitution-making Process', *Social Politics* 12:3, 412–32.

Lovenduski, J. (1986), *Women and European Politics. Contemporary Feminism and Public Policy* (Brighton: Wheatsheaf Books).

— (1997), 'Sex Equality and the Rules of the Game', in Gardiner.

Ludlow, P. (1991), The European Commission, in: R.O. Keohane and S. Hoffmann (eds), *The new European Community. Decisionmaking and institutional change* (Boulder: Westview Press).

MAE (Ministère des Affaires Etrangeres), Documents from the European Community Archives, Florence.

Marjolin, R. (1986), *Le travail d'une vie. Mémoires 1911–1986* (Paris: Robert Laffont).

Marks, G. et al. (1996), 'European Integration from the 1980s: State-Centric v. Multiple-Level Governance', *Journal of Common Market Studies* 34:3, 341–78.

Mattli, W. and Slaughter, A. M. (1998), 'Revisiting the European Court of Justice', *International Organization* 52:1, 177–209.

Mazey, S. (1998), 'The European Union and women's rights: from the Europeanization of national agendas to the nationalization of a European agenda?', *Journal of European Public Policy*, 5:1, 131–52.

— (2002), 'Gender Mainstreaming Strategies in the EU: Delivering on an Agenda?', *Feminist Legal Studies* 10, 227–40.

— and Richardson, J. (eds) (1993), *Lobbying in the European Community* (Oxford: Oxford University Press).

Mazur, A. (1991), 'Agendas and 'Egalité Professionelle': Symbolic Policy at Work in France', in E. Meehan and S. Sevenhuijsen, *Equality Politics and Gender* (London: Sage).

McCrudden, C. (ed.) (1987), *Women, Employment and European Equality Law* (London: Eclipse Publications).

— (1994) *Equality in Law between Men and Women in the European Community. The United Kingdom* (Dordrecht/Luxemburg: Martinus Nijhoff Publishers/Office for Official Publications of the EC).

Meehan, E. (1985), *Women's Rights at Work. Campaigns and Policy in Britain and the United States* (Houndmills: Macmillan).

— (1993), 'Women's rights in the European Community', in Lewis.

Menschik, J. (1971), *Gleichberechtigung oder Emanzipation? Die Frau im Erwerbsleben der Bundesrepublik* (Frankfurt: Fischer).

Meyer, M. K. and E. Prügl (eds) (1999), *Gender Politics in Global Governance* (Lanham: Rowman and Littlefield).

Millar, J. (1989), 'Social Security, Equality and Women in the UK', *Policy and Politics* 17:4, 311–19.

Milward, A. S. (1992), *The European Rescue of the Nation-State* (London: Routledge).

Moravcsik, A. (1993), 'Preferences and Power in the European Community: A Liberal Intergovernmentalist Approach', *Journal of Common Market Studies* 31:4, 473–524.

— (1997), 'Taking Preferences Seriously: A Liberal Theory of International Politics', *International Organization* 51:4, 513–53.

— (1998), *The Choice for Europe: Social Purpose and State Power from Messina to Maastricht* (Ithaca: Cornell University Press).

More, G. (1999), 'The Principle of Equal Treatment: From Market Unifier to Fundamental Right?', in P. Craig and de Búrca, G. (eds), *The Evolution of EU Law* (Oxford: Oxford University Press).

Nödinger, I. (1983), 'Für Frieden und Gleichberechtigung: Der Demokratische Frauenbund Deutschland', in Hervé.

Nonon, J. (1979), 'Het Bureau voor de problematiek van de vrouw in het arbeidsproces', in *Europese vrouwen over Europa* (Brussel: Ministerie van Buitenlandse Zaken).

— and Clamen, M. (1991), *L'Europe et ses couloirs. Lobbying et lobbyistes* (Paris: Dunod).

Northcutt, W. and Flaitz, J. (1985), 'Women, Politics and the French Socialist Government', *West European Politics* 8:4, 50–70.

NRC-Handelsblad (several years), Dutch daily.

Official Journal (several years), Official Journal of the European Union.

Ostner, I. (1993), 'Slow motion: Women, work and the family in Germany', in Lewis.

— and J. Lewis (1995), 'Gender and the Evolution of European Social Policies', in Leibfried and Pierson.

Outshoorn, J. (1997), 'Incorporating feminism: the women's policy network in the Netherlands', in Gardiner.

Pettiti, Chr. (1995), 'L'égalité de rémunération en France', in F. Eyraud et al., *Égalité de rémunération entre hommes et femmes dans les pays industriels* (Genève: Bureau International du Travail).

Pfarr, H. M. and Bertelsmann, K. (1985), *Gleichbehandlungsgesetz. Zum Verbot der unmittelbaren und der mittelbaren Diskriminierung von Frauen im Erwerbsleben* (Wiesbaden: Hessendienst).

Pierson, P. (1996), 'The Path to European Integration. A Historical Institutionalist Analysis', *Comparative Political Studies* 29:2, 123–63.

Pillinger, J. (1992), *Feminising the Market. Women's Pay and Employment in the European Community* (Houndmills: Macmillan).

Plantenga, J. (1993), *Een afwijkend patroon. Honderd jaar vrouwenarbeid in Nederland en (West-)Duitsland* (Amsterdam: Sua).

Pollack, M. A. (1997), 'Delegation, agency, and agenda setting in the European Community', *International Organization* 51:1, 99–134.

— and Hafner-Burton, E. (2000), 'Mainstreaming Gender in the European Union', *Journal of European Public Policy* 7:3, 432–56.

Popper, K. R. (1980ed), *The Logic of Scientific Discovery* (London: Hutchinson).

Prechal, S. (1995), *Directives in the European Community Law. A Study of Directives and their Enforcement in National Courts* (Oxford: Clarendon Press).

— and Burrows, N. (1990), *Gender Discrimination Law of the European Community* (Dartmouth: Aldershot).

Randall, V. (1987), *Women & Politics. An International Perspective*, 2d edition, (Houndmills: Macmillan).

Reinalda, B. (1997), 'Dea ex Machina or the interplay between national and international policymaking. A critical analysis of women in the European Union', in F. Gardiner.

— and Verhaaren, N. (1989), *Vrouwenbeweging en internationale organisaties 1868–1986. Een vergeten hoofdstuk uit de geschiedenis van de internationale betrekkingen* (Nijmegen: Ariadne).

Reuter, S. and A. G. Mazur (2003), 'The Dynamics of French Equality Discourse', in Liebert.

Risse-Kappen, T. (1995), 'Structures of governance and transnational relations: what have we learned?', in Risse-Kappen, T. (ed.), *Bringing Transnational Relations Back In: Non-State Actors, Domestic Structures, and International Institutions* (Cambridge: Cambridge University Press).

— (1996), 'Exploring the Nature of the Beast: International Relations Theory and Comparative Policy Analysis Meet the European Union', *Journal of Common Market Studies* 34:1, 53–80.

Rosamond, B. (2000), *Theories of European Integration* (Houndmills: Macmillan).

Ross, G. (1995), 'Assessing the Delors Era and Social Policy', in Leibfried and Pierson.

Rossilli, M. (ed.) (2000), *Gender Policies in the European Union* (New York: Peter Lang).

Rowbotham, S. (1972), 'The Beginnings of Women's Liberation in Britain', in Wandor.

Rubenstein, M. (1987), 'The Equal Treatment Directive and U.K. Law', in McCrudden.

Rutherford, F. (1989), 'The proposal for a European directive on parental leave: some reasons why it failed', *Policy and Politics* 17:4, 301–10.

Sabourin-Ragnaud, A. (1993), 'Equality between men and women in the workplace', in F-G. Dreyfus, J. Morizet and M. Peyrard (eds), *France and EC Membership evaluated* (London: Pinter).

Sandholtz, W. (1996), 'Membership Matters: Limits of the Functional Approach to European Institutions', *Journal of Common Market Studies* 34:3, 403–29.

— and Stone Sweet, A. (eds) (1998), *European Integration and Supranational Governance* (Oxford: Oxford University Press).

— and Zysman, J. (1989), '1992: Recasting the European Bargain', *World Politics* 95–128.

Saunders, C, and Marsden, D. (1981), *Pay inequalities in the European Communities* (London: Butterworths).

Scharpf, F.W. (1988), 'The joint-decision trap: lessons from German federalism and European integration', *Public Administration* 66, 239–78.

Schimmelfennig, F. (2001), 'The Community trap: liberal norms, rhetorical action, and the eastern enlargement of the EU', *International Organization* 55:1, 47–80.

Segers, M.L.L. (2006), *Tussen Verzoening en Verval* (Nijmegen: Radboud Universiteit, dissertation).

SER (1953), *No. 9, Advies inzake het vraagstuk van gelijke belonging van mannen en vrouwen voor gelijkwaardige arbeid* ('s-Gravenhage: SER).

— (1966a), *No. 3, Advies inzake de regeling van het minimuminkomen* ('s-Gravenhage: SER).

— (1966b), *No. 15, Advies over de arbeid van vrouwen in Nederland* ('s-Gravenhage: SER).

— (1973), *No. 13, Advies inzake gelijke beloning voor mannen en vrouwen.* ('s-Gravenhage: SER)

— (1977), *No. 13, Advies met betrekking tot het ontwerp van een EEG-richtlijn inzake de gelijke behandeling van mannen en vrouwen op het gebied van de sociale zekerheid* ('s-Gravenhage: SER).

Serra, E. (ed.) (1989), *Il Rilancio dell'Europa e i Trattati di Roma* (Bruxelles: Bruylant).

Shanks, M. (1977a), *European Social Policy, Today and Tomorrow* (Oxford: Pergamon Press).

— (1977b), 'Introductory article: the social policy of the European Communities', *Common Market Law Review* 375–83.

Shaw, J. (2000), 'Importing gender: the challenge of feminism and the analysis of the EU legal order', *Journal of European Public Policy* 7:3, 406–31.

Sifft, S. (2003), 'Pushing for Europeanisation: How British Feminists Link with the EU to Promote Parental Rights', in Liebert.

Sjerps, I. (1988), 'Indirect Discrimination in the Netherlands: Demands of the Dutch Women's Movement', in Buckley and Anderson.

— (2000), 'Contribution to public hearing on equal treatment for men and women', <http://www.e-quality.nl/sjerps.html>.

Snoy et d'Oppuers, J.-C. (1989), *Rebâtir l'Europe. Mémoires. Entretiens avec Jean-Claude Riquier* (Paris: Editions Duculot).

Spaak, P.-H. (1969), *Combats inachevés. Vol. 2. De l'espoir aux déceptions* (Paris: Fayard).

Stienstra, D. (1994), *Women's movements and international organizations* (Basingstoke: Macmillan).

Strange, S. (1988), *States and Markets* (London: Pinter Publishers).

Stratigaki, M. (2000), 'The European Union and the equal opportunities process', in L. Hantrais (ed.), *Gendered Policies in Europe. Reconciling Employment and Family Life* (Houndmills: Macmillan).

— (2005), 'Gender mainstreaming versus positive action: an ongoing conflict in EU gender equality policy', *European Journal of Women's Studies* 12:2, 165–86.

Sullerot, E. (1970), *De vrouwenarbeid en de daarmee verbonden problematiek in de lidstaten van de Europese Gemeenschap* (Luxemburg: Bureau voor Officiële Publikaties).

Thatcher, M. (1993), *Mijn jaren in Downing Street 10* (Amsterdam: Uitgeverij Balans/Kritak).

Thüne, A. and Olfe-Schlothauer R. (eds) (1980), *FrauenBilder LeseBuch* (Frankfurt am Main: Büchergilde Gutenberg).

Urwin, D. W. (1995), *The Community of Europe. A History of European Integration since 1945* (London: Longman).

Usher, J. (1987), 'European Community Equality Law: Legal Instruments and Judicial Remedies', in McCrudden.

Vallance, E. and Davies, E. (1986), *Women of Europe. Women MEPs and equality policy* (Cambridge: Cambridge University Press).

Van Arnhem, C. (1984), 'Méér dan gelijk loon voor gelijk werk. Vrouwen op de arbeidsmarkt', in *Socialisties-Feministiese Teksten 8* (Amsterdam: Feministische Uitgeverij Sara).

Van Bergen, A. (1984), 'Ambtenaren knokken door tot het Europese Hof', *Opzij* 5, 37–8.

Van der Vleuten, A. (2001), *Dure vrouwen, Dwarse staten. Een institutioneel-realistische benadering van de totstandkoming en implementatie van Europees beleid* (Nijmegen: Nijmegen University Press).

— (2004), 'De loze reflexen van de vakbeweging', *Lover* 31:3, 52–3.

— (2005), 'Pincers and Prestige: Explaining the Implementation of EU Gender Equality Legislation', *Comparative European Politics* 3:4, 464–88.

Van Ooijen, M. et al. (eds) (1996), *Bouwen aan Europa. Het Europese integratieproces in documenten* (Nijmegen: Katholieke Universiteit Nijmegen).

Van Praag, Ph. (1985), 'Tien jaar emancipatiebeleid', *Beleid en Maatschappij*, 1:2, 3–12.

Van Rossum, H. (1992), 'De gesubsidieerde revolutie? De geschiedenis van de vrouwenbeweging, 1968–1989', in: J.W. Duyvendak et al., *Tussen verbeelding en macht: 25 jaar nieuwe sociale bewegingen in Nederland* (Amsterdam: SUA).

Verloo, M. (2001), 'Another Velvet Revolution? Gender mainstreaming and the politics of implementation', *IWM Working Paper* No. 5/2001 (Vienna).

Vogel-Polsky, E. (1994), *La citoyenneté européenne et les femmes, in: Les Femmes et la Construction européenne. Egalité? Parité?* (Paris/Bruxelles: Cahiers du Grif).

Volkskrant (several years), Dutch daily.

Wandor, M. (ed.) (1972), *The Body Politic. Writings from the Women's Liberation Movement in Britain 1969-1972* (London: Stage 1).

Warner, R. H. (1984), 'EC Social Policy in Practice: Community Action on behalf of Women and its Impact in the Member States', *Journal of Common Market Studies* 23:2, 141–67.

Weatherill, S. and Beaumont, P. (1999), *EU Law* (London: Penguin Books).

Weiler, J.H.H. (1993), 'Journey to an Unknown Destination: A Retrospective and prospective of the European Court of Justice in the Arena of Political Integration', *Journal of Common Market Studies* 31:4, 417–46.

— (1999), *The Constitution of Europe. "Do the new clothes have an emperor?" and other essays on European integration* (Cambridge: Cambridge University Press).

Wendt, A. (1994), 'Collective Identity Formation and the International State', *American Political Science Review* 88:2, 384–96.

Werner, W. G. and De Wilde, J. (2001), 'The Endurance of Sovereignty', *European Journal of International Relations* 7:3, 283–313.

Wiggershaus, R. (1979), *Geschichte der Frauen und der Frauenbewegung in der Bundesrepublik Deutschland und in der Deutschen Demokratischen Republik nach 1945* (Wuppertal: Peter Hammer Verlag).

Wiener, A. and Diez, T. (eds), *European Integration Theory* (Oxford: Oxford University Press).

Index

Gender in a Global/Local World

Also published in the series

The Gender Question in Globalization
Changing Perspectives and Practices
Edited by
Tine Davids and Francien van Driel
ISBN 0 7546 3923 1

Turkey's Engagement with Global Women's Human Rights
Nüket Kardam
ISBN 0 7546 4168 6

Vulnerable Bodies
Gender, the UN and the Global Refugee Crisis
Erin K. Baines
ISBN 0 7546 3734 4

Fashioning Inequality
The Multinational Company and Gendered Employment in a Globalizing World
Juanita Elias
ISBN 0 7546 3698 4

Setting the Agenda for Global Peace
Conflict and Consensus Building
Anna C. Snyder
ISBN 0 7546 1933 8

(Un)thinking Citizenship
Feminist Debates in Contemporary South Africa
Edited by
Amanda Gouws
ISBN 0 7546 3878 2

For Product Safety Concerns and Information please contact our EU representative GPSR@taylorandfrancis.com
Taylor & Francis Verlag GmbH, Kaufingerstraße 24, 80331 München, Germany

www.ingramcontent.com/pod-product-compliance
Ingram Content Group UK Ltd.
Pitfield, Milton Keynes, MK11 3LW, UK
UKHW021303190926
475701UK00009B/621
9780367605742